LANDSCAPE ANALYSIS

A key aspect of town planning, landscape planning and landscape architecture is to identify and then use the distinctive features and characteristics of space, place and landscape to achieve environmental quality. *Landscape Analysis* provides an introduction to the field both in theory and in practice. A wide range of methods and techniques for landscape analysis is illustrated by urban and rural examples from many countries.

Analysing landscapes within a planning context requires both skill and insights. Drawing upon numerous concrete examples, together with an examination of some theoretical concepts, this book guides the reader through a wide range of different approaches and techniques of landscape analysis that may be applied at different scales, from elementary site analysis to historical and regional studies. This is an essential book for students and graduate practitioners working in landscape architecture, planning and architecture.

Per Stahlschmidt is a Landscape Architect and until 2008 was partner in a landscape firm and Associate Professor at the University of Copenhagen, Denmark. He worked mainly with landscape planning and landscape design. Now he is retired.

Simon Swaffield is Professor of Landscape Architecture at Lincoln University in New Zealand, and from 2011 has been Honorary Professor at the University of Copenhagen, Denmark. He is also a registered Landscape Architect in New Zealand.

Jørgen Primdahl is a Landscape Architect and Professor of Countryside Planning at the University of Copenhagen, Denmark. He works mainly with rural landscape policy and planning.

Vibeke Nellemann is a Landscape Architect and was responsible for research, development and teaching in methods for landscape analysis, planning and management at the University of Copenhagen, Denmark, until her retirement in 2015.

LANDSCAPE ANALYSIS

Investigating the Potentials of Space and Place

Per Stahlschmidt, Simon Swaffield,
Jørgen Primdahl and Vibeke Nellemann

Routledge
Taylor & Francis Group

LONDON AND NEW YORK

First published 2017
by Routledge
2 Park Square, Milton Park, Abingdon, Oxon OX14 4RN

and by Routledge
711 Third Avenue, New York, NY 10017

Routledge is an imprint of the Taylor & Francis Group, an informa business

© 2017 Per Stahlschmidt, Vibeke Nellemann, Jørgen Primdahl and Simon Swaffield

British Library Cataloguing-in-Publication Data
A catalogue record for this book is available from the British Library

Library of Congress Cataloging-in-Publication Data
Names: Stahlschmidt, Per.
Title: Landscape analysis : investigating the potentials of space and place / Per
    Stahlschmidt, Vibeke Nellemann, Jørgen Primdahl and Simon Swaffield.
Description: Abingdon, Oxon ; New York, NY : Routledge, 2017. | Includes
    bibliographical references and index.
Identifiers: LCCN 2016031112 | ISBN 9781138927148 (hardback : alk. paper) |
    ISBN 9781138927155 (pbk. : alk. paper) | ISBN 9781315682792 (ebook)
Subjects: LCSH: Landscape assessment.
Classification: LCC GF90 .S77 2017 | DDC 304.2—dc23
LC record available at https://lccn.loc.gov/2016031112

ISBN: 978-1-138-92714-8 (hbk)
ISBN: 978-1-138-92715-5 (pbk)
ISBN: 978-1-315-68279-2 (ebk)

Typeset in Frutiger LT Std
by Apex CoVantage, LLC
Printed by Ashford Colour Press Ltd

CONTENTS

List of illustrations   *ix*
Foreword   *xiii*
Preface   *xv*
Acknowledgements and credits   *xvi*

1 **Landscape change and the need for analysis**   **1**
   Introduction 1
   Content and structure 3
   The landscape concept – origins and definitions 4
   Analysis 5
   Changing landscapes 6
   Landscape policy, planning and design 10
   Landscape analysis in a decision-making context 11
   The nature of landscape analysis 11
   Scope and settings of landscape analysis 15
   Applications of landscape analysis 16

2 **Framing analysis: values, experts and citizens**   **18**
   Introduction 18
   Framing values 19
   Types of values 22
   Karby – an example of managing values 23
   Identifying citizens, communities and stakeholders 27
   Collecting information on values 29
   Conclusion 32

3 **Analysis of natural factors, biophysical attributes and land use**   **33**
   Introduction 33
   Natural factors 35

Land cover 36
Land use 38
Main case: biophysical analysis, Kaloe 39
Variations 45
    Geomorphology 45
    Terrain 46
    Soil 52
    Hydrology and drainage networks 52
    Land cover and land use 54

4   **Historical analysis**   **61**
Introduction 61
Relevance to planning solutions 63
Sources for historical analysis 63
Three methods 64
    The retrospective method 65
    The retrogressive method 67
    The chronological method 69
Variations 71
    Historical series of topographic maps 71
    Historical series of thematic maps 73
    Comprehensive mapping 73
    Landscape biography 75

5   **Spatial analysis**   **78**
Introduction 78
Main case: The Image of the City *80*
Variations 84
    Visibility analysis 85
    Eye-level analysis 85
    Figure ground 88
    Serial vision 89
    Nolli's analysis 91
    Higuchi analysis 92
    SAVE structural analysis 93
    SAVE urban edge analysis 93
    LCA (DK) spatial-visual analysis 94
    Infrastructure analysis 95

6   **Regionalisation and landscape character assessment**   **99**
Introduction 99
Regionalisation and land classification 99
Equivalent or nested hierarchical classification 102

Landscape ecological classification 102
Procedure for regionalisation 103
Thematic approach 104
Topographic approach 106
Nested hierarchical classification into landscape
*   areas/types, England 106*
Main case A: nested hierarchical landscape
*   analysis Skive 109*
Main case B: the Danish LCA approach Svendborg 116
    Landscape characterisation / phase A 118
    Landscape judgement / phase B 122
    Landscape strategy / phase C 125
    Implementation / phase D 126

7 **Site selection and landscape potential**   **129**
Introduction 129
Procedure 133
Identifying and grouping selection factors 135
    Development requirements and landscape potentials
        or constraints 136
    Definitive or relative site constraints 138
    Reciprocity in potentials and constraints 139
    Zones of influence around sensitive locations 140
    Future site possibilities 141
    Scale 142
Main case: McHarg's overlay analysis 142
Variations 146
    Skovbo site-selection analysis 147
    Danish LCA site-selection analysis Randers Bay 149

8 **Impact assessment and futures analysis**   **153**
Introduction 153
Impact assessment (IA) 154
Environmental impact assessment (EIA) reporting 156
Landscape visual and aesthetic assessment 157
Main case: aesthetic EIA assessment Frederikssund
*   Motorway 159*
Variations 164
    Representing change 164
    Analysing change 166
    Futures analysis and alternative futures 170
Case A: alternative futures, Oppdal 171
Case B: alternative futures, Willamette Valley 173

Contents

9   Landscape analysis in research and practice   176

Introduction 176
Landscape analysis and landscape democracy 177
Improving landscape analysis – research into process,
   methods and techniques 179
Landscape analysis as research 181
Conclusion 184

References   *185*
Glossary   *195*
Index   *200*

ILLUSTRATIONS

Figures

1.1	Medieval farming	2
1.2	Palazzo Farnese, Italy	5
1.3	Driving forces of landscape change	7
1.4	Rural landscape, Northern Jutland	9
1.5	Ratio scale example	13
1.6	Interval rating example	13
1.7	Ordinal ranks example	14
1.8	Nominal categories example	14
2.1	Distribution of NATURA 2000 sites across the EU, 2012	20
2.2	Karby village	24
2.3	Favourite places in Karby	25
2.4	Strategy for Karby	26
2.5	Focus group interview	30
2.6	Options	31
3.1	La Palma, Canary Islands	34
3.2	Landforms, South Djursland – Kaloe and Mols Hills	40
3.3	Topography, Kaloe	41
3.4	Geomorphology, Kaloe	41
3.5	Terrain heights, Kaloe	42
3.6	View to Mols Hills	42
3.7	Terrain gradient and geophysical regions, Kaloe	43
3.8	Sub-soils, Kaloe	43
3.9	Hedgerows, Mols Hills	44
3.10	Top-soil classification, Kaloe	44
3.11	Block diagram coast profile, Svinkloev DK	45
3.12	Terrain inventory	47
3.13	Shaded contour lines	48
3.14	Digital terrain model	49

3.15   Vaux-le-Vicomte, France   49
3.16   Categorical terrain model, Vaux-le-Vicomte   50
3.17   Cross section of railroad line   50
3.18   Cross section with perspective   51
3.19   Longitudinal profile of road   51
3.20   Terrain model of catchment area   53
3.21   Risk area for flooding   54
3.22   Aerial photo, rural landscape   55
3.23   Detailed inventory, vegetation structure   56
3.24   Detailed inventory, forest structure   57
3.25   Vegetation record of a park   58
3.26   The Copenhagen Zoo – before renovation   59
3.27   The Copenhagen Zoo – after renovation   59
4.1   Historical layers   62
4.2   The retrospective method   65
4.3   Illustration of the retrospective method   66
4.4   The retrogressive method   67
4.5   Illustration of the retrogressive method   68
4.6   Use of the retrogressive method, Villa Lemm Berlin   68
4.7   The chronological method   69
4.8   Illustration of use of the chronological method in teaching   70
4.9   Time series of topographic maps, Sdr. Felding DK   72
4.10   Time series of thematic maps   73
4.11   Land-use transformation in the Solano Basin, Italy – four parallel themes   74
4.12   Comprehensive time series of a waterfront   75
4.13   Comprehensive time series of forests   76
5.1   Hammershus Castle – a spatial view   80
5.2   Kevin Lynch analysis, Boston   82
5.3   Five symbols to characterise the spatial pattern of a place or a landscape   83
5.4   Digital visibility analysis, Randers Fjord   86
5.5   Eye-level analysis, Hellerup Beach Park   87
5.6   Hellerup Beach Park   88
5.7   Cullen's serial vision of a hypothetical mountain village   90
5.8   Nolli's map of Rome, 1748   91
5.9   Higuchi-analysis of Japanese mountain landscape   92
5.10   Structural analysis of city   93
5.11   City-edge analysis   94
5.12   Vaeth farming plain   96
5.13   Spatial-visual analysis, Vaeth   97
6.1   Detailed level of landscape character areas   101
6.2   Regionalisation of a valley   103
6.3   Delineation based on contour lines   105
6.4   Landscape character areas at national scale, England   107
6.5   Hierarchic landscape character mapping, England   108
6.6   Regionalisation of Hoejslev, map   111
6.7   Regionalisation of Hoejslev, air photo   112
6.8   Regionalisation of Hoejslev, ground photo   113

6.9   Regionalisation of Skive Municipality   114
6.10   Phases in landscape character assessment LCA (DK)   117
6.11   Physiographic regions, Svendborg Municipality   119
6.12   Landscape character areas, Svendborg Municipality   120
6.13   Spatial-visual analysis, Egense   121
6.14   Characterisation, Egense   122
6.15   Judgement, Egense   124
6.16   Policy objectives, Svendborg Municipality and Egense   127
6.17   Egense agricultural plain   128
7.1   Feeling of being well situated in the landscape   130
7.2   The relationship between new development and
       existing landscape   131
7.3   The process of site-selection analysis   132
7.4   Building integrated in the existing landscape pattern   134
7.5   Good and poor site selection for landscape development   137
7.6   New farm buildings out of scale of existing landscape   139
7.7   Positive or negative factors   140
7.8   Surrounding zone for wetland   141
7.9   Protected zone around protected habitat   141
7.10   Existing and planned projected site-selection factors   141
7.11   Scale as a determining factor   142
7.12   Slope, Richmond Parkway   143
7.13   Surface drainage, Richmond Parkway   144
7.14   Overlay techniques, Richmond Parkway   145
7.15   Proposal for alignment, Richmond Parkway   146
7.16   Landscape areas and site-selection factors, Skovbo   147
7.17   Characterisation of site-selection factors, Skovbo   148
7.18   Adjustment of classification into landscape areas, Skovbo   149
7.19   Sensitivity study, Randers Bay   150
7.20   Mapping of constraints and site-selection options, Randers Bay   151
7.21   Albk Village   151
7.22   Scenario of relocated farms, Randers Bay   152
8.1   Raippaluoto Bridge   154
8.2   Generalised model of Impact Assessment (IA)   155
8.3   Dynamic of vegetation succession   158
8.4   a–c: Aesthetic assessment, Frederikssund Motorway   160
       d: Red and green alternatives at Hove   161
       e–g: The current landscape at Hove; photomontage, red alternative;
       photomontage, green alternative   163
8.5   Wind farm, Evanstown   166
8.6   Gap between illustrations of the project and the reality   167
8.7   Separated aspects recreation plan   168
8.8   Environmental conflicts regional plan   168
8.9   Mock-up building extension, DK   169
8.10   Impacts of different development plans, Oppdal   172
8.11   Alternative landscape futures, Willamette Valley   174
9.1   Conceptual framework of landscape democracy   178

Tables

1.1	Four scales of measurement	12
3.1	Categories of land cover	37
6.1	Strategic options future management	126
9.1	Levels of analysis	180
9.2	Types of knowledge used in practice	181
9.3	Analysis as part of landscape architectural research	181

FOREWORD

A long time ago, in what now seems like a galaxy far, far away, the then 'Countryside Commission for England and Wales' asked the University of Manchester to develop what was hoped would be a 'definitive' approach to landscape assessment. They were looking for a reliable and reproducible expert method for evaluating 'landscape quality' at the county (sub-regional) scale. This was in response to a requirement of the newly introduced structure planning system to be able to identify those areas of high quality landscape which should be protected from the negative impacts of economic development. After five years of intensive research and testing, the 'Manchester Method' was finally published (Robinson et al, 1976) – and promptly put in a drawer to be rapidly forgotten.

Landscape analysis has come a long way since the demise of the method supposed to supersede all methods, as is born witness by the current volume, not just in terms of the increased diversity and the range of methods and approaches presented, but also in terms of the questions society is asking of the landscape.

Two main criticisms brought about the rapid downfall of the Manchester Method. One was largely pragmatic – it required disproportionate amounts of time and human resources in order to be applied in real life situations, and relied upon the extensive use of computers at a time when they were not widely available. The other criticism was based on what was perhaps more of a 'gut reaction': how, it was asked, could aesthetic judgements be reduced to objective measurements and statistical treatments and expressed in computer print-out answers? Even today, however, the ubiquity of computers and their vastly enhanced power, has not – or at least not yet – led to any widespread professional uptake of quantitative approaches to landscape aesthetics as those embodied in the 'Manchester Method'. Modelling is widely used in research, and professional assessments certainly utilise digital technologies for mapping and visualisation, but assessments continue to be based upon expert weighing up of multiple factors through logical argument, rather than by application of a given formula.

Within Europe, the European Landscape Convention (ELC) has been an important factor in driving the further development of landscape analysis, not least by confirming the role of the observer as an integral part of the very definition of landscape, as well as reaffirming the fact that the landscape covers the whole of a country's territory. But even before the advent of the ELC the 'landscape question' had already moved on from being a simple concern with "where are the best bits?" to a more nuanced approach asking "what types of landscapes are we dealing with, what factors are determining their character, what is their condition, and what are the implications for future landscape management?".

It is not just the questions posed to landscape analysis which have become more varied and sophisticated. The broadening range of expert approaches required is also highlighted by the ELC definition of landscape, which stresses that the character of a landscape is essentially an interdisciplinary matter, namely "*. . . the result of the action and interaction of natural* (the province of the natural sciences) *and/ or human factors* (the province of the humanities)."

Widely adopted and much praised as it is, the ELC also contains some provisions that might be interpreted as being somewhat contradictory. The importance afforded to general awareness raising and the role of the wider public in determining landscape values is present throughout the text, and Article 6 in particular asks signatory states to take account the values attributed to landscapes by the general public. The same article, however, promotes the need for the international exchange of experts and technical experience, and the importance of research – so 'top-down' and 'bottom-up' approaches to landscape analysis seem to be given similar levels of importance.

It is an important achievement of this book that as well as illuminating the wide range of questions we now ask of the changing landscape, it also helps to square the circle of balancing the treatment of important topics such as landscape values with a wide variety of other landscape analysis methods and techniques aimed at meeting a broad range of needs and objectives. These range from visibility analysis to character assessment, from typologies to preference studies, and incorporate approaches and concerns from disciplines such as landscape ecology and landscape archaeology into those of landscape planning. The field of landscape analysis as represented in this volume has become nearly as many layered as the landscape itself. *Landscape Analysis* provides both a rigorous theoretical underpinning and richly illustrated practical examples to give students and practitioners the necessary grounding to be able themselves to develop the field further in future.

Richard Stiles
Professor of Landscape Architecture at Vienna University of Technology, Austria, and long-time Coordinator of the LE:NOTRE Thematic Network in Landscape Architecture

PREFACE

The idea to write this book evolved from Per Stahlschmidt and Vibeke Nelle-mann's Danish textbook *Methods in Landscape Analysis* (2009). The original book was published in two editions and is widely used by practitioners and students in Scandinavia. This English-language text is an extended version of the Danish book with a wider scope, and we hope that international readers find the text and the examples at least as useful and inspiring as Scandinavian readers have found the original version.

Landscape-planning practice, as well as the technical capacity to analyse land-scapes in space and time through GIS and CAD, has changed dramatically in recent years. New and more integrated and inclusive planning processes have evolved, and new approaches to landscape analysis have been demanded by clients and communities. This book provides theoretical background as well as practical exam-ples of some of the new demands for landscape analysis, as well as an overview of established needs and principles of the field. The focus remains at the landscape scale, rather than at site or regional level.

It has been challenging to combine theoretical foundations with very specific examples from analysis practice within a relatively short and basic textbook. We hope the book will contribute to students' and practitioners' understanding of needs and approaches to landscape analysis, and that the examples serve as useful sources of inspiration, as well as helpful guidance on choices that must be made about analytical approach as well as representation technique.

ACKNOWLEDGEMENTS AND CREDITS

This book is to a large extent based on Per Stahlschmidt and Vibeke Nellemann's Danish book *Metoder til Landskabsanalyse* ('Methods in Landscape Analysis'), published in 2009 by Groent Miljoe Publishing, Copenhagen. We are grateful to the Danish editor, Soeren Holgersen, for supporting this international and extended version and for providing figures. We thank Dorte Silver for the first translations to English and to the Foundation for Garden Culture ('Havekulturfonden') and to the Margot and Thorvald Dreyer Foundation for sponsoring the translation. Thanks to two anonymous reviewers for comprehensive and useful comments on our proposal.

We wish to thank Dr. Morten Stenak from the Danish Agency for Culture and Palaces for his extensive expert input to the section on historic analysis in Chapter 4. Thanks also to landscape architect Uffe Wainoe for providing and processing the maps used in Figure 8.4, to Melanie Downes and Eckart Lange who arranged and granted permission to use Figure 8.6, and to architect Morten Stahlschmidt for his comments on the final script.

Thanks also to our colleagues at Planning and Landscape, University of Copenhagen; in particular to Dr. Ole Hjorth Caspersen who together with Dr. Patrick Karlsson produced the maps in Figures 3.4–3.10, to Prof. Anders Busse who did the translation to Figure 3.24, to landscape architect Sara Folvig who improved several of the figures and compiled the reference list, and to Kamilla Hansen Moeller for advice and support.

Finally, we wish to thank Sadé Lee and Christina O´Brien from Routledge for their engagement and patience in the project.

1

LANDSCAPE CHANGE AND THE NEED FOR ANALYSIS

Introduction

In the famous story by Daniel Defoe, after arriving on an island as a castaway Robinson Crusoe decided to find the right location for his camp:

> I soon found the Place I was in was not for my Settlement, particularly because it was upon a low moorish Ground near the Sea, and I believ'd would not be wholsome, and more particularly because there was no fresh Water near it, so I resolv'd to find a more healthy and more convenient Spot of Ground.
>
> I consulted several Things in my Situation which I found would be proper for me, 1st. Health, and fresh Water I just now mention'd, 2dly. Shelter from the Heat of the Sun, 3dly. Security from ravenous Creatures, whether Men or Beasts, 4thly. a View to the Sea, that if God sent any Ship in Sight, I might not lose any Advantage for my Deliverance, of which I was not willing to banish all my Expectation yet.
>
> In search of a Place proper for this, I found a little Plain on the Side of a rising Hill; whose Front towards this little Plain, was steep as a House-side, so that nothing could come down upon me from the Top; on the Side of this Rock there was a hollow Place worn a little way in like the Entrance or Door of a Cave, but there was not really any Cave or Way into the Rock at all.
>
> (Defoe 1719)

Robinson decides upon the criteria for a camp location, interprets the landscape using these criteria, and identifies a site that responds to his requirements.

Robinson's needs, considerations, approach, and decision deal with the same basic issues as this book.

The wonderful diversity of landscapes in the world may be urban, rural or wilderness, but one feature is common – all landscapes change, sometimes fast, sometimes more slowly. Increasingly the changes are driven by people. We have entered the 'Anthropocene', when human population growth and actions are a major factor in landscape change at multiple scales, from individual sites, to watersheds, cities, regions, and the whole earth. Landscape change may be intentional, creating places for people to live, work, play, or visit, or producing energy, food, timber, or other resources. Other changes may be unintended, such as human-induced climate change. It is clear, however, that our future wellbeing depends upon making wise decisions about how all landscapes will change, in order to ensure that the health of the planet is sustained and the needs of people now and in the future can continue to be met.

To make wise decisions, we need to understand how landscapes are structured, function, are changing, and might change for the better. Many past decisions about

FIGURE 1.1 Medieval farming
The appearance of the landscape at any particular time reflects social, economic and technical conditions. Wider society and the local inhabitants influence the landscape and the landscape influences society and the local inhabitants.
Source: Pieter Bruegel the Elder (1565): *De Hooioogst / Hay Harvesting*. Oil painting 117 x 161 cm. © The Lobkowicz Collections, Czech Republic.

landscape change have been based upon accumulated everyday knowledge of local communities, and this grounded knowledge remains vital. However, rapidly growing scientific understanding, the complexity of modern technologies, economies and societies, and interconnected global processes mean that it is impossible for any individual or small group to fully understand landscape change without a more systematic approach. This requires a process of analysis.

This book is about analysing landscapes in a decision-making context, as part of policy, planning and design decisions of various kinds and forms. It offers guidance to students, their teachers, and new professionals about practical ways to undertake landscape analysis in a range of settings and applications. The primary goal is educational and non-technical; it does not offer detailed instruction on all the specific analysis techniques used in landscape architecture, but aims to provide an overview of the types of analysis and their characteristics, with examples, to help those starting on their professional careers to understand the possibilities and potentials of systematic analysis.

Content and structure

This practical and educational aim is expressed in the content and order of the chapters in the book. Chapter 2 is focused on the question of landscape values, and what and whose values should be considered. Chapters 3 to 8 then discuss procedures and techniques relevant to specific types of analysis. The aim of this structure is to guide the choice of appropriate methods for work- or study-related assignments that would benefit from landscape analysis. The different types of analysis discussed are suited for different tasks. Each can be used to examine a given landscape that is the object of analysis.

The task may be to examine natural factors, biophysical attributes and land cover of the landscape in question (Chapter 3), its history (Chapter 4) or the spatial patterns and their visual expression (Chapter 5). The assessment of landscape character is addressed in Chapter 6, Chapter 7 focuses on site selection, and Chapter 8 discusses impact assessment and futures analysis. Finally Chapter 9 draws the technical chapters together, and discusses contemporary developments which are broadening citizen involvement in analysis as it becomes part of the discourse of landscape democracy. The final chapter also considers how analysis can be a form of inquiry that creates new knowledge in the same way or as part of a research project.

Each of the Chapters 3–8 features a case based on a published text that describes and explains a specific method and the relevant techniques. The case example is supplemented with variations that illustrate different techniques, each illustrated with one or two examples. The main cases have been selected for their usefulness, level and documentation. *Usefulness* means that the example is a helpful tool in relation to the task that is discussed in the chapter. *Level* implies that the technique is suitable for beginner's courses. Finally, *documentation* means that the main example has come from a source that explains the method and the system from which the technique is drawn.

Variations are selected to be useful, representative of an application field, and simple and straightforward illustrations. The priority is to provide a clear presentation of the principle and idea of the method, rather than sophistication in visual appearance. Often, the examples illustrate the outcome of the analysis rather than the analytical process, but the intention is to enable the reader to gain insight into the process by studying the outcome.

The terminology is based upon contemporary northern European practice, influenced particularly by the European Landscape Convention and related practice guidance documents, including the landscape character assessment procedures in the UK and Denmark. We include specific definitions in relevant chapters, starting below with the concepts of landscape and analysis.

The landscape concept – origins and definitions

There are many definitions of landscape and interpretations of its multiple meanings. A useful and influential framework is the European Landscape Convention (ELC 2000) which defines landscape as 'an area, as perceived by people, whose character is the result of the action and interaction of natural and/or human factors' (Figure 1.2). By this definition the delineation of a 'landscape' is contextual, and depends on how people perceive what belongs to their particular 'landscape'. The broad landscape concept expressed in the ELC is used in this text. It differs from some disciplines and other contexts which focus *either* on physical patterns and attributes only, with little attention to the cultural dimension, *or* upon perceptual and scenic dimensions, which deal only with landscape as a pictorial visual phenomenon.

There is extensive scholarship tracing the linguistic and cultural development of 'landscape' from its North–European origins expressing collective management of an area of land and water (Olwig 1996), which has since evolved along multiple intersecting pathways. Many contemporary writers focus on landscape as a living place, with growing interest in the relationship between landscape and personal and community identity, and in landscape functioning as a dynamic socio-ecological system. Relevant essays on the landscape concept and its analysis and representation from different disciplinary perspectives can be found in Jackson (1984), Olwig (1996), Corner (1999), Antrop (2000), Buttimer (2001), Jones (2003), Mitchell (2001), Wylie (2007), and Howard (2011).

The landscape concept is also scale-dependent. Framstad and Lid (1998, p. 267) define landscape as 'an area large enough to contain patterns and processes that are necessary for the ecological or administrative issues that are of interest'. They suggest that in practice landscapes may range from a few hundred square metres to hundreds of square kilometres. This covers a wide range of scales and reflects the diversity of definitions and meanings of landscape – indeed some usages extend even larger, talking of landscapes that may extend over millions of square kilometres. Antrop (2000) distinguishes between thinking of landscape as a *type* of area (e.g. agricultural landscapes) and the landscape of a *particular* area (e.g. the Argentine Pampas) and this is a useful reminder of how analysis can be both general and particular depending on its purpose.

FIGURE 1.2 Palazzo Farnese, Italy
Formalised landscape analysis has a short history, but landscape considerations have always been part of settlement and building. Palazzo Farnese north of Rome was formerly a stronghold which was reconstructed by Vignola as a summer residence in the 16th century. The house sits on a sloping crest above the village of Caprarola with a view of the countryside – useful both for defence and pleasure.
Source: Photo by Stahlschmidt, P.

Analysis

Analysis means conceptually separating the parts of the whole (such as a landscape) and examining their interrelationships, in order to improve understanding. *Analysis* derives from Greek *analusis*, from *analuein* 'unloose' (*ana* 'up' + *luein* 'loosen'), and means 'detailed examination of the elements or structure of something' (Oxford Dictionaries 2011) by separating its constituent elements. It is often contrasted with *synthesis*, which refers to 'putting things together', and synthesis typically follows analysis. Indeed, most if not all professional 'landscape analyses' include a synthesis stage, or are closely linked to a synthesis process, as they are typically focused upon some need and opportunity for action. While scientists may use analysis to improve knowledge, landscape architects and spatial planners are committed to helping people and communities improve their lives in a practical way. Landscape analysis in the sense used in this text is therefore an examination of a landscape with the purpose of understanding its character, structure and function, *in order to make policy, planning or design decisions concerning its future condition and management.*

There are many ways to undertake landscape analysis. One early but still useful classification of land analysis (Mabbutt 1968) distinguishes between a *parametric* approach (i.e. looking at what Antrop (2000) describes as themes or components, such as soil, geology, etc.); a spatial or areal approach (sometimes described as the *landscape* approach), which looks at what makes particular areas distinctive; and a *genetic* approach, which looks at how land (or landscape) has become the way it is – that is, a historical analysis. These are not mutually exclusive, and a landscape analysis may usefully incorporate several different types of analysis.

All these evolving understandings create a rich field for landscape analysis, but they may also represent potential confusion. Different analysts frequently bring different understandings of the nature of landscape, and promote different methods of analysis, and different ways of representing the findings. It is therefore essential when embarking upon a landscape analysis project to be clear about the definition of landscape that is being used and the nature and intent of analysis. A good place to start is by asking why the analysis is being undertaken, and this inevitably relates to landscape change.

Changing landscapes

Landscapes are always changing, incrementally, and occasionally in dramatic steps. The causes of change are as diverse as landscapes themselves, and so analysis about how to intentionally shape and direct landscape change requires understanding about the nature of landscapes and about the causes and drivers of change. Central to this understanding is the fact that every landscape represents *both* an entity in itself – a whole which can be characterised in terms of its structure, function, and change processes (Forman and Godron 1986) – *and* a local area which is part of wider networks, in which decisions and actions affect and are affected by decisions and action going on in other – often distant – places (Giddens 1990). Key drivers of contemporary landscape change include biophysical processes and events – both naturally occurring and those influenced by humans (the biophysical aspects include terrain, elevation, soil types, drainage networks, vegetation cover, ecotones, built infrastructure, etc.). Other key drivers are the actions and intentions of local landscape agents whose everyday activities continually reshape landscapes.

An analysis framework based upon change 'drivers' and responses developed by the OECD (1997) and subsequently expanded by the European Commission (2006) is useful to describe landscape change at regional scale and in a longer timeframe (Figure 1.3). According to this model:

- *the driving force* (substantial increase in grain price, for example) results in a
- *pressure* (expansion of fields with annual crops, for example), which in turn changes the
- *state of the landscape* (reducing the proportion of the area with perennial vegetation, for example) resulting in

- *impacts* on the biodiversity (fragmentation and reduction of semi-natural habitats, for example), which then trigger
- *responses* from an environmental policy regime (amending the Nature Conservation Law with better protection of valuable semi-natural habitats, for example), and this new improved legislation then finally represents a new
- *driver* of landscape change (for example, the effect of new policies that provide incentives for farmers to retire land from production).

Key drivers of landscape include both natural factors such as erosion and coastal transformation, and human factors such as technological change, markets, urbanisation, and public policy interventions, including landscape planning. The biophysical character of landscapes is shaped by their geological, geomorphological and bio-geographical history and dynamics, and landscape change driven by natural factors tends to be episodic, with long periods of incremental evolution punctuated by major events such as drought and floods, landslips and earthquakes. *Natural factors* are the first driver for landscape change. Understanding the way that natural factors have shaped biophysical patterns and processes is crucial to all decisions on landscape, and biophysical surveys and analyses are therefore part of most landscape assessment.

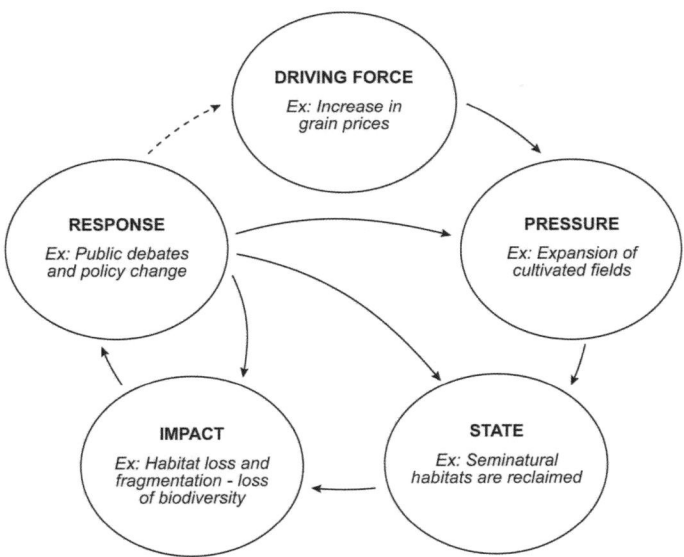

FIGURE 1.3 Driving forces of landscape change
Framework illustrating how the Driving force starts the process: Pressure–State–Impact–Response (DPSIR).
Source: Figure moderated from European Commission (2006).

The second driver, *technology change,* may relate to:

- new systems and techniques of agricultural production (such as pasture management, irrigation systems or more efficient ploughs and tractors)
- new modes of transportation or changes in efficiency
- new modes of information technology
- changed sources of energy or industrial production
- changed habitation or leisure.

New technologies tend to be introduced in waves, and particularly influence the scale and pattern of land-use practices. Analysis therefore needs to include understanding of the management systems affecting a landscape.

Markets for finance, food, minerals, energy or land are a third driver of change, and market dynamics have profound consequences for landscapes. The European grain market opened for overseas imports in the 19th century, and was accompanied by technological innovations in transport (trains and cargo ships) and infrastructure (silos). The result was that agricultural landscapes changed dramatically all over Europe, but also changed around the world in colonies and countries which could now supply food to Europe. Similar widespread change is occurring today under the contemporary phase of globalisation, due to new markets, organisational systems and information flows. This shapes the use values attached to landscapes.

Urbanisation (including counter-urbanisation and new infrastructures) is a fourth key driver of landscape change. When rural populations leave their land and move to towns and cities, as urban populations grow, and as urban dwellers travel out into rural areas for leisure or to live, so landscapes change in character. The changes occur both subtly and quite dramatically. Analysis of urban–rural interactions and relationships is therefore vital.

The fifth driver, *public policy interventions* (including spatial planning), may influence landscape change in a number of ways. Public policy may be directed at managing the condition of particular landscapes or types of landscape – for example, protection of landscapes valued for their natural or cultural heritage – an approach that Selman (2006) described as policy *for* landscape. More typically, however, public policy is aimed at other goals for society, which may have unintended landscape consequences. The landscape change can be direct, caused by new agricultural production incentives (such as the North American and European Union frameworks that support or encourage particular types of crops or cropping practices). Or the change can be indirect, resulting in zones for new activities (such as a tourism resort which may also stimulate other developments). An emerging approach is to attempt to achieve wider public policy goals *through* landscape (Selman 2006, Primdahl et al. 2013b), for example using landscape management to deliver 'services' (such as recreation or biodiversity). This requires analysis of the relationships between landscape structure and function and the values and benefits that are important to people (Termorshuizen and Opdam 2009).

Landscape change is also driven by *local actions* – the sixth driver. It is vital to understand the role and intentions of local landscape agents – the land owners, farmers, foresters, communities, businesses, conservation groups, and visitors whose actions cumulatively lead to landscape change. The individual agent may participate in landscape change through different roles, which is important to keep in mind when the landscape analytical task includes preference studies or direct participation of stakeholders. A farmer, for example, affects the rural landscape through roles as a *producer* of food, fibre and energy (undertaking farming practices related to tillage, livestock management, use of chemicals, etc.), as an *owner* of a farm property (afforestation and other major changes in land use, for example), and as a *citizen* (considering the views of their neighbours or agreeing to public walking access on their land, for example) (Primdahl et al. 2013a).

It is clear that the analysis of past, current and possible future conditions of landscape change can be complex, and involves careful teasing apart of change drivers

FIGURE 1.4 Rural landscape, Northern Jutland
This countryside on the island of Mors, Denmark contains a number of geological and historic layers and has always been in change caused by natural and cultural driving forces. Among current changes are the restorations of former wetlands partly driven by aims to improve their capacity to absorb nutrients (nitrogen and phosphate). The fields in front of the village will be a lake in few years from now (2016). Outmigration, especially of young people, and a gradual aging and gradual reduction of the rural population is another driver of landscape change.
Source: Photo by Primdahl, J.

and their interrelationships. In the next section the nature of landscape policy and planning and design is briefly addressed.

Landscape policy, planning and design

All of the human dynamics that influence landscape change are mediated to some degree by public policy. Spatial and landscape planning activities in particular have a more or less immediate influence on landscape change. This has been the case historically where regulations of 'rights' and 'duties' concerning landscape occur in the earliest forms of legislation (Olwig 2002). A global landscape policy domain is now emerging (Primdahl and Swaffield 2010), in which change in one driver or location has potential effects across the world. One of the reasons is developments in environmental, agricultural and heritage policy from the 1970s and onwards in Europe, North America and Japan. A second reason is the internationalisation of policy institutions such as the UN, and a third reason is the globalisation of markets and technologies. To understand landscape change, what it is caused by, and how changes are interlinked, it is therefore necessary to consider wider policy, planning and design contexts, and to consider the changes at a range of scales.

It is important to keep in mind the distinction made earlier, that public policies or plans seldom affect landscapes directly – instead, they affect the myriad of human decisions and practices that make landscape. This is a critical relationship to understand in landscape analysis. It is important to understand both the values and aims behind the policies, *and* the values, behaviours and decisions of people, organisations and communities, which are crucial for the implementation of policy and plans. Even the consequences of natural landscape factors such as floods are framed by public policy and plans. Such frames may regulate how and where people are able to live and work, and hence how they are likely to influence and be influenced by natural 'hazards'. As climate change becomes more apparent, and its effects more widespread, understanding 'natural hazards' and their management through landscape plans will become an ever more significant dimension of landscape analysis.

Two public policy agendas of particular relevance for landscapes worldwide are the market policy agenda and the sustainability agenda (Dwyer and Hodge 2001). Market policies determine how nations, corporations and communities trade goods and services with each other. Since the 1980s the focus has been upon deregulation and liberalisation of trade, and decisions are shaped at international and national level with relatively little consideration for the environmental and landscape consequences. The sustainability agenda in contrast is focused upon ensuring that development and urbanisation do not undermine and degrade the long-term function and integrity of societies, cultures and the environment. The sustainability agenda operates at multiple levels, from the global to the local. The 2001 Rio Declaration by the United Nations is a global initiative. Legislation and programmes are done at federal and national level. Regions, municipalities and territorial authorities make strategies, policies and plans, and local actions are made at community level. Landscape analysis is frequently undertaken to attempt to better reconcile the practical effects of market-driven changes upon the sustainability of local landscapes. Recognition of these wider dynamics is an essential context to the analysis process and its outcomes.

Landscape analysis in a decision-making context

When undertaking landscape analysis in relation to a policy, planning or design task it is therefore vital to ask what role the analysis plays and how it fits into a wider decision-making process. This will help us decide how to approach the analysis. Should we focus on the needs and visions of the people most directly involved, and base our analysis upon their knowledge and direct experience of the site? Or should we base our analysis upon our own 'expert' understanding and response to the site? Should we employ different analytical tools, and if so in what order? Or should we develop a process that is a discussion between all the different people and organisations that may have an interest in the future of the site or landscape? The answer depends upon the context, including the nature, scale and scope of the task, the number and types of people involved, and the time and resources allocated to the job.

The American landscape planner Carl Steinitz (1990) has developed a framework for landscape planning structured through six questions, which provide a useful checklist to guide analysis:

- How should the landscape be described?
- How does the landscape operate?
- Is the landscape working well?
- How might the landscape be altered?
- What differences might the changes cause?
- Should the landscape be changed? How is the decision to be made?

The first three questions are focused upon understanding the existing situation, and the second three are focused upon how to respond to the situation – and they all require analysis in order to be answered. Later in the chapter we differentiate situational analysis, relating to the first three questions, and action-oriented analysis, relating to the second three questions, and they will be dealt with in different chapters in the book.

The nature of landscape analysis

As will have become clear already, the subject of landscape analysis is the rich and complex phenomenon of landscape. It is frequently focused directly upon the observed biophysical landscape (in space and time). However, landscape analysis may also consider various representations and images of the landscape, including people's understandings, preferences, or values. Indeed, it is impossible to directly 'see' human values or preferences in landscape. The relationship between different perceptions and experiences of landscape and their representation (such as the diagrams by Kevin Lynch 1960, see Figure 5.2), and the material landscape and its representation in the forms of maps, photos and drawings, is a complex philo-sophical issue, and beyond the scope of this book (see Nijhuis et al. (2011) for a collection of theoretical and practical approaches to the visual landscape). Here we have tried to make clear when the analysis deals explicitly with people's individual and collective perceptions of landscape and the representation of these percep-tions (for example, in Kevin Lynch's 'Image of the City', see Chapter 5), and when it deals with expert or scientific records. The records could be maps, spatial data and layers, air or satellite images, photos and drawings.

Another important practical distinction that is frequently drawn is between *quan-titative* analysis, which is based on measurable dimensions of a landscape and its components, and *qualitative* analysis, which involves assessing the properties of a landscape and its components directly, without using instruments, standard mea-sures or calculations. However, the distinction between quantitative and qualitative analysis is a false dichotomy. Quantitative and qualitative analyses are part of a con-tinuum and depend on the type of measurement used in the analysis (Table 1.1). *Ratio scales* (Figure 1.5) represent the most sophisticated level of measurement, in which the measures include type, rank, relative proportions, and absolute size in rela-tion to a baseline – for example, the metric system used to measure mass and length. This allows a wide range of statistical calculations and mathematical analyses associ-ated with quantitative studies. At the other extreme, the *nominal scale* (Figure 1.8) is the simplest form of measure, and signifies membership of a certain category – for example, forest, field and wetland. It is characteristic of analysis at the qualitative end of the continuum. In between it is possible to use the *interval scale* (Figure 1.6) which is a ratio scale with no absolute zero, which rates items evenly on a scale of 1–5 for example, and the *ordinal scale* (Figure 1.7) which merely ranks items in order – for example, high, medium or low visual quality (Stevens 1946).

All the four scales of measurement are used in landscape analysis, although nominal and ordinal scales are most typical and will be emphasised in this book. Quantitative analysis using ratio and interval measures, including different types of modelling and statistical analysis is of growing importance particularly at grad-uate level, but requires a significant degree of specialised skills and knowledge which are beyond the scope of this text. However, quantitative analyses can use-fully underpin and put into operation many of the approaches and techniques that are included here, and we make reference to this where appropriate.

TABLE 1.1 Four scales of measurement.

Scale	Ratio: Precise numerical relationship	Interval rating	Ordinal ranks	Nominal categories
Example	Elevation above sea level	Exam grades	High, intermediate and low landscape quality	Woodland, grassland and arable land use
Quantitative .... Qualitative				

Source: Based upon Stevens 1946.

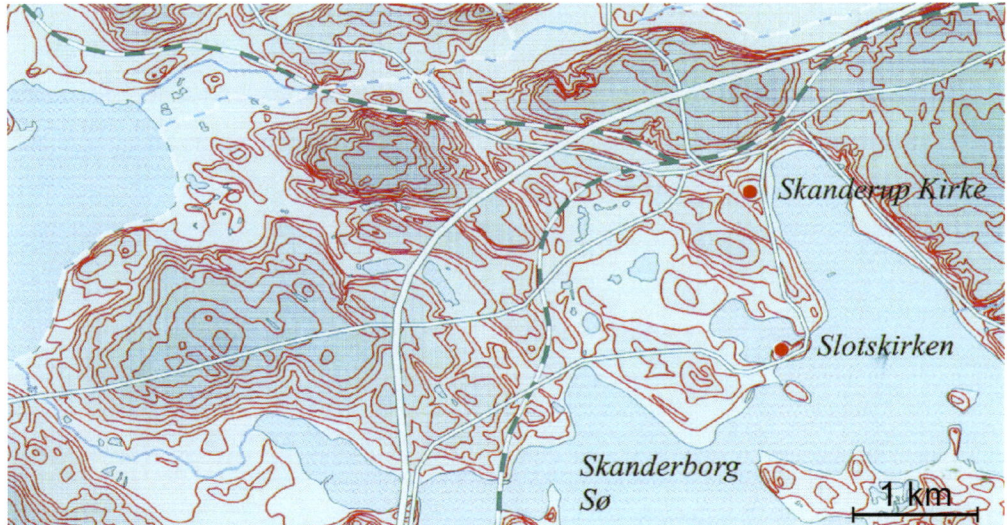

FIGURE 1.5 Ratio scale example
The form of the terrain is expressed by red contour lines, supplemented by toned elevation layers which get darker with increasing height (from 25 to 65 metres above sea
level), a new tone for every 5 metres. The base map is a terrain map supplemented with
lakes and water courses, major roads and with two churches indicated with red dots.
No contour lines are shown below the lake surface. The tones make it easy to recognise
the complexity of the terrain forms in Skanderborg, Eastern Jutland, Denmark.
Source: Danish Ministry of Environment (1997): *Kommuneatlas Skanderborg*, p. 4.

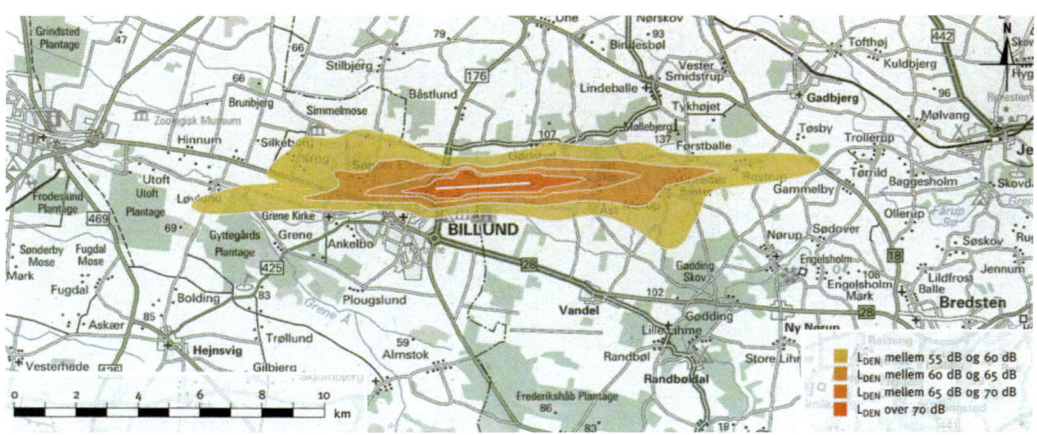

FIGURE 1.6 Interval rating example
The intensity of noise from Billund Airport in Denmark is calculated and represented by
zones, based upon projected maximum traffic volumes.
Source: Ribe County og Vejle County (1998): *VVM-redegørelse for Udvidelse af Billund Lufthavn*.
Ribe og Vejle, p. 54.

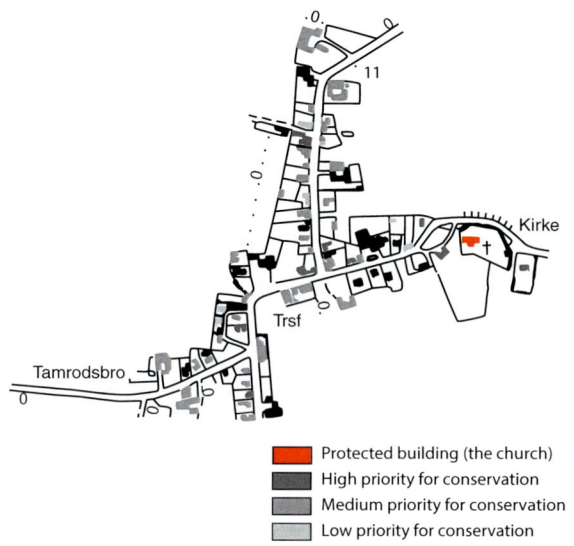

Protected building (the church)
High priority for conservation
Medium priority for conservation
Low priority for conservation

FIGURE 1.7 Ordinal ranks example
The buildings in the Danish village are ranked by priority for conservation. Houses built after 1939 (pale grey) are outside the evaluation.

Source: Danish Ministry of Environment (1993a): *Kommuneatlas Nysted*, p. 32.

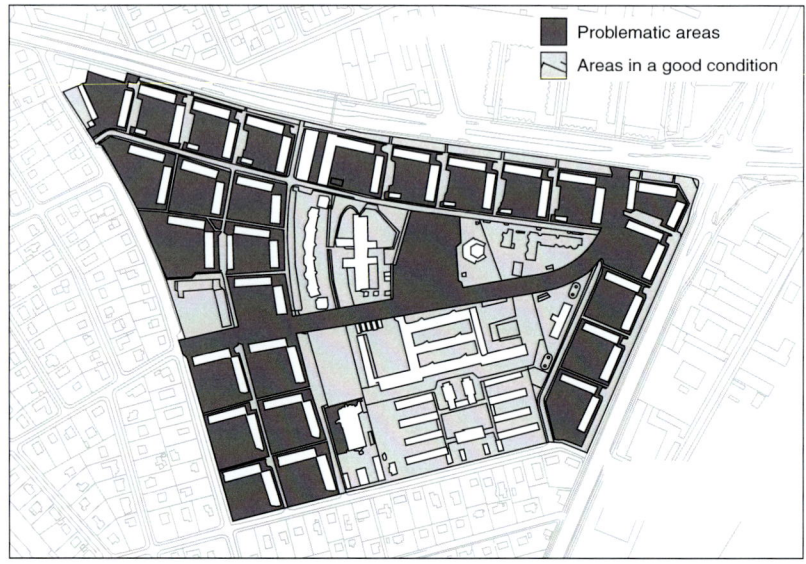

Problematic areas
Areas in a good condition

FIGURE 1.8 Nominal categories example
In a project for improvement of a residential area in Valby, Copenhagen, the initial task was to identify where to focus the effort in the planning process. Housing was therefore divided into two categories: good and problematic. The problematic areas were to be improved in the proposal, whereas areas in good condition were unchanged.

Source: Knudsen, T.T. (1999): *Renovering af boligbebyggelsen Folehaven i Valby*. Master thesis, p. 38. Institute for Economy, Forest & Landscape, Royal Danish Veterinary and Agricultural University. Unpublished.

Scope and settings of landscape analysis

'Landscape' refers to an urban or rural *area* (as defined in the ELC). The scope of landscape analysis can be broken down into a number of dimensions:

- *natural factors* (climate, hydrology, ecology, etc.)
- *biophysical attributes* (terrain, elevation, soil types, drainage networks, vegetation cover, ecotones, built infrastructure, etc.)
- *spatial patterns*, *elements* and *features* (linear, areal, point, etc.) which combine to create landscape *character*)
- *human functions* (food production, recreation, etc.)
- *human interests* (ownership, customary use, etc.)
- *sensory qualities* (visual, sound, smell, etc.)
- *associated meanings* (history, names, etc.) and *values* (price, identity, spiritual, etc.).

It is vital to undertake analysis with a consistent typology of descriptions, and that these are conceptually coherent. In the landscape character assessment (LCA) approach (Swanwick 2002) (see Chapter 6), for example, *character* is defined as 'a distinct, recognisable and consistent pattern of elements in the landscape'. *Characteristics* are 'elements, or combinations of elements, which make a particular contribution to distinctive character'. *Landscape elements* are 'individual components which make up the landscape', such as trees and hedgerows. *Landscape features* are 'particularly prominent or eye-catching elements', like tree clumps, church towers, or wooded skylines. The LCA guidance also includes checklists and worksheets that help assessors maintain consistency when investigating different landscapes. There is a glossary of terms at the end of the book.

Analysis can be applied to a range of *landscape types* (e.g. wilderness, rural, coastal, peri-urban, suburban, urban, etc.) and in each type there may be different distinctive patterns, features and processes. Location and scope of the analysis and whether it is part of a larger comparative investigation is therefore an important consideration in determining which analytical concepts to apply. Many researchers have put forward different systems of analysis each with their own typology of concepts and descriptors, and there is no universally accepted system. This reflects differences in disciplinary approach referred to earlier, differences in culture and native language, and indeed different priorities associated with the range of possible landscape types. Whatever terms are used, it is wise to specify the concepts used in a study at an early stage, and to include this in the final report. Comparisons are also easier if analysts use already established categories.

One analytical approach is to adopt a standard system developed for a particular country or region or profession, such as the LCA. Another is to develop a system specifically for the job at hand, drawing upon relevant research that has been published. Some professional practices and academic institutions promote particular systems of analysis, and it is also important to consider previous work undertaken in the landscape under investigation. This text does not propose a single system: rather it provides examples from a range of applications.

Applications of landscape analysis

This book recognises two broad applications of landscape analysis. *Situation analyses* are aimed at gaining knowledge and understanding of a landscape in advance of any specific proposals, and are not linked to specific plans or actions. A subset of this may be an *analysis of natural factors, biophysical attributes, and land cover* as the basis for asking "What is the connection between the natural factors and the current land use in the site?" Similarly, a *historical analysis* considers the landscape in a time perspective, asking "What has been the trajectory of change in this landscape?" A contemporary way to integrate these situational analyses is through landscape biography, telling the stories of a landscape.

A spatial *analysis* views the landscape in three dimensions, asking "What is the spatial structure and expression of the landscape?" This may lead to *classification into landscape areas* where each piece is a unit that has its own, homogeneous character, and can in turn lead to a *landscape assessment* which considers the dynamics, condition and development of the landscape in terms of its values, potentials, problems and sensitivities.

In contrast to situational analyses, *action-oriented analysis* is guided by the specific planning task at hand. A *site-selection analysis* views a landscape or region as the potential site for a specific development or designation. The question addressed is "Where in the landscape do we find the best possible sites for the proposed development or designation?" The challenge is to sort the possible sites systematically to achieve a logical connection between the goal and the outcome of the analysis. In a *site planning* context, action-oriented landscape analysis may involve site selection, development feasibility, or design feasibility. The perspective will often vary throughout the course of a planning process. *Impact assessments* are carried out once there is a draft (or several alternative drafts) for a plan or a project. "What are the most likely impacts if the proposed plan or project is carried out here or a given development takes place?" The challenge is to assess a future proposed situation to minimise unintended surprises and may lead to the modification of a proposal to avoid, remedy or mitigate its effects. *Futures analysis* undertakes this assessment at a landscape scale, investigating different possible landscape trajectories under different assumptions.

In landscape planning it has been common to distinguish between the phases of survey, analysis and design. Tom Turner criticises this 'SAD-approach' for being too linear, for being based on an underlying assumption that surveys and analyses lead more or less directly to design concepts and solutions. Instead such an approach leads to mechanistic and 'sad' results according to Turner (1996, p. 146). Although Turner has a point – survey and analyses are not enough to produce good design and planning solutions – they may be needed as a foundation on which such solutions can be based. For an interesting discussion of landscape analysis and intuition see Turner's (1991) and Richard Stiles' (1992a and 1992b) debate in the journal *Landscape Design*. In our view the need for landscape analysis is determined by the complexity and scale of the design and planning task, and landscape analyses must not be added as dead weight in reports. Analyses which are of no functional relevance but which are included to make the project *appear* well grounded should be avoided.

In this chapter we have introduced the basic aims, types and concepts of landscape analysis. The scope is shaped by practice and theory in landscape architecture and landscape planning, drawing upon these and closely related disciplines. In the next chapter we consider the nature of landscape values and their role in landscape analysis.

2

FRAMING ANALYSIS

Values, experts and citizens

Introduction

The different demands upon landscapes mean that analysis of landscape characteristics must extend beyond consideration of the condition of the landscape, and how it is changing, to also include assessment of the values associated with landscape structure, function and process. The recognition of values within a landscape analysis requires a careful and clear organisation of the process of spatially explicit mapping and assessment. Many analysis systems involve a step-by-step process of:

Description (what are the landscape attributes, elements, features and patterns?)

Characterisation and classification (what are the distinctive attributes, elements, features and patterns that make this a particular type of landscape?)

Valuation (what qualities does the landscape offer, what functions and benefits does it provide, and hence how do people value this landscape?)

Evaluation (what is the comparative value of this landscape compared with others?).

Choosing the way to assess the values in any particular landscape is not something we can take for granted. Nor can we assume whose voice or expertise should undertake or influence the assessment process or the decisions about outcomes.

This chapter considers the nature of landscape values, how they may be categorised and framed, and considers how this relates to the people involved. We start the chapter with a brief consideration of how different ways of landscape planning make different assumptions about who makes decisions, and about whose values should influence the decisions. We then review the stages and ways of involving citizens – owners, users and other stakeholders – in the analysis process. Finally, the process of collecting information on values and preferences is considered, including the role of experts and local knowledge and values. We use the term assessment to refer to the overall process of considering landscape values. This includes specific tasks of valuation (identifying and measuring values), evaluation (comparing values), and judgements of which values to highlight or prioritise.

Framing values

A simple definition of planning is 'linking knowledge to action' (Friedmann 1987). 'Knowledge' in this context includes values associated with the region, landscape or site in question, and 'linking' refers to the overall process of preparing for action. The way the landscape planning process is understood and undertaken inevitably shapes how values are defined and identified, and hence whose values are taken into account. This can be illustrated by a comparison of two contrasting models of planning. Planning theorists have made a long-standing distinction between *substantive* theories, which are concerned with what planning is or should be about, what the content of good places should be, and what planning solutions should look like, and *procedural* theories which deal with how the planning process should be organised and who should be involved (Davoudi and Strange 2009; Hall and Tewdwr-Jones 2010; Healey 1998). Different types of value are relevant to each perspective.

From a substantive perspective, our focus will be upon landscape character, condition and use. We might be concerned with identifying values that relate to the Potschin ecological function of a landscape, or what heritage features are significant and should be preserved, or how public open space is used. Such substantive values are linked to or produced by landscape 'functions' and 'services' (Potschin and Haines-Young 2006; Termorshuizen and Opdam 2009; Selman 2009). In a landscape analysis context this will open questions about how to identify, describe and measure landscape values.

From a procedural perspective, on the other hand, we are concerned with determining who should be involved, when and how. The decision here will be determined by the political values, laws and institutions of the country and place in which we are working. It may be framed through classifications of who has different kinds of interest in a particular landscape – such as residents, land owners, citizens, etc. – and will consider the way the planning process is organised. The decision-making should take place in respect to consensus building, the role of the experts, openness towards other's viewpoints and values and allocation of powers (Healey 1993).

In the real world, substance and process are typically intertwined, as are assumptions about the relationship of the planning activity to the wider political economy and culture. These conditions frame the values that are of relevance and crucial for how they should be determined. There is a spectrum of possibilities. Some decisions over landscape change are made 'top-down', and the values that predominate are the values determined by those in power. Woodrow Wilson, who was later to become President of the USA, argued that public administration should

promote the interests of the state, with decisions made by professional administrators (Wilson 1887). The 19th century designation and compulsory acquisition of
the early national parks and reserves is an example of this type of planning, where
a government *bureaucracy* decides on a course of landscape-related action and
the values that are relevant. The European strategy for a continental network of
habitats, the NATURA 2000 Network, is another example of a top-down decision
mainly influenced by administrators, in this case the EU Commission in cooperation
with national experts in the member states (see Figure 2.1).

'Top-down' perspectives are needed to shape and validate legislative or strategic action that may commit major public expenditure or changes to individual's
rights, or to make commitments to long-term programmes. Locating a new town
for instance is an example of a planning task in which top-down decision-making
is likely to dominate due to the complex technical dimensions of such a project
and its high costs. However, it is also clear that top-down decision-making is open
to abuse and failure, and by the 1970s an alternative to traditional government

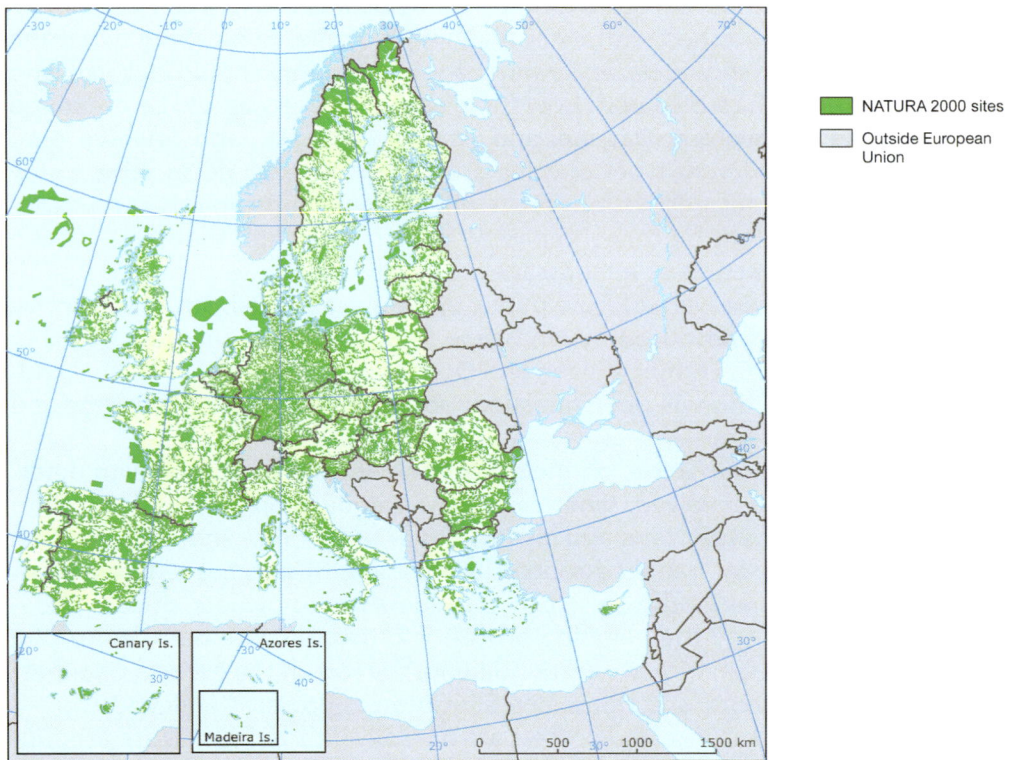

FIGURE 2.1 Distribution of NATURA 2000 sites across the EU, 2012
NATURA 2000 is a network of important habitats across the EU. Habitats designated
and protected through the EU Bird Protection Directive and Habitat Directive are
included in the network.
Source: European Environmental Agency (2014).

bureaucracy had developed, called 'public choice' theory (Ostrom and Ostrom 1971). Public choice places emphasis on the need for effectiveness in meeting clearly stated public goals, and is intended to constrain the actions of government agencies and departments and steer them towards narrower and more transparent outcomes. Environmental assessment (Chapter 8) is an example of a process developed initially as a way to ensure that the actions of government agencies were accountable to the wider public interest in relation to the environment.

A focus on action by public agencies tends to emphasise *technical* expertise in assessment, and early work on landscape assessment was based upon the assumption that it required expert knowledge (Zube, Sell and Taylor 1982). The assessment role was therefore assigned to technical experts, such as landscape architects, who use their professional knowledge and training to identify, measure and compare values. A focus on expertise tends to privilege the idea that values are generic in character, are associated to different degrees with particular places and phenomena, and can be identified by those with the right professional skills.

Place-making (through site design, for example) and conflict management (through environmental assessment, for example) are two common and equally important dimensions in spatial planning, including landscape planning, where the first dimension traditionally has been focused on substance and the second on processes. For planning to be effective, however, both dimensions should be considered (Healey 1998).

However, the mid-20th century was also a time when the power of community and local democracy was becoming more widely recognised in developed countries, and local social movements became more active in environmental advocacy and debate. The era of *'public participation'* had begun, where citizens demanded and governments slowly provided increased opportunity to become involved in planning processes for landscape change (Hester 1984). Hence valuation also became 'bottom-up', as different groups and communities expressed the matters that concerned them. The idea that values are closely connected with and expressed by individuals and communities leads to a need for processes to identify who has a potential interest, and what it is that they specifically value.

At the same time, improved understanding of the decision-making process regarding public policy has made clear that the process of shaping and making policy is more subtle and complex than *administrative, technical* or *participatory* models imply. In a modern democratic country, power is distributed widely and constantly renegotiated (Forrester 1989). In order to take action, decision-makers need to persuade others, and two powerful ideas become central to the process. First is the notion that *planning is discursive* – that is, it is not primarily a bureaucratic or technical procedure, but an open process in which different groups, interests and agencies engage in dialogue about what might and should happen (Drysek 1990, 2000; Fischer and Forester 1993). Second, in order for decisions to be made and enacted, there needs to be sufficient support and agreement from a network of groups, who create coalitions of interest (Sabatier and Jenkins-Smith 1993) to promote and implement particular types of change. So values become part of a conversation, and may be shaped and reshaped through *discourse.*

Types of values

What are values? Values are concepts or beliefs about outcomes that transcend specific situations, guide evaluation and action, and are typically ordered in relative importance (Schwartz and Bilsky 1987). The *Oxford English Dictionary* identifies three broad value categories: *worth; preference/opinion;* and *morality*. Values may therefore be expressed in many ways, and can (Dietz et al. 2005) refer to:

- fundamental or intrinsic worth, both human and non-human
- instrumental usefulness
- exchange value in monetary terms
- individual preferences
- principles that underpin social and cultural norms and activity.

Landscape values have also been classified in a range of ways. Some authors distinguish between natural and cultural values. Others distinguish between monetary values – landscape attributes to which an exchange value can be assigned – and non-monetary values that cannot be measured – for example, spiritual values (Millennium Ecosystem Assessment 2005). A common working distinction is between values that are related to the use of particular *landscape attributes* (e.g. ecosystem functions), values that express *social or cultural norms and expectations*, and *individual preferences and interests* (Andrews 1979; Swaffield 2013).

Some researchers have investigated the degree of commonality between different types of value – for example, ecological and visual values (Tveit et al. 2006). An important insight has emerged which suggests that the way people understand and value landscape features (such as conservation reserves) depends upon how they are 'framed' through landscape management (Nassauer 1995, 1997). The evidence of stewardship increases perceived value. Landscape character assessment (Swanwick 2002) brings another new dimension to analysis in which the focus is upon the distinctive identity of *every* landscape, not just those that stand out as valuable. This concern for everyday landscapes highlights the importance of the collective values that shape landscape management practices, and the particular local values recognised by communities (Stephenson 2008).

An influential contemporary approach to understanding conditions and values in landscape is the idea of ecosystem services, which identifies and evaluates the benefits that ecosystems are believed to provide for communities (Millennium Ecosystem Assessment 2005; Potschin and Haines-Young 2006). The MEA distinguishes between *provisioning services* (e.g. food), *regulating services* (e.g. flood control), *supporting services* (e.g. biodiversity) and *cultural services* (e.g. aesthetics). Each of the services is 'delivering' different kinds of benefit or value to people. Hence analysis should distinguish between the *biophysical attributes of a landscape* (e.g. soil and landform structure and condition), *the services it can supply* (e.g. agriculture) and *the benefits that particular people receive* (e.g. income, food, aesthetic enjoyment of views) (Swaffield and McWilliam 2014).

However, Antrop (2000) has shown how the value of a landscape component depends both upon its inherent characteristics *and* its context in the wider landscape. A rock face may be one of many in a large mountainous area, and of little specific significance, but if the same type of rock face is a unique feature within a rolling down land it may assume much greater significance – that is, it has a different value. Hence value depends upon location. Termorshuizen and Opdam (2009) have therefore developed the concept of landscape services, with explicit recognition of spatially expressed values. Their model proposes that particular landscape structural attributes provide functions which have specific value to particular people or communities. Landscape thus becomes conceptualised as a spatially explicit system of structure–function–value.

One of the biggest challenges in landscape analysis and assessment is that values associated with landscape therefore depend upon the perspective from which they are assessed. The assessment determines both the values of relevance and how they are evaluated compared with other values and other landscapes. A particular river may have different values for a local fisherman than for a national hydropower company, and a particular type of river may have different values depending on where it is located. Comparing and weighing up values that are significant for different communities is one of the hardest tasks in landscape analysis.

KARBY – AN EXAMPLE OF MANAGING VALUES

The example of the landscape strategy for Karby on the island of Mors, Northern Jutland, in Denmark illustrates the challenge of identifying local and wider landscape values, and shows how a discursive process can lead to a solution that is appropriate to the context. In 2010 the Karby parish participated in an experimental programme on new ways to include local communities in rural landscape planning. The parish is located along a fjord with relatively large salt marsh lands along the coast (Figure 2.2). Historically these salt marshes were naturally *fertilised* through nutrients left by the fjord during frequent flooding, and were a valuable resource for the farmers. The marshes produced fodder for cattle, which in turn – during winter time in the barn – produced dung to be spread on the arable fields. Today there is no economic value in the salt marshes for the farmers. A few of the marshes have been converted into arable fields, and more have been abandoned. However, the salt marshes are now recognised to represent semi-natural bird habitats of international importance and most of the Karby salt marshes are designated as NATURA 2000 areas, which means that they are highly protected according to European Union law, and must be maintained according to an approved management plan.

The nature value of the salt marshes is their function as feeding grounds for migrating birds from northern Scandinavia when they pass by during spring and autumn, or when they use the salt marshes as their winter quarters during mild winters. However, the geese and wading birds can only benefit

FIGURE 2.2 Karby village
The village on the island of Mors, Denmark, is situated in between arable loamy soils and extensive salt marsh areas along a fjord, representing a classical 'edge' location for an old village. Until the middle of the 20th century the salt marshes were valuable and integrated parts of the farm systems, providing grass for the livestock which in turn produced manure to use on the fields. Today the salt marshes have lost economic importance for farms. Grazing is, however, very important for the maintenance of the semi-natural habitat. Without grazing the marsh would lose its international importance as a feeding ground for birds migrating from North Europe to the South.
Source: Photo by Primdahl, J.

from the salt marshes if they are grassed. Here is the dilemma, as there is a contrast between the farmers' view of the salt marshes as a local agricultural asset and European society's view of the salt marshes as an internationally important habitat. Usually this type of issue is solved in a European context through offering the individual farmer a voluntary management agreement which will provide some financial compensation to manage the salt marsh in a way that is suitable for the birds. But it can be hard to coordinate the outcomes. In the Karby planning process the dilemma was solved in an exemplary way.

First, a common understanding of the rural landscape and its values was developed through a process that involved external experts, excursions to other rural landscapes, interview surveys, and a workshop. All farmers were interviewed about their farm, their landscape practices, and the valuable sites in the area as they perceived them (Figure 2.3). Following the workshop the

FIGURE 2.3 Favourite places in Karby
During personal interviews concerning the farmers themselves, their farm properties and their land use, the persons interviewed were asked to mark his or her favourite places in the parish. The questions, deliberately broadly formulated, were: *"Which areas do you find particularly valuable in relation to nature and landscape? Where do you prefer to go for a view or a walk?"* Here all of the answers are put together on one map.
Source: Nellemann et al (2015): *Strategi for Karby Sogn – landskab og landsby*. In Kristensen, Primdahl and Vejre (eds), Dialogbaseret planlaegning i det aabne land – om strategier for kultur-landskabets fremtid, p. 75. © BOEGVAERKET, authors and photographers, 2015. ©GST. Contains data from the Danish Geodata Agency.

15 farmers who owned salt marsh land made a collective management agreement involving all the 250 ha of salt marsh, which also included the establishment of a walking trail and construction of a bird-watching tower (Figure 2.4).

In this example the individual farmers each got support though EU agri-environmental measures as part of an area-wide agreement for all the 250 ha of salt marsh. The agreement was relatively attractive because the various use rights were combined into larger, more economic units. Wider society benefited from the simple solution which reduced the costs of negotiation, etc., and the pasture management became more sustainable and resilient because

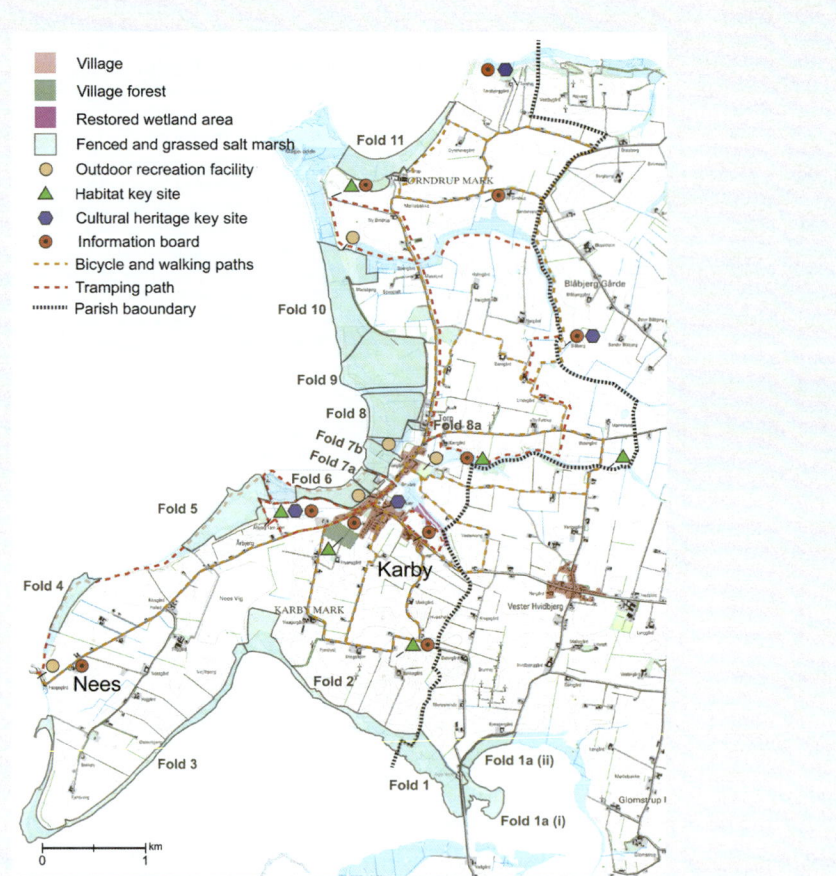

Village
Village forest
Restored wetland area
Fenced and grassed salt marsh
Outdoor recreation facility
Habitat key site
Cultural heritage key site
Information board
--- Bicycle and walking paths
-·-· Tramping path
········ Parish baoundary

FIGURE 2.4 Strategy for Karby
The Strategy for Karby includes a number of actions and projects including new walking paths, a bird-watching tower, wetland restorations and a salt marsh management plan including fencing and a grassland management scheme covering almost all the salt area in the parish. 'Fold' on the map means 'enclosure'.

Source: Nellemann et al (2015): *Strategi for Karby Sogn – landskab og landsby*. In Kristensen, Primdahl and Vejre (eds), Dialogbaseret planlaegning i det aabne land – om strategier for kultur-landskabets fremtid, p. 75. © BOEGVAERKET, authors and photographers, 2015. ©GST. Contains data from the Danish Geodata Agency.

farmers cooperated in allocating the cattle to the different fens. Outdoor recreationalists also benefited from the project due to new access provisions and a bird-watching tower donated by a foundation which also owns salt marsh land in the area.

The Karby example illustrates how careful and inclusive analysis of landscape conditions and of values held by different people and at different levels can lead to solutions that both protect existing values and add new values to the landscape.

Identifying citizens, communities and stakeholders

As the Karby example shows, there are a number of ways to define the people who have an interest in the landscape, and the values that shape public planning action. The most inclusive category is to talk about *humans*. Egoz et al. (2011) have developed an idea of landscape 'rights' to sit alongside other statements of human rights, in which they focus on landscape rights as a critical nexus in linking universal human rights (human wellbeing and dignity) with particular landscape resources and landscape values. The 'right to landscape' approach is conceptually and morally connected to the way the European Landscape Convention has evolved and is applied (Chapter 9).

A slightly less broad category which is widely used in landscape planning is the role of *citizens*. Citizenship implies a set of rights and responsibilities that individuals may hold in relationship to a defined political entity or territory. Originating from Greek city states in the ancient world, citizenship is now most commonly formally associated with having rights to vote in some level of representative democracy, such as a nation state or a particular town or city, and confers a strong sense of belonging and mutual obligation. Many governmental processes requiring involvement of people in planning and assessment assume a constituency of citizens whose views and values need to be identified and taken into account. However, citizenship may exclude visitors or those who do not have full rights of residency. At the same time, not all citizens have equal capacity to become engaged – children, for example, may not have the skills needed by some forms of engagement (such as a public meeting) – and special processes may be needed.

Community is also widely used to describe who should be involved in landscape planning and decision-making, but has many possible interpretations. The common feature of all communities is their collective nature, as they always comprise a group of people who have some measure of shared experience, knowledge, or interests, and collaborate in some way to achieve a collective goal or action. However, the reasons for particular communities to evolve are different.

Three types of community are especially relevant to landscape analysis. The first is *communities of place* – the people who live together in a particular place or landscape. This type of community is defined by space or territory. However, in an increasingly mobile world, this is not as simple as it sounds. Some people have more than one home, or may have moved away from their childhood home but still retain strong connections. Are they members of the community of that particular place?

Communities of practice are people who share distinctive knowledge, skills and habits of action. In landscape analysis it is important to understand how particular landscapes are managed, and this may involve people from different place communities who collaborate in some way to manage a particular landscape in a distinctive way. It could be hunters who collectively manage a game resource, or farmers who share certain styles of farming (organic dairy farmers, for example). Landscape architects are also a community of practice in the way we share particular knowledge and skills.

Communities of interest are people who share a material, financial, spiritual or other interest in the outcomes of landscape management and landscape change.

They may be land owners, or members of a conservation society. Descendants of earlier inhabitants who live elsewhere but retain a concern and feeling for a landscape could also be part of a community of Interest. Members of a community of interest may not live together or even act together; indeed they frequently have conflicting views. Defining the relevant community or communities of place, practice and interest is a critical part of identifying relevant landscape values.

Stakeholder is a relatively new term that is increasingly used in planning, and has gained wide currency in approaches that emphasise defined interests rather than a general citizenship or place community. Stakeholder implies someone with a legitimate interest in a situation, and that may include legal or financial interests exercised at a distance, even from different constituencies, as well as place-based interests. Hence global consumers, or shareholders in a transnational company, may be considered stakeholders in a local landscape from which they purchase goods or in which they invest. It is clear that stakeholders can be a very elastic term depending on how legitimate interest is defined. Equally, a tight definition of stakeholders can exclude people who feel they have a right to be involved, but may not be acknowledged or recognised by a planning authority.

In a landscape-analysis context it may be useful to include a systematic analysis of the stakeholders who have an interest in the project in questions. Who are they? What power do they have? What is their role, what 'hat' are they wearing? To what networks and alliances do they belong? What interest would they have in the landscape analysis in question? Such questions may be of relevance to many kinds of landscape analysis. Ramirez (1999) and Reed et al. (2009) provide systematic and practice-oriented overviews of the relevance of and methodological approach to stakeholder analysis.

Ownership is a specific form of interest in landscape, and is normally associated with a title to exercise a set of rights of some kind on a defined area of land, such as use, occupancy, and the ability to sell and to take certain resources. There are also a wide range of other customary-use rights that may link individuals or groups of people to a particular landscape without conferring land ownership in the modern legal sense, but which nonetheless may involve legal rights (e.g. hunting) and give rise to a strong sense of moral or psychological interest.

In some landscapes, ownership, customary or use rights may be held by people who are not resident and who may only visit very occasionally, or even not at all. They may also change over time – for example, leasehold rights typically have a defined time limit. On the other hand, sustained involvement in landscape practices over a period of time – such as walking across a field – may lead to new rights being acquired. In some situations those with a right to be consulted or heard are defined by statute or local laws. In other situations it may be less clear, and defining those who may have an interest in a landscape is difficult. Analysis can therefore be a challenging and far from straightforward task, and deciding who has a legitimate voice in identifying landscape values can be a significant part of the analysis process. Relationships between indigenous cultures or long-time citizens and more recent arrivals in a country or landscape can be a particular source of friction and contest, and other tensions emerge between 'city' and 'country' and different communities of interest.

Most landscape-planning tasks involve issues where there are different judgements by experts and communities about particular landscape values, and different interests in the outcomes. If these differences are to be dealt with in a fair and democratic way it is vital that all legitimate interests are heard, and conflicts over existing values are dealt with in comprehensive, balanced and just ways. However, as the Karby example showed, landscape planning is about more than dealing with conflict resolution and protecting existing values. It is also about creating new values and shaping change in positive directions – for example, making new residential areas, creating new public squares, or establishing green infrastructure. In short, it is also about place-making. A typical landscape analysis task involving both conflict-management and place-making dimensions therefore requires involvement of different communities – not only to be fair, but also to be effective (Healey 2009).

In addition to a range of possible ways to define *who* might be involved, there is also a range of potential *levels* of involvement in identifying landscape values. Arnstein (1969) suggested a 'ladder of involvement' in planning which is still widely quoted today. The lowest levels of involvement are described as *non-participatory*, being focused upon manipulation of sentiment and reassurance using public media to shape and steer opinion. Intermediate levels might involve *providing information about a proposed change,* or *asking for opinions.* A very high level could mean giving people the *power to decide,* either in partnership, through delegation, or at the highest level, by *empowerment to act.*

Critics argue that Arnstein's model is insufficient to describe the nature of contemporary participatory planning, which is a much more complex and dynamic process involving social learning, deliberation and adaptation. Selman (2004) therefore sees the range of possible involvements more as a continuum of possibilities rather than a ladder, from minimal participation, to participation for material incentives, to interactive participation, and then self-mobilisation, where other landscape agents – such as land owners, communities or businesses – take action independent of government agencies. The emerging area of landscape democracy and co-management, and its implications for analysis, is discussed in Chapter 9.

Collecting information on values

There are a number of texts that provide knowledge and advice on *how* to undertake different types of engagement about landscape with people and communities, and the social and policy sciences have large bodies of theoretical and applied knowledge about the different methods and their assumptions, strengths and weaknesses. A simple basic distinction is between *direct* and *indirect* methods. *Direct* methods involve the landscape analyst in communications or face-to-face meetings with citizens, stakeholders or communities. *Indirect* or secondary methods rely upon some intermediate filter – for example, an analyst might use data from a census undertaken by government in order to derive or infer information about landscape values of a particular community.

Direct methods can be *individual*, one-on-one, or can involve *groups* of people. There are advantages and disadvantages of each. *Individual* methods allow detailed investigation of personal or sensitive issues – for example, through in-depth interviews which also enable a high level of confidentiality to be provided. Other types of one-on-one direct contact such as questionnaires can be distributed to large numbers of people, and a good sample design enables statistical analysis of the results, which may support the development of predictive models.

Group methods involve people being engaged with an assessment process in some collective way – for example, in focus group interviews, workshops, or public meetings such as those used in the Karby example. Group methods can be very creative and also enable social learning to take place easily (Figures 2.5 and 2.6).

FIGURE 2.5 Focus group interview
Focus group interviews can be efficient ways to collect information about values and at the same time be integrated parts of the collaborative planning process. The picture was taken during a coffee break at a workshop with full-time farmers. The aim was to identify valuable landscape issues for commercial farmers to be dealt with by a coming planning process. The size of the group – 15 participants – enabled a direct semi-structured debate and systematic 'rounds' where every participant was expected to express his or her view of the issue in question.
Source: Photo by Primdahl, J.

FIGURE 2.6 Options
People gathered to get information of the results of a survey they had participated in. During the presentation of the results they were frequently asked what they believed would be the overall results of certain questions – before these results were presented. This procedure subsequently triggered engaged discussions, including debates about landscape values, discussions which are often difficult to start up.
Source: Photo by Møller, K. H.

However, they may also reveal conflicting values or divisions over preferred courses of action and require careful management. What people say is heard by others in the community, which can disadvantage people with minority views or who feel uncomfortable about speaking in public. They can also result in more weight being given to a limited number of articulate or forceful individuals within the group. Management of group processes is therefore a skilled role.

The direct, indirect, individual and group approaches can sometimes be combined. When people are gathered at public meetings they can be confronted with analysis already done (or done in another place with a value context similar to the one in question), and values identified though indirect methods can be discussed by people. In the Karby example, visiting experts added their understanding to that of local farmers. If there is a concern that strong voices may dominate, people can be asked to reply individually to questions by filling out questionnaires, or by anonymously pressing buttons (Figure 2.6).

Irrespective of the type of approach used, there is an expectation that the consultation should be genuine and open, timely, and carefully planned with clear objectives (Landscape Institute 2013). Having clear objectives is vital to avoid wasting people's time and to ensure that the methods are appropriate to the task. All research institutions such as universities have protocols to ensure that research involving people is ethical. Private consultants or public authorities may not have such formal processes, and it is sensible to seek guidance from experienced researchers before launching into a major participation exercise.

In addition to ensuring that the process is ethical and will not result in harm, it is also important to avoid raising expectations about what the outcomes might be. Asking people what they would like for their community is fine provided that there is a possibility of their replies having some practical effect. This is where Arnstein's ladder retains its value, as a critical check to ensure that the process being proposed is appropriate and defensible, and is not just a 'tick in the box'.

What makes participation exemplary rather than good? Hester argues that it means dealing with difference, engaging community with expert, engaging citizens with complexity, and engaging local communities with their wider region. In other words, it is a challenge in any landscape-planning project to raise the engagement beyond personal and local self-interest and to recognise the wider range of considerations involved.

Conclusion

In this chapter we have considered the nature of landscape values, the importance of the decision-making context in determining how to investigate landscape values, and the question of whose knowledge and values might and should inform landscape analysis. We have argued that contemporary landscape planning has moved beyond bureaucratic and technical analysis and decision-making, and is now recognised as a discursive activity; an activity that involves a range of participants, each with different interests, knowledge and values that they bring to the process. As experts within a discursive process, landscape architects must develop skills in becoming collaborators in the co-production of knowledge and solutions. In the following chapters we examine the technical aspects of analysis in detail, but in every case the discursive context will be vital in shaping how the analysis is designed and implemented. In the final chapter we return to the question of citizen involvement in analysis through the concept of landscape democracy.

3

ANALYSIS OF NATURAL FACTORS, BIOPHYSICAL ATTRIBUTES AND LAND USE

Introduction

Consideration of natural factors, biophysical attributes (including land cover) and land use has several roles in landscape analysis: it provides an objective context for analysis of cultural social and visual aspects of landscape; provides vital evidence for understanding landscape history, dynamics and change; is a vital part of landscape character assessment, as well as assessment of possible biophysical impacts of proposed development; and provides vital data for planning and design.

Natural factors refer to the fundamental natural drivers that shape the underlying structure and dynamics of landscape systems: climate, geology and geomorphology, hydrology and ecology. These natural factors in the landscape are increasingly affected to some degree by human activity – whether past or present. Thus, natural factors are seldom free or independent of cultural influences, but comprise systems, forms, processes and features in a landscape that are predominantly natural rather than cultural in origin and character. *Biophysical attributes* are the specific conditions in a particular landscape such as terrain, elevation, soil types, wetlands and waterway networks, vegetation and habitat, built infrastructure, etc. Biophysical analysis therefore includes consideration of both human and non-human features and patterns, but is focused upon the material landscape, rather than the social or experiential landscape. *Land cover* refers to the biophysical surface conditions of a landscape. *Land use* refers to the human activities undertaken to produce, change or maintain particular land cover.

As noted in Chapter 1 there are several ways to undertake classification of biophysical data related to land and landscape analysis (Mabbutt 1968). Natural factors such as geology, geomorphology, and river systems – whose character is strongly shaped by their formative processes – are typically classified according to their origins (*genetic*). *Parametric* classification is commonly used for landscape attributes such as terrain, land cover, and infrastructure networks that can be accurately recorded using higher levels of measurement. '*Landscape*' characterisation is typically used for assessment of 'landscapes as perceived by people' (Council of Europe 2000) and is influenced by natural factors, biophysical attributes including land cover, and land use. A comprehensive analysis of natural factors, biophysical attributes, land cover and land use may therefore include different types of classification systems and data.

The extensive scientific knowledge base relating to natural factors, land cover and land use means that landscape architects undertaking landscape analysis as a professional activity seldom need to undertake primary-field research to gain data on these aspects. Rather, the task is primarily one of accessing, collating, interpreting and synthesising existing sources of information, and checking its accuracy and relevance on site in the context of the project. Geographic information systems are now a dominant mode of mapping different information layers. A practical challenge in biophysical landscape analysis is the transformation of the different sources into a common data set that is spatially and temporally integrated

FIGURE 3.1 La Palma, Canary Islands
Grazing is abandoned on the steep slopes of the ravines and the forest has taken over. Only a few of the best terraces are still intensively cultivated. Constraints due to natural factors, especially the terrain form, combined with social factors will cause fundamental changes in land use and land cover in this landscape.
Source: Photo by Stahlschmidt, P.

and consistent across scales. However, the assessment of data availability; coverage and age, validity (whether data actually relates to the phenomenon it claims to describe), reliability (whether the data is described consistently) and spatial calibration; and combination of different types of data are a major research topic and beyond the scope of this text.

The purpose of this chapter is therefore to convey a practical rather than technical and scientific understanding of biophysical landscape analysis. The majority of examples use traditional modes of integration based on layered maps, sketches and diagrams, and annotated photos, in order to focus upon analysis fundamentals. The cases that serve as variations on the main case are arranged under the headings of terrain, soils, hydrology and land use.

Natural factors

Geology refers to the underlying structure of the earth. Geological maps for public use typically show the rock type closest to the earth's surface. Geology is a driver of landform at a macro scale – shaping mountain areas and uplands, major valley systems, and in some cases particular landscape features – for example, where major fault lines break the surface. In the UK the landscape character areas identified in sources such as the Natural Areas of England (Swanwich 2002) correspond broadly with the type of geology maps familiar to generations of students, which themselves were developed in the early 19th century by William Smith, an early surveyor working on canals (Winchester 2001). However, while geology is helpful in understanding the overall patterns of a landscape, the deep geological structure is frequently overlaid by surface deposits, and at a project scale it is often more helpful to focus upon geomorphology.

Geomorphology is the branch of geology that deals with the earth's surface and refers to the study of surface terrain and its formation. Typically, this relates to processes in the past such as glaciation and fluvial processes, but it also includes contemporary processes related to influences from sea and climate – for example, the formation of dunes and land spits. Regardless of the purpose of the landscape analysis, knowledge about the geomorphological formation of the landscape is almost always a good basis for developing a background understanding of the site, and when describing a landscape it is useful to begin with a geomorphological description – for example, by stating that the city of Amsterdam is located in a major river delta or that Stockholm is part of a large archipelago in the Baltic Sea. Using such terms provides a link to the general formation of the landscape and gives indications of more general biophysical conditions of the landscape character and processes.

Hydrological systems are crucial components of every natural landscape, and also every human–ecological system, as they shape land cover and in particular habitat and biodiversity, influence land use and the potential for agriculture, provide critical resources (irrigation, drinking water, industry, etc.) and have a major influence on the perceptual experience of the landscape. Presence of surface water is a key determinant of scenic quality. Improved planning standards – including requirements regarding water quality and discharge of rainwater and storm water from development – mean that knowledge of hydrological conditions is critical to:

- the assessment of environmental impacts of projects
- ecological restoration projects, and to projects that seek to enhance the resilience of settlements
- climate change, increasing sea levels and more frequent extreme rainfall events.

The classification of surface terrain according to its formation is a critical indicator of many landscape attributes, potentials and limitations – including characteristic terrain form, ground stability and erosion status and potential, hydrology and surface-water networks and soils as well as spatial features and appearance. Understanding the geomorphological history of a landscape also provides a conceptual framework that is often more tangible than deep geology, and use of scientific knowledge about the types of surface terrain and their formation that are common in a landscape can help engage local communities with the analysis process – for example, through landscape biography (Roymans et al. 2009). After all, in the final assessment, landscape analysis is about telling stories that help communities and decision-makers determine a future course of action. While knowing that a feature was created by a glacier may not change a decision, it can help provide an informed, meaningful, engaging and hence evocative context for decision-making.

Land cover

The Food and Agriculture Organization (FAO) of the United Nations defines land cover as 'the observed (bio)physical cover on the earth's surface' (Di Gregorio and Jansen 2000). The science of landscape ecology has developed a sophisticated spatial language to describe and analyse patterns of land cover (Forman 1995) involving concepts of patch, edge, corridor, and matrix or mosaic (a combination of patches and corridors). Landscape analysis as a professional activity also makes extensive use of the concept of landscape features, which refers to particular parts of the land-cover mosaic such as hedges, woods, roads and buildings. These features may be point, linear, or areal features. It is vital to clarify the spatial language being used in an analysis and to be consistent in its application.

Land-cover information may be sourced from a range of organisations, depending upon the country you are working in. It is now usually in the form of a digital database, or digital maps, which can also be supplemented with air photos or satellite images. This allows for a more precise interpretation of land cover than a topographic map. With software programs such as Google Earth™ it is possible to combine terrain models, satellite photos and aerial photos. The programs also make it possible to look at areas in a vertical or an oblique perspective and to rotate the images and view them from different angles. A European land-cover database, the so-called Corine Land-Cover maps are available from the European Environment Agency (www.eea.europa.eu).

Land cover largely comprises different types of vegetation, but also includes bare natural areas and constructed surfaces such as buildings and roads. Land cover may be either natural or cultural, or a combination created by human management of natural vegetation and animals. As with soil classifications, there have been many land-cover classification systems developed in different countries and for different purposes, and much effort has been devoted to developing a more standardised system for global comparison. The FAO classification has eight categories (Table 3.1), which are summarised below. Within these categories there are many national and regional variations, but the FAO provides a broad framework useful worldwide.

Terrestrial natural /semi-natural vegetated areas are areas where the vegetative cover is in balance with and an integral part of the abiotic and biotic systems, or where vegetation is naturally occurring but influenced by human actions, such as open dunes or moorlands used for grazing.

Terrestrial cultivated and managed vegetated areas are where the natural vegetation has been removed or modified and replaced by other types of vegetative cover of human origin. This vegetation requires cultural activities such as agriculture to maintain it in the long term, and includes agrarian landscapes, intensively managed and planted forests, and open recreation areas including parks. It is the largest and most common category in many temperate countries.

Aquatic or regularly flooded areas with vegetation can be natural or semi-natural. They are transitional between terrestrial and aquatic systems, and are where the water table is usually at or near the surface, or the land is covered by shallow water and the vegetative cover is significantly influenced by water and dependent on flooding (e.g. salt marshes and wetlands). Cultivated aquatic areas are where an aquatic crop is purposely planted, cultivated and harvested, and which is standing in water over extensive periods during its cultivation period – such as paddy rice. They are less common in temperate countries. Figure 3.23 is an example of a detailed survey of a wetland biotope.

TABLE 3.1 Categories of land cover.

The FAO subdivide Land Cover into eight main types							
Primarily vegetated areas				*Primarily non-vegetated areas*			
Terrestrial		*Aquatic or regularly flooded*		*Terrestrial*		*Aquatic; snow and ice*	
(Semi) Natural	Cultivated and managed	(Semi) natural	Cultivated	Bare areas	Artificial surfaces	Natural	Artifical

Source: Di Gregorio, A., and Jansen, L.J.M. 2000 *Land Cover Classification System (LCCS): Classification Concepts and User Manual*. UN Food and Agriculture Organization, Rome.

Terrestrial and primarily non-vegetated areas comprise two types: natural bare areas with little vegetation, such as high mountain areas of rock and scree, sands and deserts, and artificial surfaces that result from human construction, such as many parts of towns and cities, transport routes, industrial areas, etc. Roads, streets, paths and railway lines can all be mapped, showing their horizontal and vertical route, their capacity (e.g. size of highway), and the visual experience of travelling on them.

Aquatic non-vegetated cover includes natural features such as lakes and rivers, or artificial features such as canals and reservoirs. Identification, mapping and classification of different types of water features can be a useful contribution to landscape characterisation (Chapter 6). Identifying different sizes and types of river can also be linked to a more comprehensive analysis of hydrological systems, showing not only where the water features are located, and their boundaries, but also how the system functions (see Figures 3.20 and 3.21). Identifying the water quality and quantity in different locations can be very important in action-oriented analysis, as this will influence possible uses – for example, recreation. In coastal locations, the salinity of water features is also important and analysis may distinguish between freshwater, such as inland lakes and rivers, brackish features which have some salinity, such as rivers that flow into estuaries, and saltwater which is fully tidal, such as estuaries, inlets, etc. As sea levels rise with climate change, the extent and salinity of coastal aquatic areas will change, and this will in turn change the nature and location of vegetation around their margins, and the wider landscape character.

Land use

Land use describes the functional role of the landscape for people, and the roles and values it provides. The FAO define *land use* as 'the arrangements, activities and inputs people undertake in a certain land-cover type to produce, change or maintain it' (Di Gregorio and Jansen 2000), which highlights the close connection between land cover and land use. For example, agriculture is a common land use, and this may be based upon different types of farming regime, which are associated with different types of land cover: either permanent cover such as meadow or woodland, or shorter-term cover such as an annual crop. Both cover and use are key aspects of the human–ecological landscape system that includes the natural factors.

While natural factors, land cover and land use are all closely related, they are not always well integrated. Certain landscape areas may indeed be characterised by a clear link between natural factors and both land cover and land use, such as a river valley with grazed meadows on the valley floor and woodland on the steep slopes where intensive farming is not a feasible land use, or urban areas with open space in valley sections and on steep slopes. Many landscape planners see this relationship between natural factors, land cover and land use as a critical factor in landscape sustainability. So, for example, Ian McHarg (1969) was particularly interested in understanding the suitability and capability of the natural landscape for different functions, and used this as a basic rationale for developing regional plans. In many landscapes, however, functional links between natural factors, land cover, and land use have become blurred or severed, and may require continual inputs of energy and other interventions to be maintained. That is the case, for example, where dikes and land draining have enabled intensive farming in former tidal meadows, or where urban neighbourhoods have been created with no regard for the underlying terrain form, soil type and hydrology. Where natural factors, functions and cover are no longer aligned, the landscape may become dysfunctional or obsolescent (Wood and Handley 2001), and this frequently stimulates further landscape change.

Land-use functions can be divided into primary and secondary uses. Primary land use is the dominant function of the area, such as agriculture, while the secondary land use refers to other functions which are also present; in an agricultural area, for example, this may involve hunting and water catchment. Land uses may be classified in a number of ways: by economic characteristics, or by planning regulations, or by cultural practices. Most countries have a national classification system for land use, and different municipalities may also have their own land-use categories as part of their planning policy. With increasing international focus upon understanding and measurement of global land resources, land scientists are developing common systems of land-use classification, which can be used for analysis of environmental trends, such as climate change, and their effects.

Main case: biophysical analysis, Kaloe

The purpose of this analysis was to provide the biophysical basis for a comprehensive landscape character assessment in the area around Kaloe Vig in the Djursland region in Jutland, Denmark. The case example is inspired by Dr. Ole Hjorth Caspersen who also together with Dr. Patrik Karlsson processed the maps shown here (Figures 3.4–3.10) to their present form. As described in Chapter 1, the *biophysical* analysis is one of the first steps in the characterisation phase of a landscape character assessment (LCA). The object of the particular analysis at Kaloe is the geomorphological formation, the terrain forms and the soil types of the landscape. In this analysis, underlying (deep) geology is not a primary factor, as the landscape has been largely shaped by glacial and fluvial deposits and processes that overlay the 'country' rock. Hence geomorphology – the formation of surface features – is the starting point. Interpretation of the geomorphological processes as illustrated in Figures 3.2 and 3.4 is an example of the retrospective historical method, which will be explained in Chapter 4. The retrospective approach involves looking back in history for the purpose of understanding the features of the contemporary landscape, and is commonly linked to genetic classifications of land cover.

The sources used in the survey are evident from the illustrations, which are all in digital form, so that they can be processed in GIS. The procedure involves comparing and interpreting the various thematic maps (Figures 3.2–3.10) in order to classify the landscape into homogeneous areas (Figure 3.7). In Chapter 6, the process of classifying a landscape into homogeneous areas is explained in more detail. What distinguishes a biophysical analysis is that the classification into homogeneous areas does not attempt to include the overall character of the area and the way it is perceived by people, but focuses exclusively on themes concerning the natural factors.

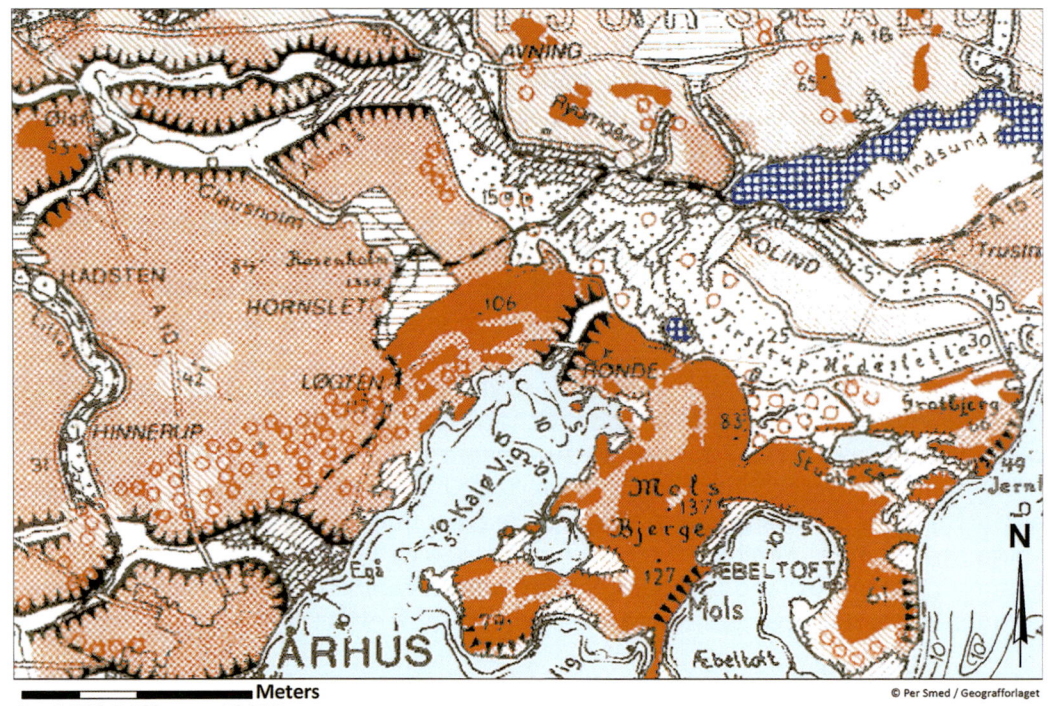

Symbol	Description		Symbol	Description
	Moraine landscape from Weichsel glaciation, mainly with clayey soil		Tunnel valley	
	Moraine landscape from Weichsel glaciation, mainly with sandy soil		Ice-lake basin or similar lake basin	
	Ice margin hills	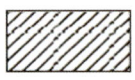	Marine foreland built up since the Atlantic transgression (5000 B.C.)	
	Landscape, hummocky or pitted due to dead-ice formation		Reclaimed area	
	Outwash plain (sandur). Rows of dots mark schematical contours.	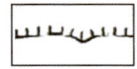	Atlantic transgression shoreline	
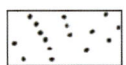	Extramarginal stream valley		Sea Cliff	

FIGURE 3.2 Landforms, South Djursland – Kaloe and Mols Hills

The Mols Hills in eastern Jutland, Denmark, are a terminal moraine landscape formed by glaciers moving from south to north. The position of the glaciers was where the two bays Kaloe Vig and Ebeltoft Vig are today. The inner (south) side of the terminal moraines consists of clay soils, and the outwash plains on the (north) outer side consist mainly of alluvial sand. North of the outwash plain is a fjord that has been reclaimed (Kolind Sund). See also Figures 3.3 and 3.4.

Source: Smed (1981): *Landskabskort over Danmark*. ©Geografforlaget/GO FORLAG A/S.

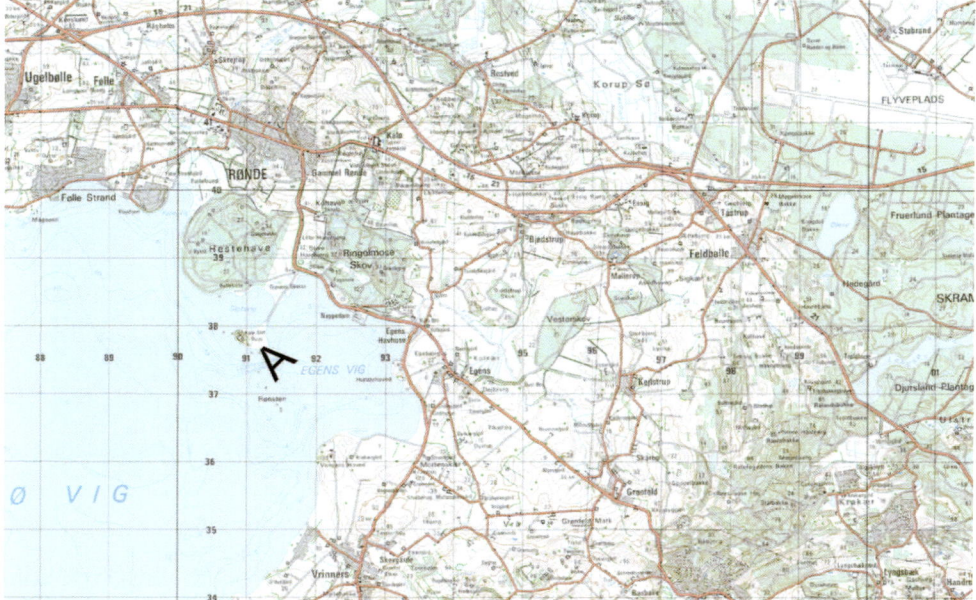

FIGURE 3.3 Topography, Kaloe

A contemporary topographic map of the same area as the following five analytical maps. The area shown here is a section of the north-east corner of the bay Kaloe Vig, part of the geomorphological map (Figure 3.2). In the south 'Mols Bjerge' means Mols Hills. The grid is 1 x 1 km. The photo position for Figure 3.6 is marked on the map.

Source: ©GST. Contains data from the Danish Geodata Agency, Kort 50 (2015).

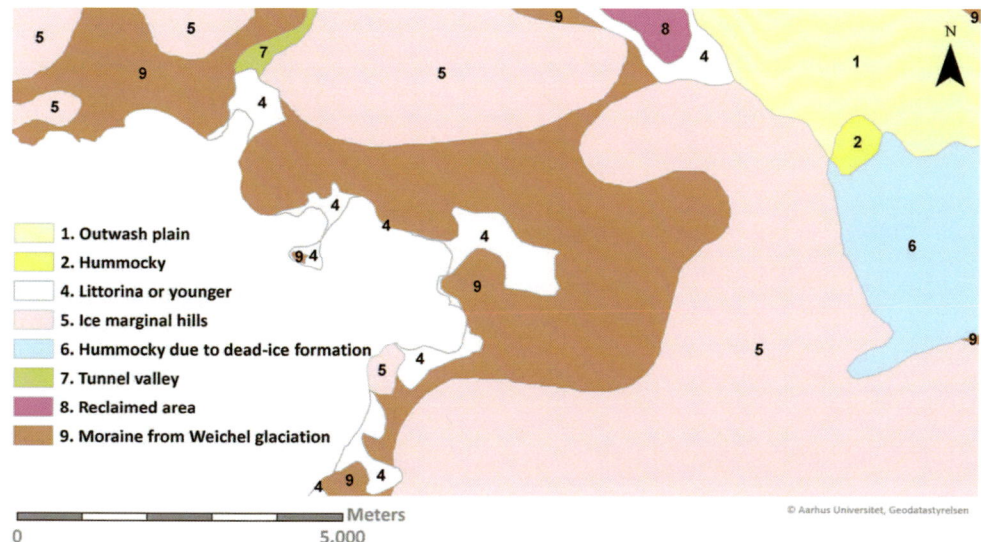

FIGURE 3.4 Geomorphology, Kaloe

A more detailed and alternatively illustrated analysis of the area shown in Figure 3.2. Littorina (4) means marine foreland formed since the Stone Age, along with the uplifted land. The terminal moraine hills (5) form a bow around the bay, and outside the moraine the outwash plain (1) and dead-ice formations (6) are located.

Source: ©Aarhus Universitet. *Atlas over Danmark: Den danske jordklassificering*. Breuning-Madsen, H. In: *Geologisk Nyt*, 2 (92), 15–17. ©GST. Contains data from the Danish Geodata Agency.

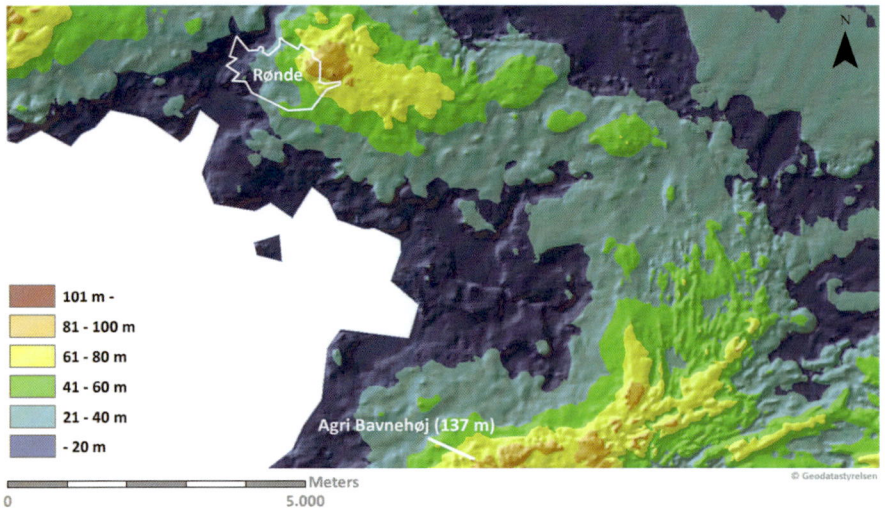

FIGURE 3.5 Terrain heights, Kaloe
By using ArcGis™ with soft shading and light direction from north-west, the colour spectrum goes from blue to brown. The representation of surface terrain can be compared with the geomorphology.

Source: University of Copenhagen and digital terrain model DMT 2007 from the Danish Geodata Agency. ©GST.

FIGURE 3.6 View to Mols Hills
The hills seen from the tiny peninsula in Kaloe Vig towards south-east. The two highest hilltops are 'crowned' by Bronze Age burial mounds, showing how human activity modifies natural factors. The land cover on the steep slopes in the background is a mixture of pasture and wood. Between the hills and the coast the terrain is less steep and intensively used for arable farming. In the foreground there are relic sea cliffs behind a wave-cut platform created by the Littorina Sea in the Stone Age. The photo position is shown on the topographic map (Figure 3.3).

Source: Photo by Caspersen, O.H.

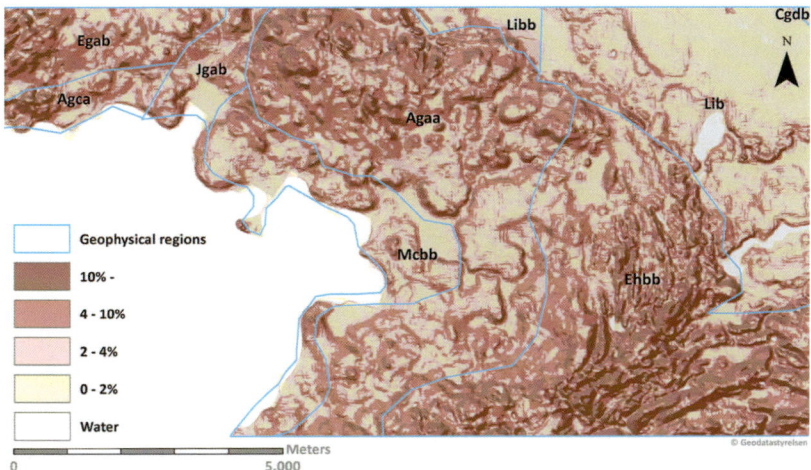

FIGURE 3.7 Terrain gradient and geophysical regions, Kaloe

The gradient of the terrain is shown as a percentage, which is more convenient than operating in degrees. The steeper slopes on the Mols Hills are highlighted, as well as the relic cliffs in the coastline. The gradient map is overlaid with physiographic regions, a 'landscape' classification of all the physiographic factors (morphology, soil type, terrain and complexity). As an example, for region *AGaa*, *A* means steep slopes (morphology), *G* means moraine clay (soil type), *a* means many small hills (terrain) and *a* means turbulent terrain forms (complexity).

Source: Caspersen & Nellemann (2004): *Landskabsanalyse – Pilotprojekt Nationalparken Mols Bjerge*. Working paper for homepage for pilot project Nationalparken Mols Bjerge. Forest & Landscape, 2004. ©GST. Contains data from the Danish Geodata Agency, digital terrain model DTM 2007.

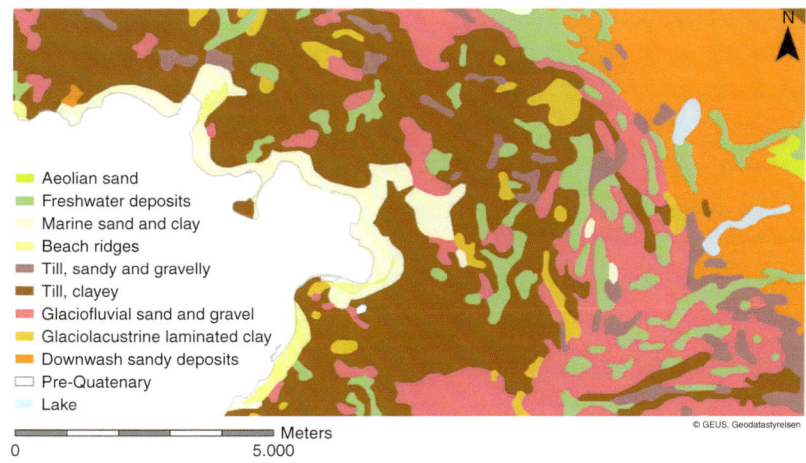

FIGURE 3.8 Sub-soils, Kaloe

The nature of the sub-soils is a result of the glacial formation. The way the glacier curved the hills around Kaloe Cove is clearly represented by the moraine clay soils (brown) and on the outside of the terminal moraine by glacial sand and gravel (purple). Intermixed with these main layers are post-glacial organic layers (green) resulting from dried-up wetlands. The sub-soil map is based on soil samples at 50cm depth combined with interpreting the process of formation. The map reflects the geomorphology map, Figure 3.4.

Source: Jacobsen, Hermansen & Tougaard (2011): *Danmarks digitale jordartskort 1:25.000 version 3.1*. Geological Survey of Denmark and Greenland (GEUS) report 2011/40. ©GST. Contains data from the Danish Geodata Agency.

FIGURE 3.9 Hedgerows, Mols Hills
Landscape view from the Mols Hills to Kaloe Cove. The land cover of permanent grassland, arable fields and hedgerows is a response to the sandy soils with risk of wind erosion. The distant Bronze Age burial mounds in Figure 3.6 are here in a close view.
Source: Photo by Stahlschmidt, P.

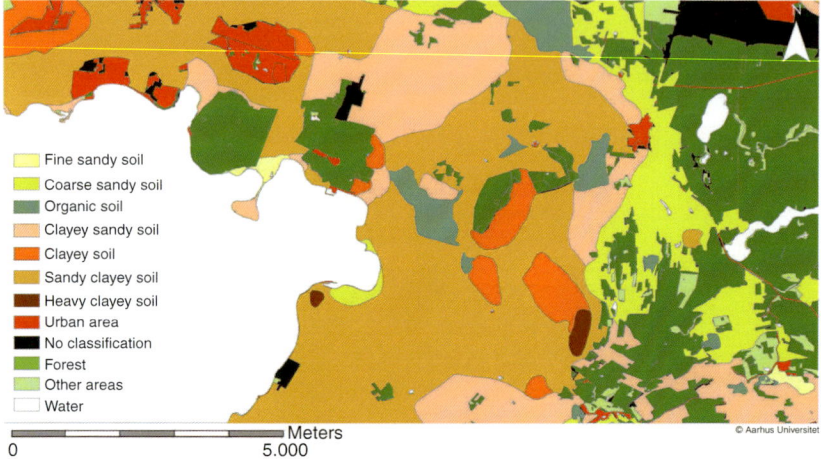

Fine sandy soil
Coarse sandy soil
Organic soil
Clayey sandy soil
Clayey soil
Sandy clayey soil
Heavy clayey soil
Urban area
No classification
Forest
Other areas
Water

Meters
0   5.000

© Aarhus Universitet

FIGURE 3.10 Top-soil classification, Kaloe
The map is based on soil samples taken at 20cm depth. The classification is based on particle size of the different soil types. Soils with small particle size – clay soils – are usually fertile soils with high capacity to retain water, whereas the more coarse-grained sandy soils have smaller capacity to retain water and lower levels of basic nutrients. The map is interesting in showing the contrast between the surface and the sub-soil conditions (Figure 3.8) and indicates suitability for farming. Therefore the top-soil map leads to further analysis of land cover and land use. Built-up areas and forests are without agricultural interest and therefore without soil classification, showing how analysis is shaped by the purpose and interests of the analysts.
Source: University of Aarhus.

Variations

In this part of the chapter we consider a number of variations on the basic analyses described above.

Geomorphology

Geomorphological data is typically based upon scientific studies at either a national, regional or local scale. For example, a comprehensive description of Denmark's geomorphology is found in Nielsen (1975) and an easily accessible source suitable for analysis is Per Smed's 'Landskabskort over Danmark' (Landscape maps of Denmark; Figure 3.2). This source also illustrates the way that knowledge is continually evolving, as Smed's maps are modified versions of Axel Schou's maps of Denmark from 1949, which used to be a fixture in the geography classroom in any school in the country, together with the block diagrams that show the relationship of terrain form and geology (Figure 3.11). Since 1949, the basic theories about the formation of the Danish landscapes during and after the Ice Age have been upheld, but subsequent drill samples and research have added modifications and detail to Schou's original maps. This continuous process of revision of science knowledge means that there is never a definitive and comprehensive database – landscape analysis involves identifying and evaluating the available sources, and extracting the data that is most up to date and relevant for the purpose of the study. The same axiom applies to other dimensions of biophysical analysis.

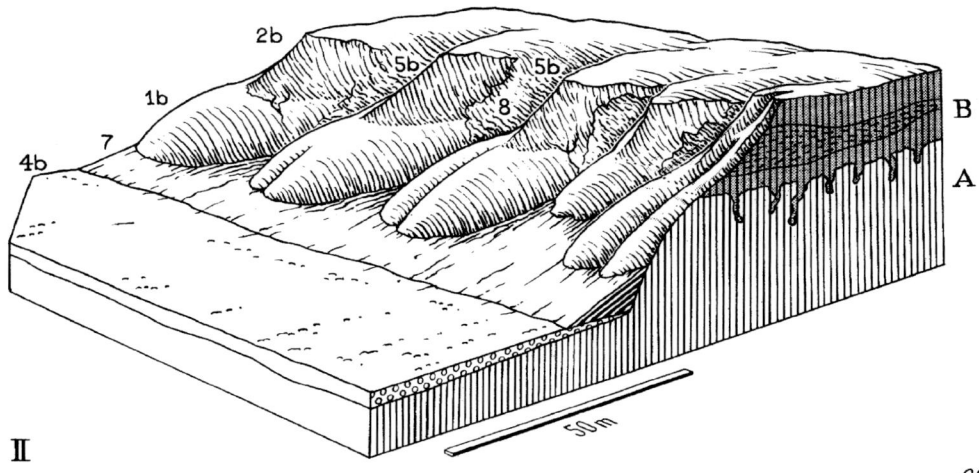

FIGURE 3.11 Block diagram coast profile, Svinkloev DK
Geomorphological patterns and features can be illustrated through a block diagram including a cross section that shows sub-surface soil layers and surface forms. The special 'cloven-footed' terrain in the North Sea coast in Northern Jutland is formed through fluvial erosion and weathering of uplifted limestone overlaid by moraine soils. A. Senonian limestone. B. Moraine and meltwater sand.

Source: Schou (1949): *Atlas over Danmark. Landskabsformerne*, p. 30. H. Hagerup ©The Royal Danish Geographical Society.

Terrain

The terrain – that is, the vertical and horizontal form of the earth's surface – is strongly influenced by geomorphology, and in turn is an essential baseline for many other aspects of landscape analysis, as slope influences drainage patterns, soil type, microclimate such as orientation to sun and exposure to wind, and thus conditions for vegetation and wildlife habitat. The terrain also affects suitability for many land uses – for example, cultivation, transport routes, settlement and building activity are generally more difficult on steeper land. The terrain also affects the overall spatial features of the visual landscape (scale, enclosed/open, linear, etc.), shapes the visual catchments of particular sites and the overall inter-visibility of different parts of a landscape, and to a large extent determines the scenic characteristics of the landscape. Elevation, in the form of steep slopes or mountains, regularly appears as a key parameter in assessments of scenic quality, both by experts and public surveys. Visually, the configuration of the terrain also shapes potential sequences of spatial experience, and provides opportunity for extensive vistas and for focused views.

Colour-coding a topographic map to reflect the relative height of the earth's surface is a common step in landscape analysis and involves assigning every level a specific colour shade (Figures 3.12 and 3.20). A common way of colouring the sequences from the bottom up is blue-green, green, yellow, brown and red. The underlying rationale behind this convention is that cooler colours are perceived as distant, while warmer colours are perceived as closer. The three-dimensional effect can be enhanced with shaded contour lines. A variation on colour-coding is the use of a screen tint that is made darker with increasing levels (Figure 1.5 in Chapter 1).

Another technique of analysis is surface shading, in order to produce a 3D representation of the terrain (Figure 3.13). Conventionally the (imagined) light source is placed in the top left-hand corner (north-west in a map where north is up). However, there is an inherent conflict in the choice of lighting, between the desire to create a particular illusion and the desire to provide information. Today this type of analysis is almost entirely based upon digital terrain models (Figure 3.14). There are two basic types: one is created by triangulating measured spot elevations; the other is grid-based (raster) where the surface is divided into square cells with assigned spot elevations. Both models have their benefits and their drawbacks. In Figure 3.14, the topographic map, with its text labels, has been converted to a 3D model. When it is only the terrain surface that is raised – and not land-cover features such as buildings and trees – the model is sometimes referred to as a 2½D model. In the model, additional woodland areas, hedges and buildings can be added in one or more standard heights. An example of a digital terrain model that is more abstract than the elevated topographical map is the *categorical elevation model*, which appears as a grid (Figure 3.16). The terrain model has been simplified by drawing a straight line from each of the cross points in the grid in a given spot elevation to four adjacent spot elevations. When the necessary data has been entered the elevations can be exaggerated if necessary – so-called vertical exaggeration – and new angles and elevations can be selected for the photo point of view. In digital models it is easy to adjust to different scales, but it is important

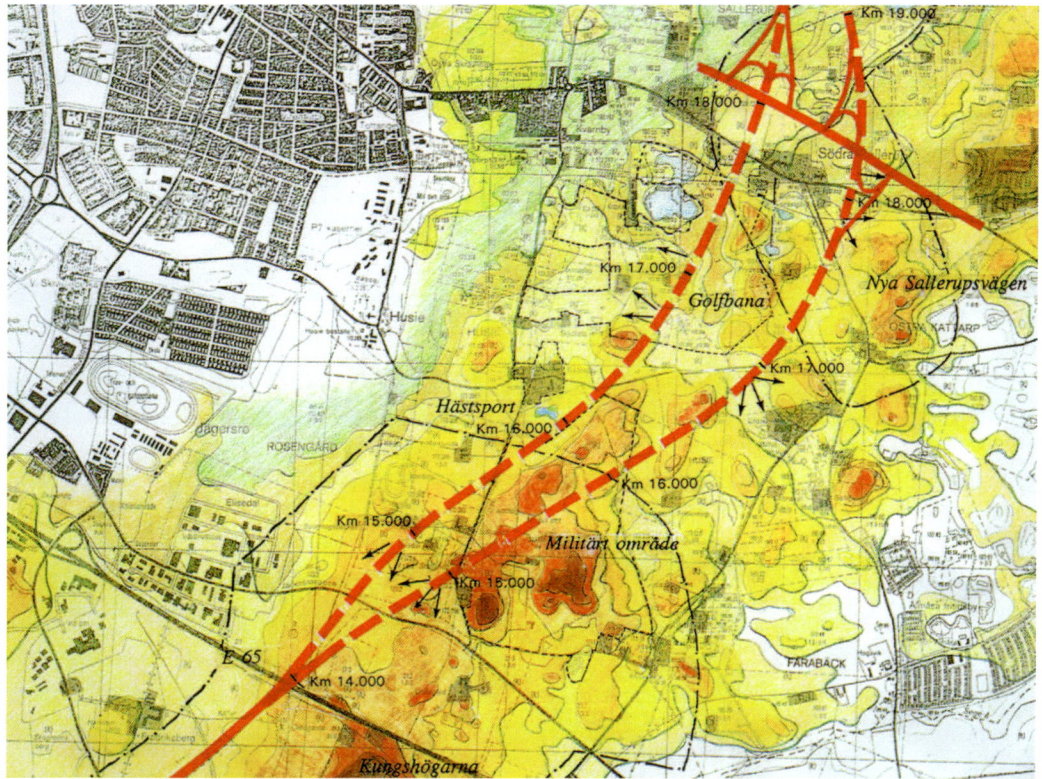

FIGURE 3.12 Terrain inventory
The elevation of the terrain is graduated at 5m intervals as part of an analysis for a Swedish highway route selection. The lowest, green areas to the west are 15–20 metres above sea level whereas the brown top layers are located 50–55 metres above sea level. The strength of the colour increases with altitude and the colours changing from (distant) cool yellow-green to (near) warm red-brown.
Source: Vägverket (1994): *Oeresundsforbindelsen Malmö*, p. 31. *Oeresundsforbindelsen Malmö. Ytre Ringvägen, Järnvaagen, Broanslutningen.* Arkitektur och landskap. Kristianstad, p. 31.

to make sure that the symbols are adjusted to match the scale that the map is printed in. Digital terrain models can be used to calculate visibility and volume – for example, in connection with impact assessments of new biogas plants and farm buildings – see Figure 5.4.

Terrain models are vital tools in risk studies of flooding caused by heavy rain, for example due to climate change. When predicting and modelling flooding of areas from streams and lakes, raised ground-water level and rainwater systems, it is important to categorise the terrain form. The different types of terrain form can be divided into simple cases, with landscapes characterised by 'isolated' low areas and basins, and more complicated cases where surface dynamics based on drainage channels (streams, ditches, sewers, etc.) play an important role in the flooding process by conducting water along to/away from the lower terrain

FIGURE 3.13 Shaded contour lines
By using a black ink pen the terrain is given a 3D appearance through shading the contour lines of a standard topographic map. The light comes from the NW – not for reasons of realism, but to make the image legible and more easily understood.
Source: Copenhagen Regional Council (1982): *Forslag til udpegning af fredningsinteresseomraader. Planlaegningsdokument PD 354*, p. 29.

(Paludan et al. 2011). As a first step in the analysis of the effect of future heavier rainfalls on the runoff systems in cities and peri-urban areas, terrain models combined with GIS data of houses and roads are used in order to map the surface low areas, named 'risk areas'. These can be combined with hydraulic assessments in advanced computer models and form the basis for climate adaptation plans, including a range of different purposes, for instance giving urban planners an idea of which areas should be kept without urban development, reserved for storage of rainwater, and combined with recreational use. They can also give environmental planners/water authorities the basis for assessment of the need for establishing wet meadows for retention of nutrients. Figure 3.20 provides an example of a terrain model of a risk area for flooding, as part of the water catchment area around the valley of Storaa and its course through Holstebro town, DK.

The perceptual experience of the landscape is often affected more by the vertical dimension than by the horizontal plane. The simplest way of conveying what happens in the vertical plane is to draw a cross section. Figure 3.17 shows a cross

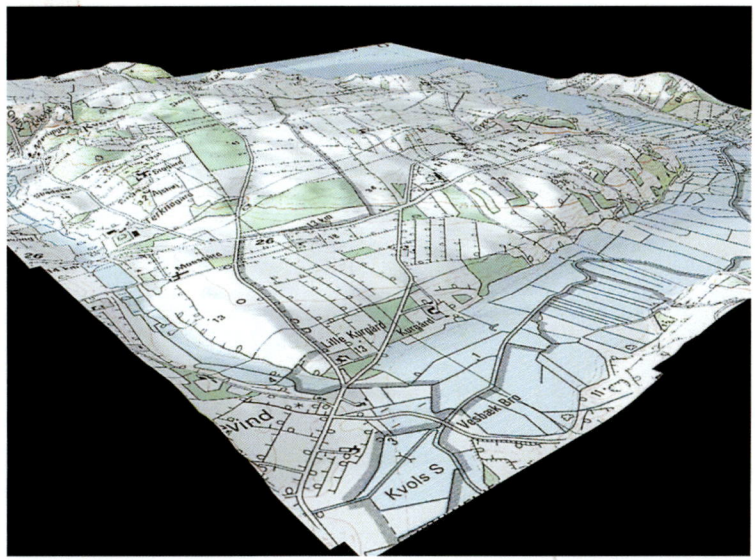

FIGURE 3.14 Digital terrain model
From the valley floor in the foreground the terrain rises on the hilly moraine in Central Jutland. The model is made by AutoCad and Quick-Surf through lifting the digital version of a standard topographic map. The height is exaggerated by a factor of five. On the computer you can freely choose the height, draping and view location to maximise the utility of the representation for the analysis at hand. A similar effect can be created using Google Maps.

Source: Joergensen et al. (1997): *Landskabsplan for Kvols-Kvosted*. Department for Economy, Forest & Landscape, Royal Danish Veterinary and Agricultural University.

FIGURE 3.15 Vaux-le-Vicomte, France
A view looking up the main axis, seen from the chateau. From this viewpoint the canal (Figure 3.16) is hidden in the valley bottom, lying in a so-called visual 'shadow'.

Source: Photo by Stahlschmidt, P.

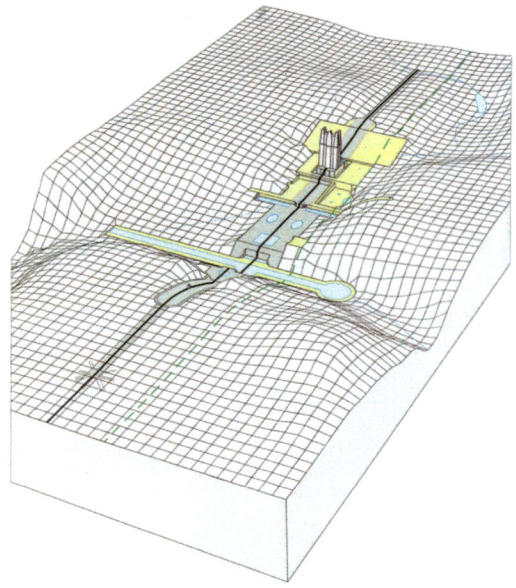

FIGURE 3.16 Categorical terrain model, Vaux-le-Vicomte
The baroque park Vaux-le-Vicomte, south-east of Paris, was constructed in 1661, located orthogonally to a tributary valley of the Seine. The block diagram reveals the paradox that the park – symbolising man's control over nature – is nicely embedded in the terrain of the natural landscape. In the 17th century a careful site analysis was crucial to ensure that the earth moving required was feasible in the pre-industrial age. In the model the heights are exaggerated by a factor of ten.

Source: Steenbergen and Reh (1996): Vaux-le-Vicomte, The balance between the geomorphology of the site and the symmetry of the design. *Architecture and Landscape* 1996, p. 22. © Thoth Publisher, Netherlands.

FIGURE 3.17 Cross section of railroad line
The cross section illustrates the relationship between the rail line and the walking tracks. People are included as a yardstick to help understand the human scale of the situation.

Source: Oeresundsforbindelsen (1993): *Oeresund Landanlaeg. Projektforslag marts 1993*. Arkitektur og landskab. Rapport A3-format.

section of an infrastructure corridor without vertical exaggeration. Figure 3.19 has a consistent vertical exaggeration. An example of a selective exaggeration of a cross section is Figure 5.11. For the purpose of clarity it may be necessary to exaggerate the elevation of the terrain form, but the distorted proportions of buildings and other features pose a problem. In Figure 3.18, the precise and technical cross section has been supplemented with an environmentally descriptive perspective. Figure 3.19 is a technical cross section of the midline of the road, a longitudinal section with a high degree of vertical exaggeration.

FIGURE 3.18 Cross section with perspective
The bold line shows the technical cross section and the relationship between the earth-work, baffle and roads. The perspectives offer an impression of the two different road environments. When illustrating projects – by drawings or photomontage – it can be tempting to exaggerate with attractive features such as trees, but the risk is that by doing so you will distort understanding of the project.
Source: A/S Oeresundsforbindelsen (1993): *Oeresund Landanlaeg. Projektforslag marts 1993. Arkitektur og landskab*, p. 34. Rapport A3-format.

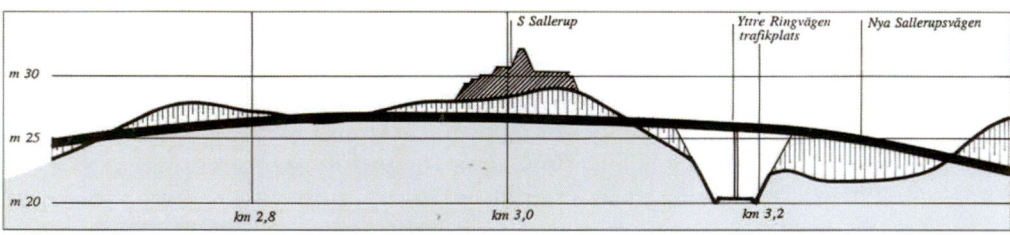

FIGURE 3.19 Longitudinal profile of road
The bold arching line marks a proposed Swedish road while the grey screen represents untouched soil. The vertical texture above or below the road line indicates cut and fill. The heights are exaggerated by a factor of ten.
Source: Vägverket (1994): *Öresundsforbindelsen Malmoe. Ytre Ringwägen, Järnvägen, Broanslutningen. Arkitektur och landskap*. Kristianstad, p. 33.

Soil

Soil is defined by the FAO (IUSS Working Group WRB 2014) as 'any material within 2 m of the Earth's surface that is in contact with the atmosphere, excluding living organisms, areas with continuous ice not covered by other material, and water bodies deeper than 2 m'. This broad definition includes a wide range of situations. Most landscape analysis is focused on soils as a key natural factor for natural and semi-natural habitats such as forests, moors, grasslands, etc. and in shaping land use, especially agriculture. The properties of the soil and sub-soils as a building material and as a foundation for buildings are also important for the location of roads, railway lines and built structures. Soil conditions may also help shed light on the historical development of a location.

In landscape analysis, two types of analysis in particular are used to classify the soil on a given site: sub-soil and top-soil. The sub-soil refers to the conditions of the ground at depths of up to two metres (Figure 3.8), but excluding the surface layer. Top-soil refers to the uppermost layer (the top 20 centimetres), which is particularly relevant in relation to agriculture and horticulture (Figure 3.10). Clay content, organic material, soil profile, and acidity are four significant characteristics of soils. Most countries have their own classifications of soils. Internationally the FAO World Reference Base for Soil Resources (2014) is the global standard intended to serve as a common denominator for communication at the international level, and complements national soil classification systems. It has two levels of categories, 32 reference soil group categories, and a set of principal and supplementary qualifiers for each main category. The first level is based largely upon formative processes except where *special soil parent materials* are of overriding importance. The *second level* is based on soil features and, in many cases, soil characteristics that have a significant effect on land use are taken into account.

Hydrology and drainage networks

In situations where scientific knowledge and mapping of hydrological systems and networks is already undertaken, the task for the professional landscape architect should be to integrate this information with other dimensions of analysis and interpret the significance for projects and policy. Historical maps and statements from locals can help define areas exposed to flood by raised water level. In urban areas it is vital to include analysis of artificial networks such as storm-water drains and pipes. Mapping can include locations of natural and artificial networks, vertical relationships and relative levels, flow capacity and flow regimes.

Figures 3.20 and 3.21 provide an example of designation of a risk area for flooding by streams and lakes, based on a terrain model combined with hydraulic assessments for the Holstebro area, Denmark. The extensive catchment area of the river Storaa sends large amounts of surface water to the valley, partly by smaller erosion valleys. In the past the farmers in the valley have benefited by having their meadows on the lowlands of the valley flooded and fertilised regularly with the valuable high-nutrient water from the river, and they have avoided constructing their farm buildings on the lowlands due to their exposure to flooding by heavy rainfalls.

However, along with the intensification of the farming systems, the hydrology of the area around Storaa has been modified through land drainage, culverting and channelisation, leading the rainwater to the streams without being delayed or reduced by storing, percolation and evaporation. Furthermore Holstebro town – which is situated as a 'plug' in the river valley – has been enlarged, and new housing areas, roads and squares have been established on the lowland. Part of the river system has been put in pipes, and many of the urban areas have been paved.

As a consequence of the increasing heavy rainfalls due to our changing climate, the urban areas of Holstebro have been prone to more and more frequent and severe flooding events, the latest in 2011. The lowest part of Holstebro is thus designated as a 'Risk Area based on assessment of the risk of flooding from streams, lakes, seas and fjords', according to the EU Flooding Directive (2007/60/EF). On this basis, careful analyses are performed to find solutions for restructuring the hydrological system, combined with redirecting, storing and evaporation of rainwater on the former wetlands, with a focus on possible recreational assets, and restructuring the urban plan to enhance the resilience of the town to extreme rainfall events.

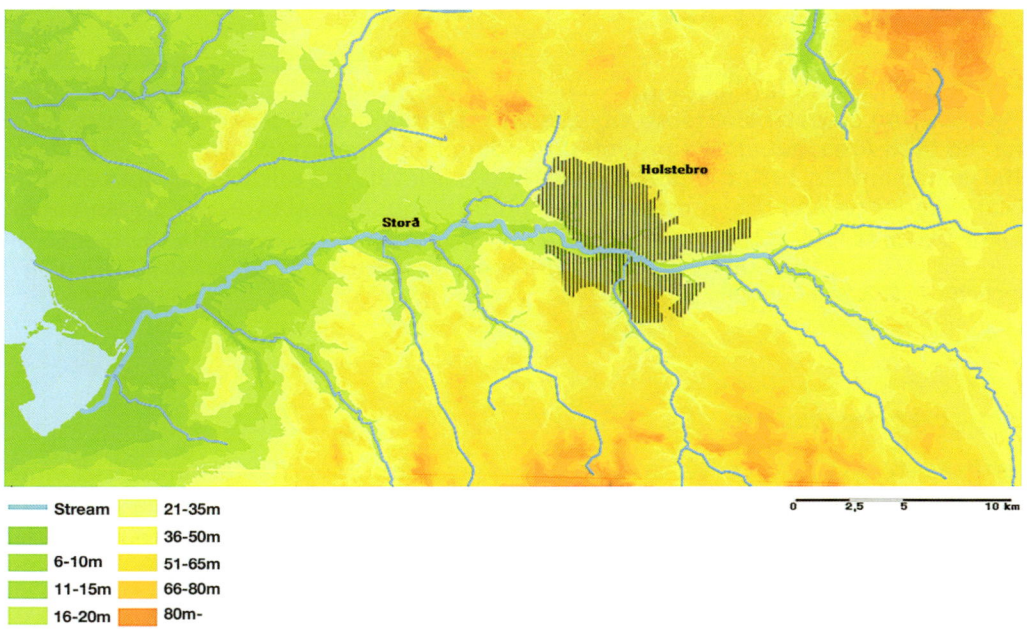

▬ Stream	☐ 21-35m		
☐	☐ 36-50m		
☐ 6-10m	☐ 51-65m		
☐ 11-15m	☐ 66-80m		
☐ 16-20m	☐ 80m-		

0   2,5   5   10 km

FIGURE 3.20 Terrain model of catchment area
The terrain model shows part of the catchment area of the second-longest river in Denmark, Storaa, and the course of the river through Holstebro city. The different shades of green and yellow/brown show the surface elevation in metres above the sea, by sections of 5 metres. The city has been prone to three major flooding events during the last 40 years.
Source: Geological Survey of Denmark and Greenland (GEUS 2016): *Maps of Denmark – Height and depth map*. Terrain model of catchment area Storaa, DK.

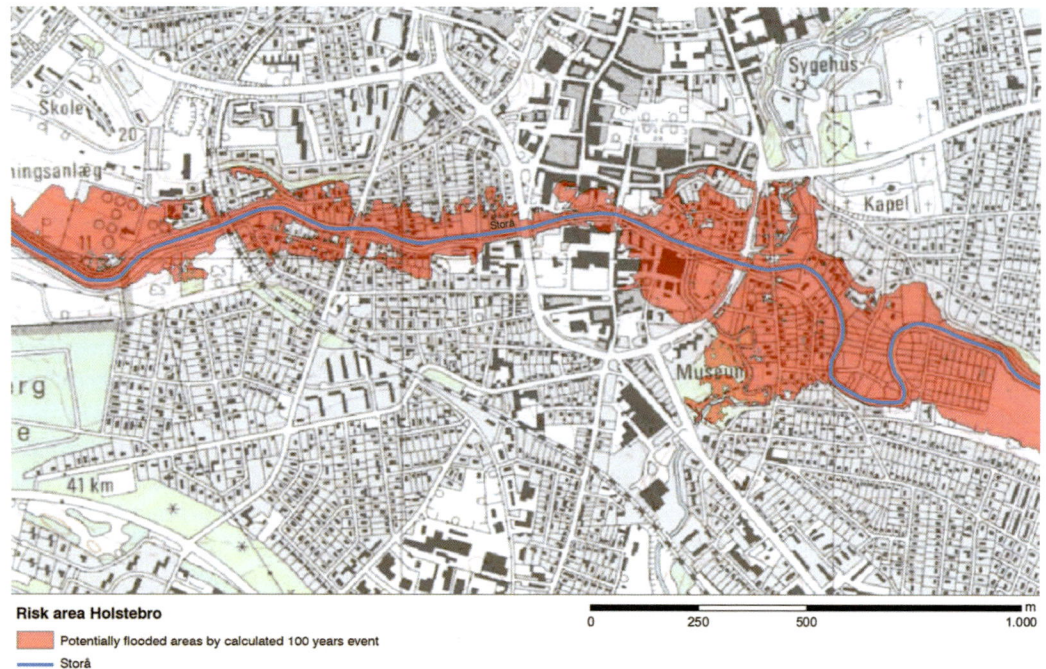

Risk area Holstebro

■ Potentially flooded areas by calculated 100 years event

—— Storå

0   250   500   1.000 m

FIGURE 3.21 Risk area for flooding
The low-lying areas of Holstebro city are an EU-designated 'Risk Area'. The extent of the red 'Risk Area' equals the potential flooding from the river Storaa by a calculated '100 year event'. In 1970 the flooding reached this level. The calculations are based on local experiences and risk assessment using terrain models and hydraulic assessments.
Source: Danish Ministry of Environment (2011): *Endelig udpegning af risikoomraader for oversvoemmelse fra vandloeb, soeer, havet og fjorde. EU's oversvoemmelsesdirektiv (2007/60/EF). Plantrin 1, Appendix A: Risk area Holstebro*, p. 101.

Land cover and land use

Particular types of land cover and land use may require specific techniques of mapping and analysis. Interpretation of air photos about land use can be added to information available on topographic maps. For instance, you can read the air photo and interpret and distinguish deciduous from coniferous forest, old from new hedgerows, and arable land from permanent grasslands. Figure 3.22 shows an example of agrarian landscapes, which are landscapes with enclosed fields, in agricultural use either for annual crops or as permanent managed grassland, and typically delineated by either hedges or fences. The features that are of particular relevance are field boundaries and the distribution of annual and perennial vegetation (see Figures 6.6 and 6.7 for other representations of same area).

Wetlands may require analysis of subtle variations in level, as this fundamentally affects vegetation cover. Figure 3.23 is a detailed survey of a wetland biotope and its surrounding area. The three-dimensional effect was partly achieved by shading

FIGURE 3.22 Aerial photo, rural landscape
The faded colour in some of the fields reveals great variations in soil type and hydrology within the field. The two dark spots in the centre of the photo are ponds surrounded by moorland with different land use (arable land, permanent grassland and shrub land). In the top-right corner a mosaic of woodland, arable land and dry pasture is obvious. Hoerslev is a case of regionalisation (Figure 6.6 and 6.7).

Source: Skive Municipality (2009): *Landskabsanalyse for Skive Kommune 09 – en intro*. Available at www.skive.dk/kommune-politik/politikker-kort-og-planer/ (accessed January 2016).

the tree areas and partly by giving the herb layer, which is more remote, a dark colour, while the canopy, which is closer, has a lighter colour.

Forests are a distinctive land cover and land use with a long and extensive history of analysis needs and techniques. An important function of most modern forests is production, and professional foresters use standard maps to show the 'stock' of timber in a forest. For example, the forest maps that the Danish Nature Agency produces for all state forests provide information about the tree species and the time of establishment for the individual forest plot. However, they lack topographic information such as contour lines and information about the spatial structure of the forest.

Gustavsson's forest analysis method (1986) provides a detailed description of the spatial structure of the forest (Figure 3.24). The description also reflects the vegetation ecology and the perceptual experience of the area. The challenge of

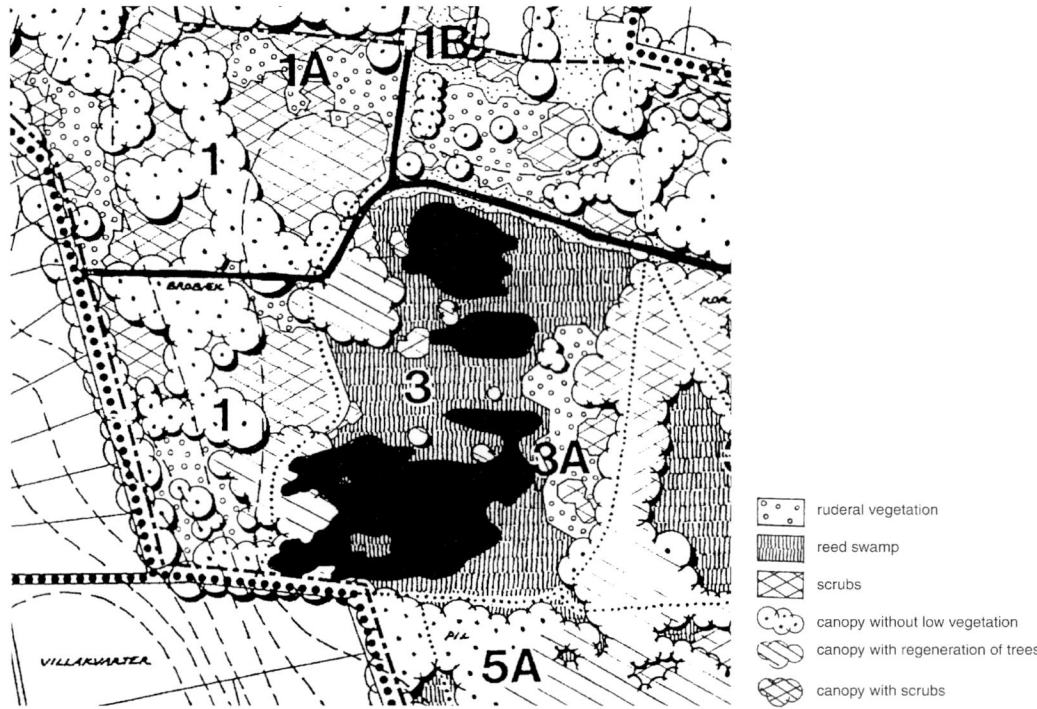

FIGURE 3.23 Detailed inventory, vegetation structure
The illustration provides – on a fine scale – a graphic overview of the spatial structure of the plant community within the wetland. Area 3 is a glade in the forest in which the small lakes are surrounded by reeds. 3A represents a transitional zone between the reed and the wooded vegetation with ruderal vegetation with patches of shrub vegetation. The dotted line through the woodland shows the traces of a former path. Area 1 is a transitional zone with regeneration of woodland and shrub land.
Source: Jensen & Thomsen (1986): *Planlaegning af bynaere moser*. Master's thesis, p. 115. Institute for Economy, Forest & Landscape, Royal Danish Veterinary and Agricultural University. Unpublished.

mapping the spatial structure of complex vegetation is that herb layer, shrub layer and canopy vary in relation to one another. These layers are therefore difficult to represent while simultaneously giving an impression of the actual appearance of the landscape as seen from above. The section gives an impression of the horizontal extension of the forest layers. The symbol for each of the three layers (plus the unlisted symbol for 'no canopy') should be legible in all eight possible combinations (four with a single legend, three with two legends combined, and one with all three legends combined). Most of the forest section features both a tree layer at a height of more than five metres and an intermediate tree layer at two to five metres. Therefore, it takes time to develop a sense of three-dimensional space while 'moving around' in the plan. The high degree of detailing in Figure 3.24 requires a considerable survey effort. For cross sections the detailing is only realistic in relatively small areas. Using drones, a high degree of detail is now available for aerial

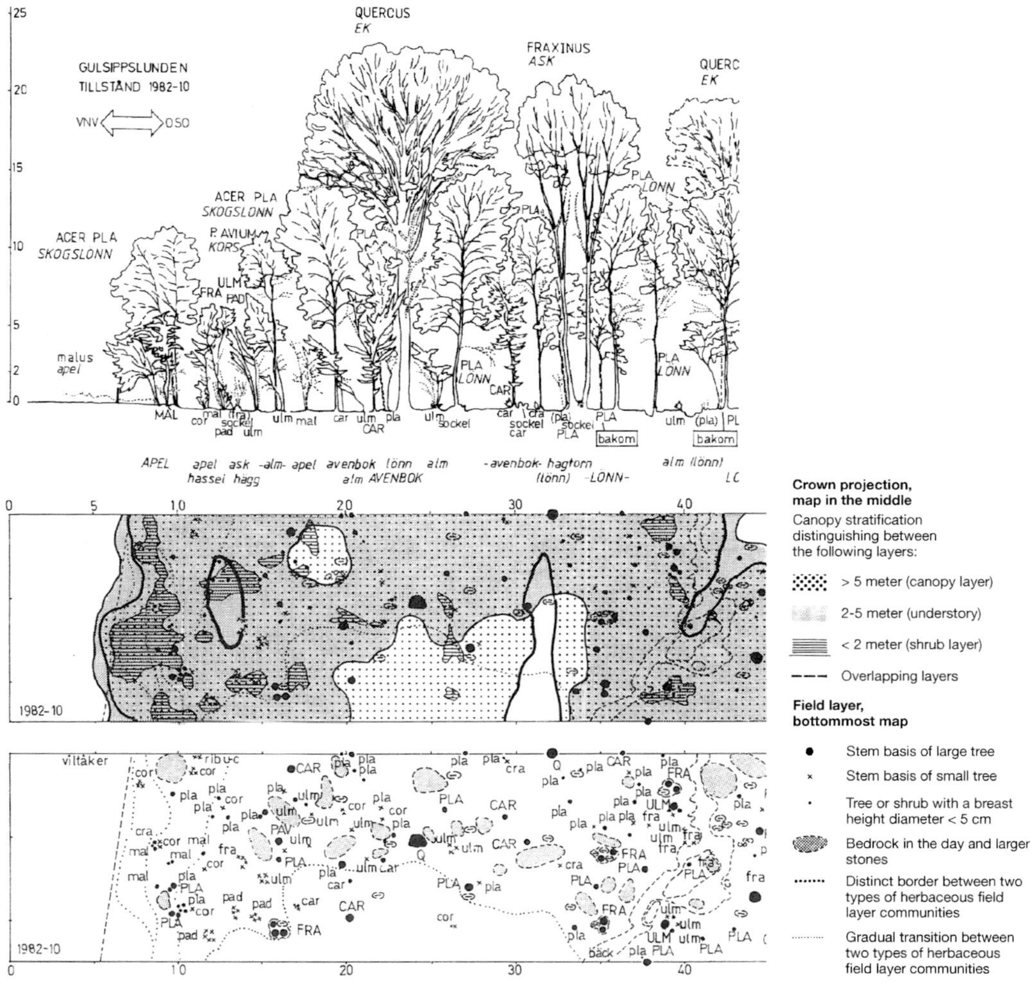
QUERCUS
EK
FRAXINUS
ASK
QUERC
EK
GULSIPPSLUNDEN
TILLSTÅND 1982-10
VNV
OSO
ACER PLA
SKOGSLONN
malus
apel
1982-10
Crown projection, map in the middle
Canopy stratification distinguishing between the following layers:
> 5 meter (canopy layer)
2-5 meter (understory)
< 2 meter (shrub layer)
Overlapping layers
Field layer, bottommost map
Stem basis of large tree
Stem basis of small tree
Tree or shrub with a breast height diameter < 5 cm
Bedrock in the day and larger stones
Distinct border between two types of herbaceous field layer communities
Gradual transition between two types of herbaceous field layer communities

FIGURE 3.24 Detailed inventory, forest structure

This 12 metre wide and 40 metre long transect of a forest edge in Sweden is recorded in a 'profile diagram' in three complementary ways: a vertical projection (cross section), a horizontal projection of layers in the canopy and a horizontal map of the forest floor. The transect has been inventoried by means of a cross section (profile diagram) shown at the top. On the central map with crown projections the horizontal expansion of tree crowns is shown in different layers and the bases of the tree stems/trunks are indicated with black dots. On the bottom map the field layer properties are recorded. The old Quercus (Q) in the middle of the map has an elevated canopy that forms the canopy layer > 5 metres (raster with black dots) together with specimens of e.g. *Carpinus betulus* (CAR), *Acer platanoides* (PLA) .

The grey raster indicates the coverage of the understory (2–5 metres) while the areas with line raster indicate the crown projects of the scattered shrub layer (< 2 metres).

Source: Gustavsson (1986): *Struktur i Lövskogslandskap. Stad & Land*, 48, p. 108–110. Alnarp.

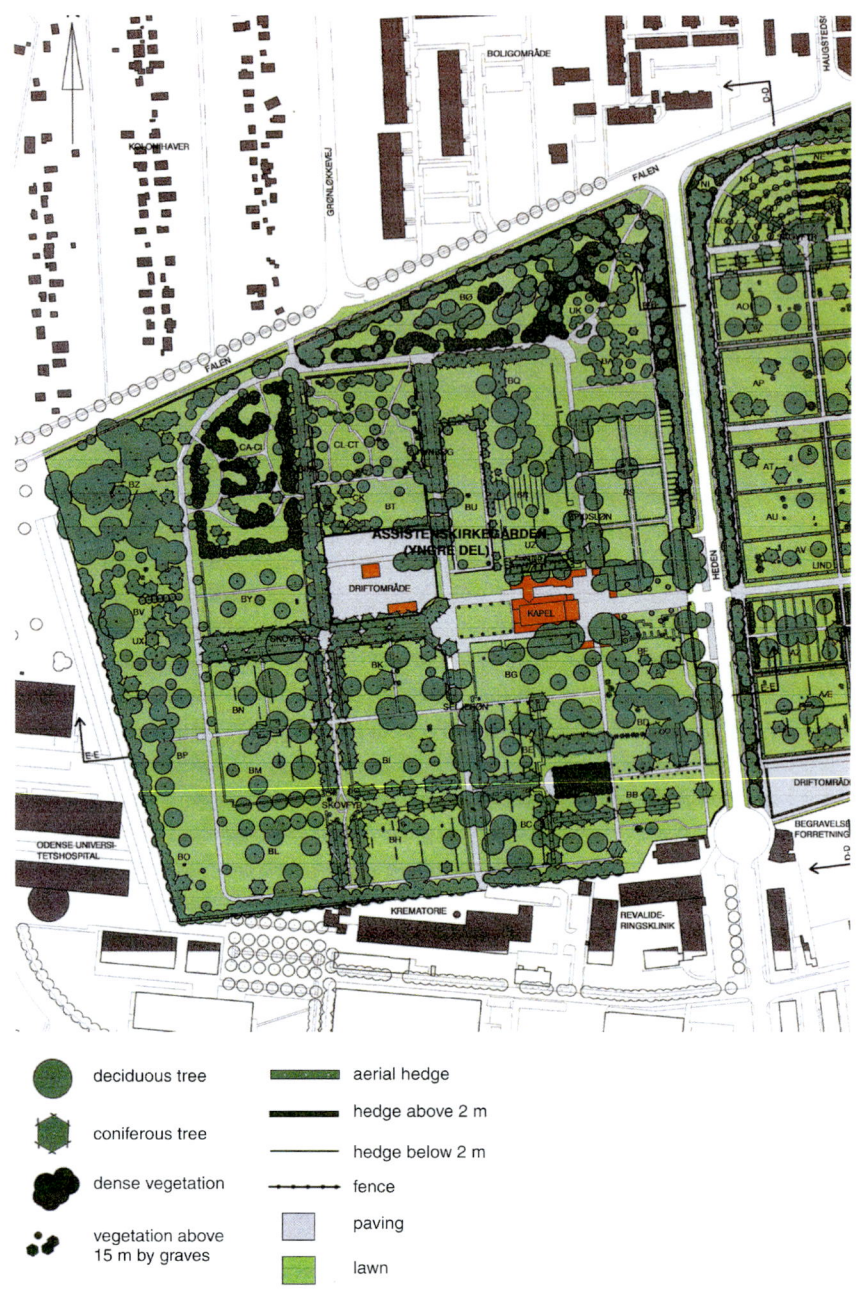

deciduous tree		aerial hedge
coniferous tree		hedge above 2 m
dense vegetation		hedge below 2 m
		fence
vegetation above 15 m by graves		paving
		lawn

FIGURE 3.25 Vegetation record of a park
The thematic map of vegetation is drawn in CAD. The digital basis of the map is extensive field records of vegetation and gravestones. The map classifies the trees and other features into a few categories suited to the planning process.

Source: Dragenberg (1999): *Helhedsplan for Assistenskirkegaarden og Ansgaranlaegget i Odense*. Master's thesis. Institute for Economy, Forest & Landscape, Royal Danish Veterinary and Agricultural University. Unpublished.

FIGURE 3.26 The Copenhagen Zoo – before renovation

For a section of the zoo the map distinguishes between white walking paths for the visitors and other-coloured open space for the animals. The shading of the buildings and tree planting with light from NW gives a three-dimensional effect which could have been intensified by contour lines.

Source: Joersboe (1999): *Vejledning i fremstilling af terraenmodeller.* Section for Landscape, Department for Economy, Forest & Landscape, Royal Danish Veterinary and Agricultural University. Unpublished.

FIGURE 3.27 The Copenhagen Zoo – after renovation

In the plan proposal the same signs and drawing technique are used as in the survey map to enable comparisons between the existing situation and proposed design.

Source: Joersboe (1999): *Vejledning i fremstilling af terraenmodeller.* Section for Landscape, Department for Economy, Forest & Landscape, Royal Danish Veterinary and Agricultural University. Unpublished.

photos. The same presentation technique, where cross sections illustrate the forest layers, was also used in the Danish Nature Agency's catalogue of 19 forest development types for nature-near forest management (Danish Nature Agency 2005).

Parks are another distinctive feature of both rural and urban landscapes, and are typically areas of managed vegetation used for a variety of non-productive purposes, primarily heritage and recreation. The patterns, nature and condition of vegetation in gardens and parks is an essential aspect of their function and value, and can be surveyed and represented using the same presentation techniques as those traditionally used to prescribe future planting. Figure 3.25 is an example of a survey of bushes and trees with regard to their spatial and structural role. Figures 3.26 and 3.27 use a similar technique to show 'before' and 'after' maps of surface cover as part of a renovation project. At this scale the mapping and analysis converges with techniques used in site design.

4

HISTORICAL ANALYSIS

Introduction

Chapter 3 highlighted the importance of understanding how landscapes change under the influence of natural factors, and how these changes are expressed in the biophysical attributes and land cover of a landscape. Landscape history can also be read as a deep-layered text – a palimpsest of human cultures and activities – where successive human generations have added, removed and changed elements, structures and patterns.

If you stand at a local viewpoint and overlook a typical landscape in Europe you will usually see a mixture of natural and cultural landscape elements, each with different ages. These elements create structures and patterns on a higher level of scale that give a landscape its overall character. Every element has a history. Some elements are new, some are quite old and some are ancient. Some elements are not visible anymore, as they are destroyed or buried under the surface, and can only be revealed by archaeology and soil science. They nonetheless form part of the history and may be expressed in different ways, such as in place names. The American landscape architect Anne Whiston Spirn (1998) also distinguished between 'enduring' and 'ephemeral' dimensions of landscape. Old geological structures together with old dominating human-installed features could be termed the 'deep' context of the landscape. Such deep context would include historic analysis of a variety of landscapes, such as terraces in Mediterranean countries, hedgerow patterns in England, or hunting forests established by the Danish Royalty more than 300 years ago. Ephemeral dimensions on the other hand are phenomena such as characteristic seasonal colours that are a distinctive part of a landscape but transient, and unmarked on most maps.

French geographer Jean Bernard Pitte noted, 'Landscape is a poem written on a blank sheet of climax vegetation' (quoted in Baker 2003, p. 140). The letters in the 'poem' are the landscape structures that have been created through time by a myriad of human adaptations or innovations to meet changes of power, economy, technology, social organisation, ideas, religion, natural disasters, etc. The combined landscape elements (letters) create patterns (sentences) that can be read as poems and interpreted with different meanings by the viewer, the land owner or the scientist.

A true historic landscape analysis must use different source materials to peel off, understand and explain the processes that change these time layers in the landscape. In that sense the landscape analyst needs to be skilled in several scientific disciplines like history, archaeology, geography, architecture and biology. In reality, very few of us are able to master all these disciplines, but a thorough historic landscape analysis will demand a multidisciplinary approach, whether you do it alone or in a team of experts.

As Figure 4.1 illustrates, landscapes continually change. Cultural landscapes typically change because they no longer function as they were intended by the people who live or visit there. This may happen because of biophysical changes – a sea inlet becomes silted and no longer suitable for shipping, or climate change may amplify flood events and in the long run cause higher sea level, and makes it necessary to improve coastal protection installations or to remove settlements from low-lying areas in the coastal zone. Technologies change – ships get too large for the inlet, new energy sources are developed (e.g. coal instead of water and wind turbines, or new machinery is developed for agriculture and the existing patterns and technologies become obsolescent for the new situation). Economies and markets also change, so that traditional ways of cultivating the land are no longer a viable way to support the community that lives there; or new people arrive, with different values and needs, such as tourists or urban commuters. There are many catalysts for change in a cultural landscape, and the historical analysis must identify critical

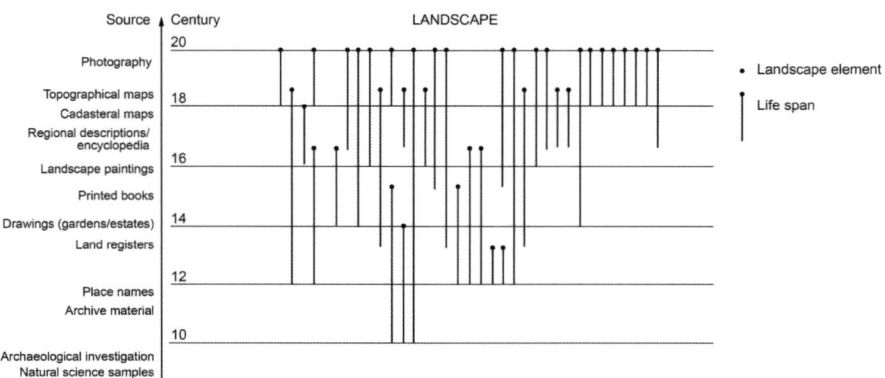

FIGURE 4.1 Historical layers
The diagram illustrates a landscape history over a thousand years – from early medieval times to the present. The left column indicates the approximate times of emergence of key sources for landscape analysis. Each landscape element is shown with a 'time-tail' referring to its emergence in the historical record and lifetime. Element-dots shown in year 2000 are still present on the surface, while element-dots in the centuries below have either disappeared or are hidden underground as potential archaeological evidence.

Source: Moderated by Stenak after Vervloet (1984): *Inleiding tot de historische geografie van de Nederlandse cultuurlandschappen. Pudoc Wageningen.*

drivers or events that cause landscapes to change quickly or significantly. From this, a landscape biography (Roymans et al. 2009) can be made – a story about the landscape just like a person's life history – except that a landscape biography never finishes, as landscapes are always evolving.

Relevance to planning solutions

Why is such an understanding of landscape history vital to landscape analysis? A common question addressed in all planning processes is "What direction do we want this landscape to go in the future and what route or pathway might we follow?" However, in order to know the goal for the plan and how best to get there, you must also know where you have been before, what resources and values you have brought with you to work with, and what the choice of a future pathway will mean for what you have already achieved. Not knowing how you came to the present situation is like having a map which clearly indicates where you want to get to, but you do not know where you are now on the map or how you got there. This calls for a historical analysis.

Historical analysis can take on different degrees of relative importance in relation to a proposed planning or design solution. In the planning of new developments, the historical analysis is usually part of a situation analysis, which is mainly used to develop an understanding of the area at hand. It may be one way of discovering the *genius loci*, the spirit of place. *Genius loci* means the prevailing character or atmosphere of a place (www.oxforddictionaries.com). The term is often used in a planning situation in association with an interpretation of a site, and the findings can have significance for the direction of planning. For example, if a landscape has remained unchanged for long periods of time this may call for a more cautious approach to proposed change than in a dynamic landscape where major changes are part of the legacy of the landscape and further change may be more easily absorbed. Kevin Lynch put the matter in a nutshell in the title of one of his books: "What time is this place?" (Lynch 1972). The analysis may also draw attention to information about changes in former land cover and land use which provide warnings of risk – e.g. flood, landslides, erosion, etc. – or may indicate potentials for habitat restoration.

The examples in this chapter are from Denmark, Italy and Germany, which are typical European landscapes with a continuous history that has not been disrupted or overlaid by recent colonisation from a very different culture, as is found in many other parts of the world. This means that the layers of cultural activity expressed in the landscapes' identity are closely related and typically build upon each other creating a rich historic fabric. In countries where colonisation has occurred, the evidence and marks of earlier phases of activity are often lost, disguised or even destroyed, which makes analysis more challenging.

Sources for historical analysis

A historical analysis may include a wide range of sources, including excavations, field studies of remains from the past, archive materials, questionnaires, interviews, statistical data, aerial photos, perspective photos and paintings. As in any other historical study, accuracy depends on the reliability of the sources. Therefore it is important to distinguish between primary sources – original historical records or field surveys – and secondary sources, such as maps produced by other scholars.

The source materials available to understand the historic landscape are not evenly distributed through time. Societies rise and fall, records are lost, new technologies are developed, and different periods of history need different analysis techniques based upon different types of available source material.

To study ancient times (pre AD 1000) before writing became common, analysts must undertake archaeological investigations, use soil or pollen samples for scientific investigations or rely upon the few surviving elements on the surface, e.g. burial mounds, megalithic tombs and remnants of ancient architecture. Only a few inscriptions and surviving documents tell us about specific landscape events or characteristics.

During the medieval period (c. AD 1000–1500) the amount of documentary evidence increases, and today it constitutes the backbone of most national/regional archives in Europe. Important sources include legislation concerning the utilisation of landscape resources, tax registers and land records. Place names of settlements, fields and other named landscape elements occupy a special role in historic analysis since they can be used to interpret the continuity and relative age of the place.

After printing technology was developed in Europe during the 15th century, the number of books and maps increased rapidly. From the Renaissance and period of Enlightenment (c. AD 1500–1800) there are increasing numbers of land registers, regional descriptions, drawings of estates and gardens, landscape paintings, cadastral maps, and the first reliable topographic maps. By careful use of these sources we can begin to create a full picture of the historic landscapes on a fine scale.

Over the last 200 years the production of detailed topographic maps has increased in number and accuracy, and today they are usually the starting point in the historic landscape analysis. During the 19th century most European countries collected census data of settlements and land use on a local scale and detailed descriptions of parishes. Since c. 1850 photography has been added to the pool of important source material that must be considered when you design the analysis.

The materials reviewed above only represent a fragment of the range of sources that will help you carry out a historic landscape analysis. Interviews, old movies or poetry might also be relevant. At the end of the day the choice of sources will depend on the purpose of the analysis, the availability of data, how you design the analysis and the amount of time available for the work. Just remember one thing: Don't miss the opportunity to do fieldwork and experience the landscape directly. Though you will only see surviving present-day elements, being in the landscape will always contribute to your sense of place and understanding of time-depth.

Three methods

Historic landscape analysis can be based on three methods – *the retrospective, the retrogressive* and *the chronological* – which are presented below as independent approaches to clarify the differences. The illustration of the three methods is based on a textbook by the Dutch historical geographer *Jelier Vervloet* (1984). To avoid blurring the message a number of scientific considerations and reflections are omitted, but they are briefly addressed for further reading by Dam and Jakobsen (2008). Just note that a historic landscape analysis must consider questions of scale, representation, interpretation, reliability, stability and rate of change for each selected landscape element. The concept of the retrospective analysis was illustrated in Chapter 3 when the existing landforms and soil types were explained by interpreting the geological processes, and is considered first. We then provide a retrogressive example. The following examples will be of the chronological method.

The retrospective method

The retrospective method (Figures 4.2 and 4.3) is a 'look back in time' method. Retrospection is often future-oriented and planning-related. It is used to map village history and cultural environments in Denmark, historic landscapes in the Netherlands, and historic landscape character in the UK (Moeller, Stenak and Thoegersen 2005; Rippon 2004). The starting point of the analysis is usually the present-day situation, but you can also start in a historic time section, where evidence is appropriate, e.g. Porsmose (1987) who used cadastral maps from c. 1800 to decipher the medieval village structure.

Retrospection is a peeling-off technique where every analysed landscape element is followed back in time through different evidence. At some point the element 'disappears' in the evidence, which can suggest the probable time period it first emerged as a continuous feature. When all elements are mapped and dated you create a picture of the different time-depth in the landscape and the dominant historic phases in selected parts of the landscape. In this way you can define historic

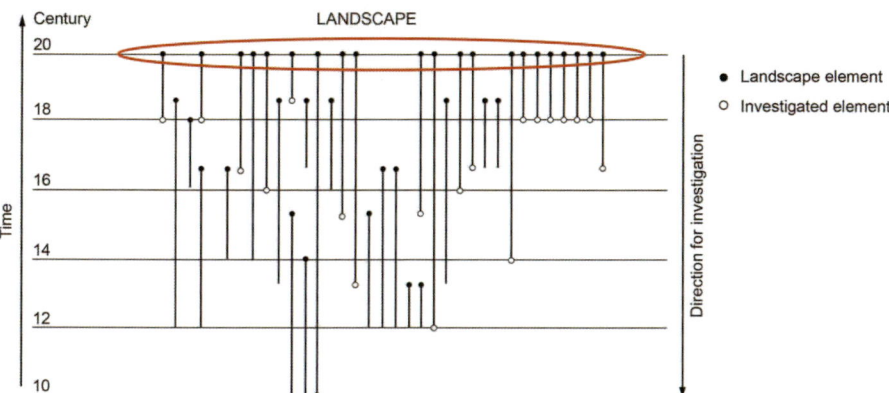

FIGURE 4.2 The retrospective method
This method looks back and investigates the history of present-day landscape elements. The notation is the same as Figure 4.1.

Source: Moderated by Stenak after Vervloet (1984): *Inleiding tot de historische geografie van de Nederlandse cultuurlandschappen*. Pudoc *Wageningen*.

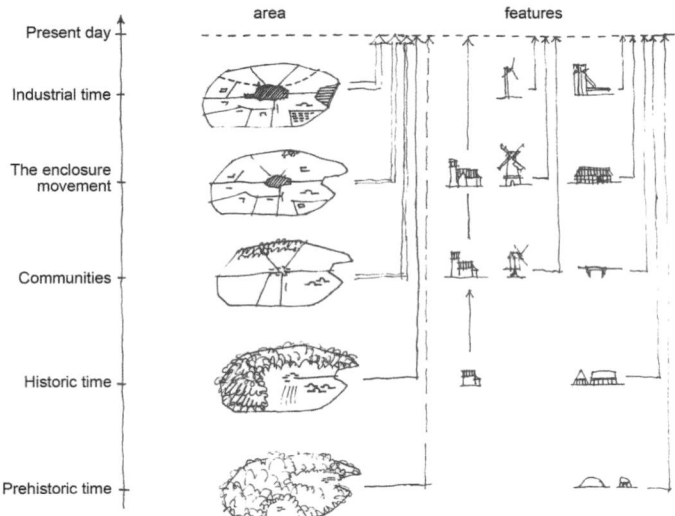

FIGURE 4.3 Illustration of the retrospective method
For a typical Danish parish the 'time-depth' is illustrated for landscape elements that have survived until now.

Source: Danish Ministry of Environment (1983): *Fredningsplanlaegning og kulturlandskab – Kulturgeografien.* Department of Geography at the University of Copenhagen and Danish Ministry of Environment, Conservation Agency.

landscapes that are well preserved, e.g. enclosed villages, ancient woodland, or landscapes with a very blurred and mixed history ('the everyday landscape').

In the previous chapter we argued that understanding biophysical landscape patterns and character needs analysis of how the patterns came to exist, and explained that a genetic approach to analysis classifies landforms and landscape elements based on the processes that created them, such as glaciation. The same applies – perhaps even more so – when seeking to understand the human dimensions of landscape.

When the analysis has built up a rich data set that can be ordered by location, age and type, it is time to craft a narrative about the landscape's history. What have been the main phases of human activity and when were there significant changes? What places and activities have continued relatively unchanged over time? What new activities, elements and values have been introduced and what have become obsolescent, been lost or destroyed? What stories does the landscape tell us? Note that we use the plural 'stories'. This is because historical landscape analysis is about the history of people, and different people and communities at different times have different experiences, different values, and different stories. Analysis therefore needs to be sensitive to the multiple histories and perceptions of the landscape and how they differ depending upon whose point of view is adopted, as well as teasing out the common threads that link these stories.

Finally, when a clear understanding of the way a landscape is changing has been achieved, then it is time to review the characterisation and to refine and sharpen the account of landscape identity and classification into homogeneous areas (see Chapter 6). It is this type of historic landscape because . . . This area differs from this because . . .

The retrogressive method

The retrogressive method (Figure 4.4) is a reconstruction method. Retrogression is often past-oriented and research-related. It is often used in a situation analysis to create an understanding and representation of a certain historic period where some evidence is missing. Reconstruction is often carried out because detailed reliable maps are unavailable. By assuming that certain landscape elements are 'constant', you can use younger maps to form the fabric of an older landscape and add historic elements that are documented in other evidence. In Denmark convincing reconstructions have been carried out by Frandsen (1983), who drew maps of field systems in the 1680s by combining cadastral maps from the late 18th century with land records from 1682–83 (Figure 4.5). Reconstructions show us how the landscape was most probably composed at a particular point in time and contribute to our understanding of historic landscapes that are difficult to imagine due to limited evidence.

In a restoration project, however, such as a habitat restoration project or the renovation of a manor house park, the historical analysis may take on a leading role and become action-oriented, and be used to identify the key elements and phases of change that can be featured and used to interpret the site for visitors (Figure 4.6). Are there subtle historical traces or elements that can be preserved and even highlighted through planning, so that they may take on renewed positive importance? Reconstruction can actually be the main principle of transformation aiming to recreate a former, documented state. The result of the historical analysis may in fact become identical to the planning proposal.

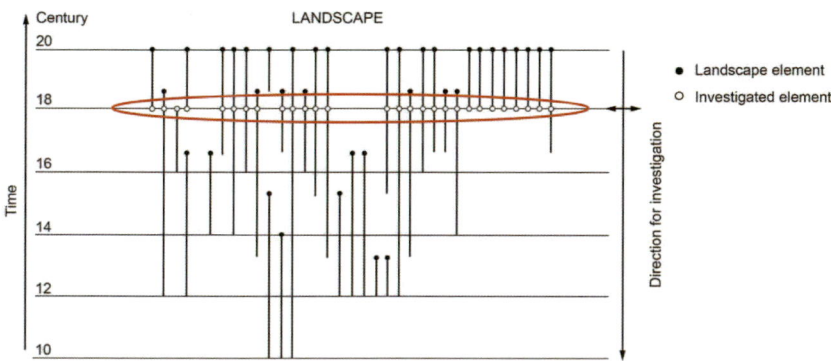

FIGURE 4.4 The retrogressive method
This method tries to reconstruct a past cross section of the landscape by combining simultaneous evidence with newer sources of landscape elements that are likely to have been 'constant' in former times.

Source: Moderated by Stenak after Vervloet (1984): *Inleiding tot de historische geografie van de Nederlandse cultuurlandschappen*. Pudoc Wageningen.

FIGURE 4.5 Illustration of the retrogressive method
The map is a reconstruction of the field system of the village, Starreklinte, Zealand, DK, based on the cadastral map from the late 18th century with land records from 1682–83. The stripes in black are arable land for one of the farms in Skarreklinte. A. Pasture, B. Property boundary, C. Farm building, D. Arable land for one of the farms.

Source: Frandsen (1983): *Vang og taegt*. Bygd, Esbjerg.

FIGURE 4.6 Use of the retrogressive method, Villa Lemm Berlin
Villa Lemm by the Havel River in Berlin is an example of use of the retrogressive method at a very fine scale. Villa Lemm was established in 1908 as a landscape garden. In 1913 a terrace section was added designed in the Italian renaissance style. In 1998 the garden was reconstructed following a detailed retrogressive analysis by the office for Gartendenkmalpflege in Landesdenkmalamt, Berlin. When the aim of a renovation is to reconstruct the historic state as accurately as possible, the historic landscape analysis becomes action-oriented.

Source: Photo by Stahlschmidt, P.

The chronological method

The chronological method (Figure 4.7) is a combination of 'looking back in time' and reconstruction, where you try to establish a full picture of several appropriate (diachronic) time sections of a landscape. The method is thus past- and future-oriented and can be applied in both planning and research. The method will usually clarify the time-depth of most landscape elements and strengthen the understanding of continuity, slow change and rapid, volatile shifts. Furthermore, it challenges your knowledge of how historic processes shape specific landscape features and vice versa. It is a very time-consuming method to carry out properly. Therefore it is usually associated with a large land development or research project and should provide detailed planning advice. Figure 8.10 (Oppdal) in Chapter 8 shows a common technique for chronological analysis. The specific visual series of Oppdal describes a future development, but in principle it might equally well have illustrated a historical development process. When dealing with past developments, it is sometimes possible to include a photo series of a development over time.

A short version of the chronological method can be applied by carrying out a landscape analysis of three time sections based on topographic and cadastral maps of the last 250 years (Figure 4.8). However, difficulties arise as soon as you go back to the periods before good maps were created.

Three choices in particular are crucial in a chronological map-based analysis: which themes are relevant (built-up structures, wetlands, fields, forests or roads, for example); which years are relevant (periods that are both interesting and accessible); and which basic map should I base my historical analysis upon (a contemporary or historical map, a toned-down map, or a blank sheet of paper).

The landscape analyst is limited in the availability of sources, and one is not free to choose what points in time to include in a historical analysis, but must rely on the years that happen to be represented in maps or other data. This is important

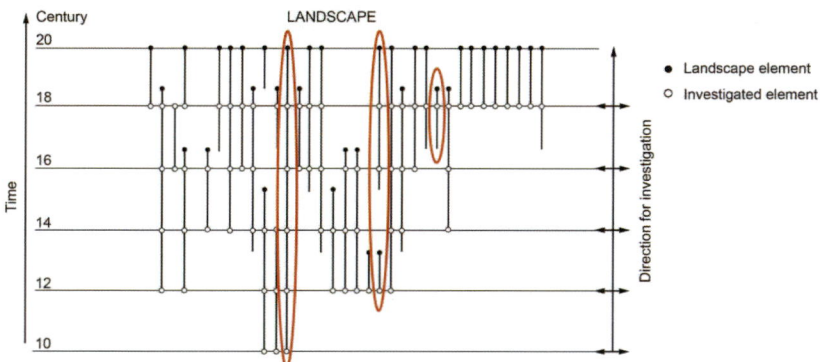

FIGURE 4.7 The chronological method
This method is a reconstruction of several historic time sections of the landscape based on numerous evidence, sources and maps.
Source: Moderated by Stenak after Vervloet (1984): *Inleiding tot de historische geografie van de Nederlandse cultuurlandschappen. Pudoc* Wageningen.

Viking age – around 900

The time around 1634

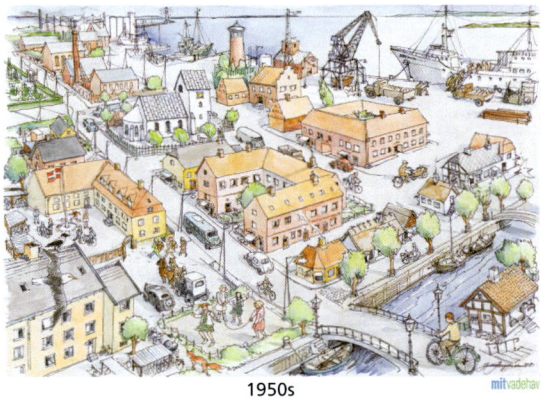
1950s

FIGURE 4.8 Illustration of use of the chronological method in teaching
Three historic landscape scenes of the 9th, 17th and 20th centuries are depicted in a
birds-eye view. The angle and mode of illustration is constant for the time series, as in
Figure 8.10 'Impacts of different development plans Oppdal'.

Source: Drawings by Joergensen, J. for www.mitvadehav.dk. From Etting (red.1995): *På opdagelse i
kulturlandskabet.* Danish Ministry of Environment and Gyldendal.

to understand, as a series of maps does not show all changes, rather they show the state of the landscape pattern at specific points in time. It is always possible that landscape elements may have been established and/or removed again in the period between two maps being made.

It is also important to be conscious of the scale and purpose of original maps that are included in the analysis, to avoid misinterpreting the maps or reading too much into them. In many topographic map series, the symbols have a fairly consistent definition and this is a key condition for carrying out a reliable historical analysis. However, it is generally a good idea to check if definitions – e.g. hedge-rows, dirt roads, wetlands, etc. – have changed during the period in question. Exact definitions of what comprises a hedge, for example, may have been recorded by the original map maker, but may have subsequently changed. Another issue concerns map revisions. Maps are revised at periodic intervals. However, sometimes only part of the map is revised – roads and urban borders, for example. Whether the map is fully or partly revised is normally mentioned on the map.

The map-based analysis reveals where and how the landscape has changed, but it does not explain why, that is, the reasons behind the developments. If no obvious explanation presents itself – for example, the presence of water by a dam – the interpretation must rely on additional sources such as statistical data or oral and written material. This is where the interweaving of the different methods comes into play, and the whole process may be drawn together as a narrative or landscape biography as explained later in the chapter.

The variations of chronological analysis that are described here are: 1) historical series of topographic maps; 2) historical series of thematic maps; 3) comprehensive mapping. While the first two involve making map series, where each map reflects its particular stage in the development process, the last involves presenting the dynamics of multiple stages in a single map. The analytical aim for the three variations is essentially the same: to demonstrate the difference between the situation at a given time, A, and the situation at a given, later time, B, within a given area. It is easier to compare the two situations if the other aspects are identical, that is, if the two maps are the same scale and the symbols have the same appearance and definition; in other words, the same principle as in the 'before-and-after plan' for the Copenhagen Zoo (Figures 3.26–3.27). In addition to these three approaches to chronological analysis, there is a further, named *landscape biography* (see page 76).

Variations

Historical series of topographic maps

In geographical terminology, a comparison of topographic maps from various periods is called a map-based analysis. 'Topographic' refers to general site description, in contrast to description of 'thematic' maps. Figure 4.9 illustrates the course of development of Sdr. Felding village, which is located in the Skjern river valley, between 1871 and 1975. Each of the three map sections illustrates the condition at a given date as a snapshot.

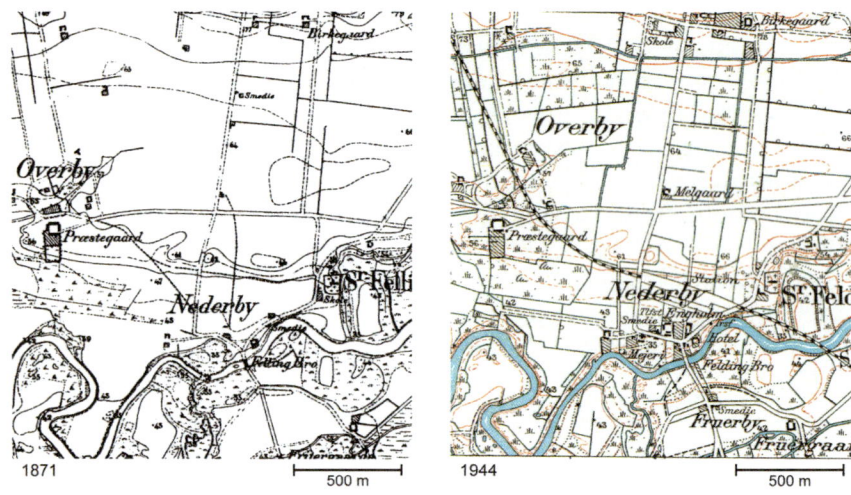

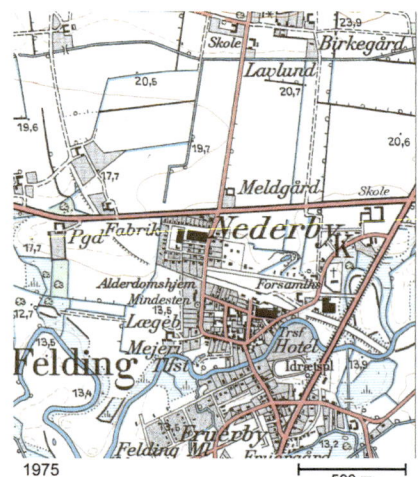

FIGURE 4.9 Time series of topographic maps, Sdr. Felding DK
Comparison of a map section from three periods provides information about changes in landscape structure and land use. The first map is from 1871, the second from 1944, and the third from 1975. During the period 1871–1944 a water race for flood irrigation is constructed along the upper edge of the map. This investment was part of a wider shift in farming systems in central Jutland, from arable production to stock raising, and enabled grassland production on the sandy river terrace where there was previously arable land. In 1871 we only find the symbol for meadow in the valley bottom along the river. On the 1944 map many meadow parcels occurred on the valley terrace, as a result of the irrigation system. During the period 1944–1975 the railroad and irrigation systems were abandoned as part of technological rationalisation, while the road system has expanded. Sdr. Felding has therefore changed over time from a village closely linked to agriculture to a rural town that is largely independent of agriculture.

Source: Jensen and Reenberg (1980): *Dansk Landbrug. Udvikling i produktion og kulturlandskab*, p. 30. Department of Geography at the University of Copenhagen. ©GST. Contains data from the Danish Geodata Agency.

Historical series of thematic maps

Comparing two or more thematic maps from different periods is often the best way of relating a given topic to other site elements based on a topographic map, perhaps in a toned-down version. The basic map may be the same throughout the stages, that is, from the same point in time, depending on the intended point of the analysis. In Figure 4.10 the basic map shows different time stages of the coastline. In Figure 4.11 you can compare the dynamic of four themes of land use in Tuscany at two stages of history (1935, 1985). In addition each theme is predicted 50 years in the future (2035). Figure 4.12 illustrates a comprehensive historic map in its simplest form. A historical sketch from Aalborg Harbour in 1798 featuring buildings and the quay has been supplemented with the contemporary edge of the quay. This not only highlights the contrast between the irregular, ragged harbour front of the past, and today's stream-lined appearance. It also indicates the land-fill area, which was established after 1798. During the working process, several stages in the development of the quay were examined, but in the final report it is enough to include the two extremes.

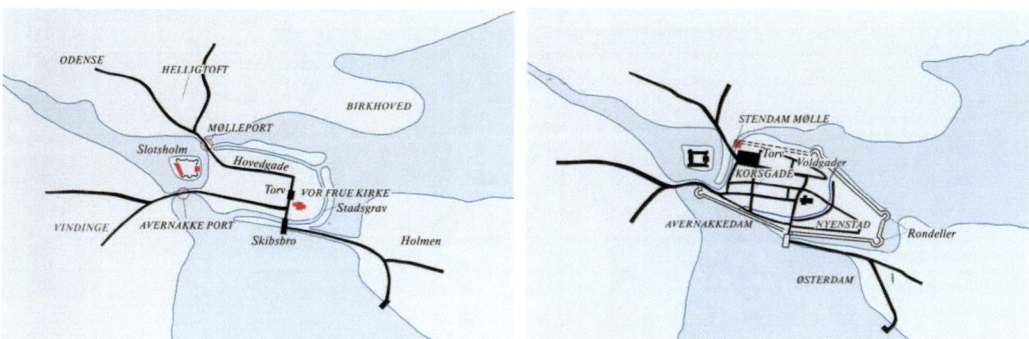

FIGURE 4.10 Time series of thematic maps
The map on the left shows Nyborg Castle in Denmark around 1450, located on a small islet west of the city island. The map on the right is from around 1550. During the 100-year period the city centre expanded towards the east, the street networks have grown, and the main square moved towards the castle. Each phase of change shapes the changes which will happen next! The streets from 1450 can be identified on the map from 1550, and also in Nyborg today. In this way the two maps provide essential information about the emergence of the city, its location in the landscape, its identity and special character. The 'theme' street network has been supplemented by other significant features such as coastline and prominent buildings of that time.
Source: Danish Ministry of the Environment (1994): *Kommuneatlas Nyborg*, p. 8.

Comprehensive mapping

This variation of historical analysis presents the dynamics of a development process in a single map, unlike the former two variations, where each map shows a stage in the process. In the comprehensive analysis symbols may refer to categories such as 'afforestation in the period 1894–1910' (Figure 4.13).

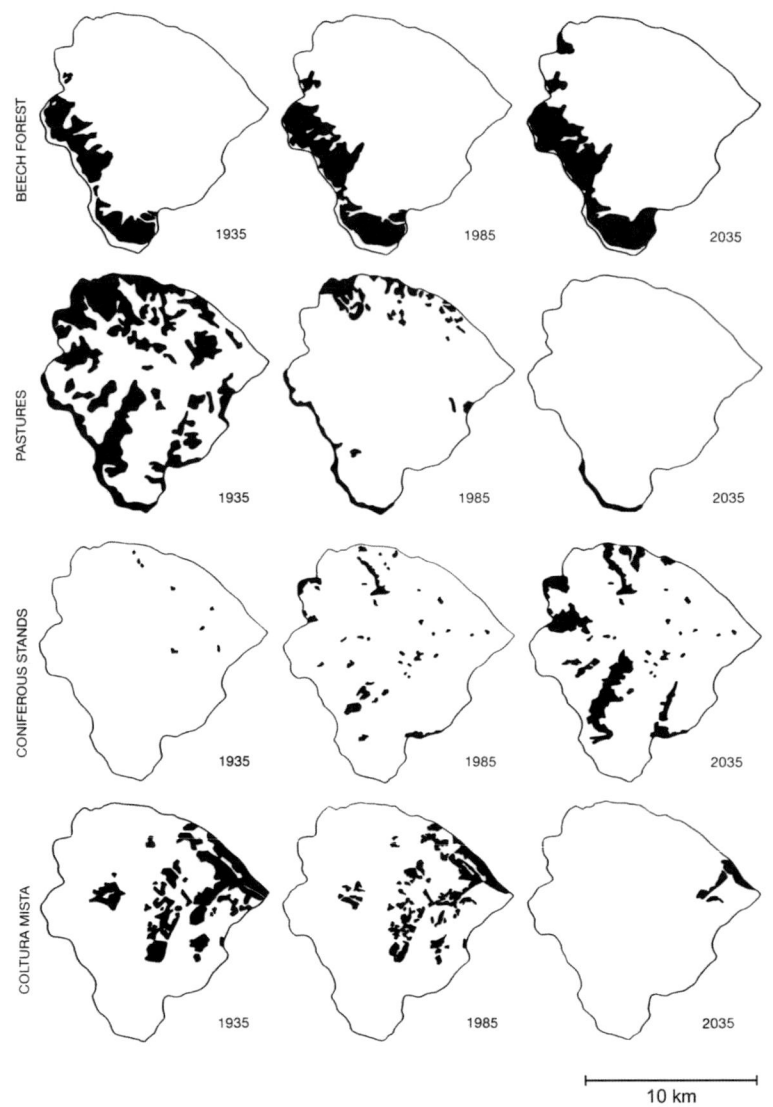

FIGURE 4.11 Land-use transformation in the Solano Basin, Italy – four parallel themes
Major land-use transformation of a heterogeneous landscape in Tuscany is shown
through four different theme maps, each representing a major land-use category:
beech forests, pastures, 'coltura mista' (a mosaic of annual and permanent crops characteristic of traditional, Mediterranean farming), and coniferous forest. The four maps
show in a simple way how the landscape from 1935 to 1985 has lost most of its pasture
land and the highly productive 'coltura mista'. Parts of the pastures have been replaced
by coniferous stands, whereas the areas covered by beech forest have been quite stable.
Through detailed analysis of the correlations between land-use changes and land types
(ecotones) it has been possible to provide a scenario for future development. Possible
changes of the four land-use types for the period 1985–2035 is therefore also shown.
However, such predictions are highly uncertain; they may be useful as background for
debate, but it is risky to base specific decisions – such as investment – on such forecasts.

Source: Vos & Stortelder (1992): *Vanishing Tuscan landscapes. Landscape ecology of a submediterranean-*
Montane area, Figure 11.13, p. 289. Pudoc Scientific Publishers Wageningen.

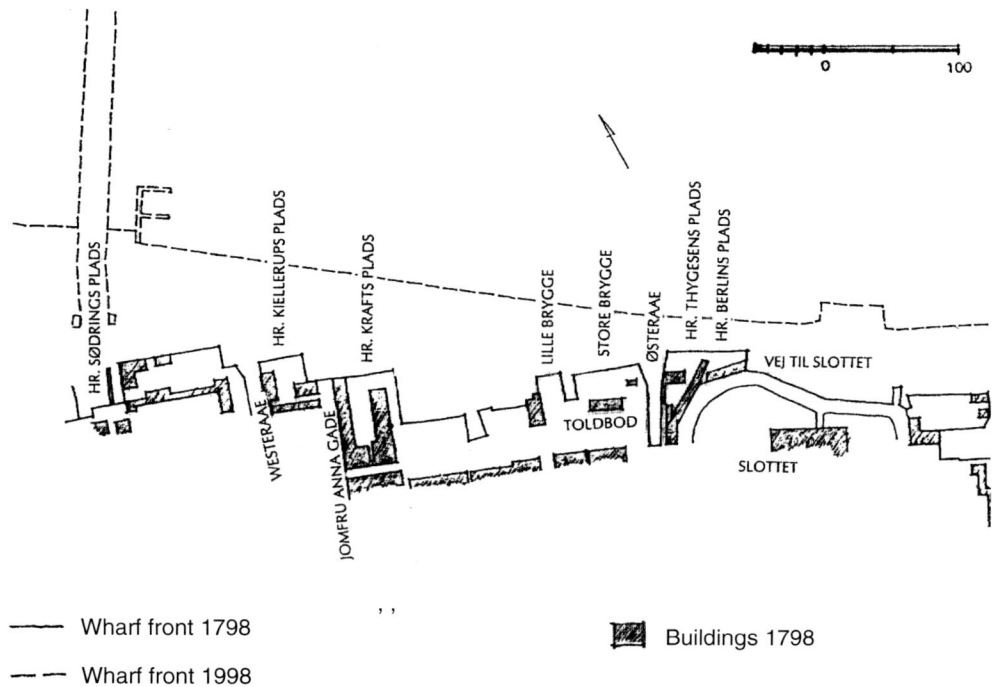

—— Wharf front 1798

— — Wharf front 1998

▨ Buildings 1798

FIGURE 4.12 Comprehensive time series of a waterfront
Land reclamation along the waterfront is changing the character and function of the city of Aalborg in Denmark. The line of the present wharf front on a simplified map showing the edge in 1798 provided useful input to a design study in 1998, aiming at designing the future relationship between the city centre and the fjord.
Source: Brandt (1998): *Aalborg – en by ved fjorden*. Master's thesis, p. 8. Institute for Economy, Forest & Landscape, Royal Danish Veterinary and Agricultural University. Unpublished.

Out of respect for the map as a historical document, historians often seek to avoid adding later developments to a historical map. Sometimes, however, a simple addition can be more informative than lengthy explanations. Figure 4.13 offers an overview of the dynamics with regard to afforestation and the clearing of wooded areas. With a topographic map as the basic map it would have been possible to compare new planting with other themes, such as the slope of the terrain, but at the cost of informative clarity.

Hägerstrand (1993, p. 27) points out that time sections, even when they are combined into a single map, are still a static depiction of the dynamics in the developing landscape. The dynamic impression emerges from the observation of a series of static images – an effect similar to film.

Landscape biography

Change in continuing cultural landscapes may occur due to biophysical events (such as a major flood), economic events or crises, technological innovations (such

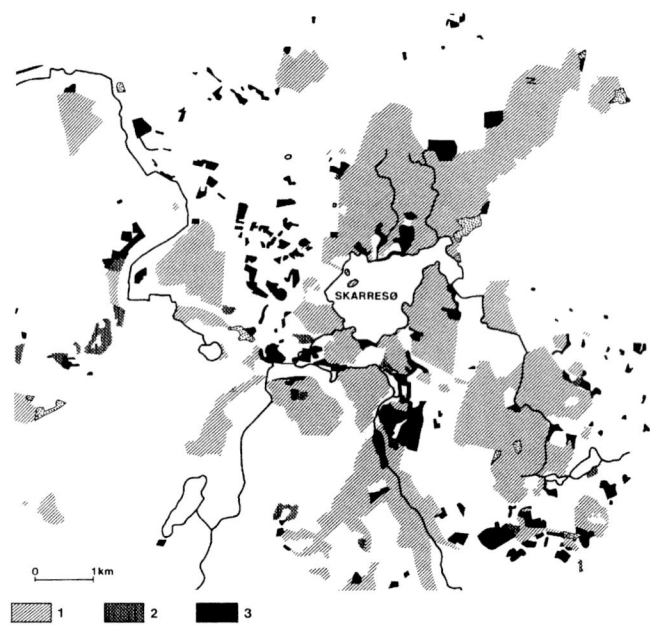

FIGURE 4.13 Comprehensive time series of forests
The dynamic of afforestation near Jyderup in Denmark is illustrated on a single map. The map is a result of close comparison between three topographic maps of different ages, 1894, 1910 and 1971. Woodland development is shown by indication of old woodland (1 – light hatch), present on map 1894, afforestation from 1894 to 1910 (2 – dark screen), and woodlands established between 1910 and 1971 (3 – black). Few and small parts of forest have been cleared between 1894 and 1910 (grey dots). Bigger new woodlands are typically located in addition to existing forests. Some areas are very dynamic in the period 1910–1971 with new establishment of one hectare or less of small woodlands. Further investigations would reveal these areas as hilly and sandy, not suited for arable farming.
Source: Danish Ministry of the Environment (1983): *Fredningsplanlaegning og kulturlandskab.*

as a new type of agricultural production), political events (such as a war), or even the actions of a single person (for example, an entrepreneur deciding to establish themselves in a particular place). Just as natural landscapes evolve in a series of pulses – periods of rapid change typically separated by longer periods of relative stability – so also do cultural landscapes, and identifying the nature and drivers of change is a central element of historical analysis.

An analysis technique that is helpful in drawing out and explaining the changes in a cultural landscape is called *landscape biography* (Roymans et al. 2009). Landscape biography takes the idea of biography from literature studies, where it refers to a description of a person's life history – where they were born, how they grew up, what influenced them, what events marked their life, and how these have shaped their character – and applies it to landscape. In the example reported by Roymans et al., the landscape biography is focused upon an area in southern

Netherlands that is undergoing rapid urbanisation. The biography uses a range of sources from different disciplines and the critical element is that, just as in human biographies, the biography focuses upon understanding the important points or phases of change – events or periods when the landscape is transformed into a new condition, or when its development path changes in some significant way. The Netherlands example of a landscape biography presents the analysis on a website for public use (www.zandstad.nl/site/ *accessed 23-11-16*), and shows that landscape biography is a powerful tool to implement the intentions of the European Landscape Convention.

5

SPATIAL ANALYSIS

Introduction

Humans have a distinctive set of physical characteristics and sensory capabilities, and these shape the way we experience the world around us and our knowledge of space. One way to better understand the consequences of this for landscape analysis is to imagine yourself as an animal such as a fox.

> You live in a fox den which is the centre of your world. This is where you sleep and raise your offspring. This burrow is carefully chosen – centrally located with multiple escape routes. From here you go out foraging, usually following specific routes which bring you through different places in the landscape with food sources, while you avoid risky places or barriers. Now imagine that you are being interviewed by two students who are undertaking a study of fox landscapes. They (kindly) ask you to draw a map of your local landscape, and when they see your map they may notice that the spatial structure of the key components is quite similar to maps drawn by humans, with paths, features, edges, etc.

Unfortunately, it is not so easy to make fox interviews and it will probably also be quite difficult for even a friendly and cooperative fox to articulate a map of its own landscape. There are nonetheless several points to make of this imagined example. Although landscape perception is an interacting process between a human brain and the outside world (and linked intimately with human consciousness), the primary senses through which humans experience the landscape are the eyes, the ears, the nose, taste and the sense of body movement – the same senses the fox is using, although with different sensitivities. The second point to make is that the fox learns about its landscape through experience, through numerous hunts – first trained through play as a fox pup, later learned the hard way in real life – through successful hunts and through failed ones. The landscape inside the head of a fox is primarily produced through practical engagement with the bio-physical world, and a fox makes itself at home in the landscape in ways similar to how humans learn to live in the world (Ingold 2000). Third, however, unlike a fox, landscape architecture students can learn from the cumulative record of symbolic (written, spoken, graphic and mathematical) knowledge that is part of human culture, using books such as this, for example. Hence analysis becomes a combination of lived experience and the application of learnt knowledge, and it is sometimes hard to distinguish between them. Experts use both seamlessly integrated together, but when we are learning it is helpful to recognise the difference. The final point to make from this example is of more general relevance to landscape analysis, namely that even though the (human) action-oriented types of landscape analyses presented in this book are linked as much to human values as to the biophysical landscape, many landscape analytical concepts have significant overlaps with landscape ecological terminology (Steinitz 1986; Gobster et al. 2007; Fry et al. 2009). This is particularly the case for what we have termed 'spatial analysis' which is the focus of this chapter. We will return to these overlaps below and discuss some of the implications for landscape analysis at the end of the chapter.

A spatial analysis is a study of the spatial relationships of a landscape. It deals with the relative location and significance of different patterns, elements and features in the landscape, and how we experience the landscape through our senses and through movement and physical engagement. The question addressed in a spatial analysis is "What is the architecture of the landscape, what is its spatial structure and what is its spatial expression?"

Spatial analysis concerns the *structure* of the landscape, how the landscape is arranged, how landscape is comprehended, and how we orient ourselves within it. Spatial analysis is therefore closely related to *visual analysis*. In a spatial analysis, the visual appearance of the landscape as seen from a particular point can be described as one would describe a building, with an account of its visible characteristics – the shape, colour and texture of its roof, facade, windows, doors, etc. However, spatial analysis is not limited to two-dimensional appearance like a picture. A third dimension is always included, as that is what creates 3D space. One of the challenges in a spatial analysis is to represent information about all three dimensions of a landscape on a two-dimensional surface – such as a screen or sheet of paper – and many different techniques of spatial projection and representation have been developed. A key step in spatial analysis is therefore deciding what representation technique to use.

Spatial analysis should not be confused with an analysis of spatial requirements, which analyses whether the size or the conditions of an area are sufficient for a given purpose, and what spatial capacity, capabilities, potentials and sensitivities the structure of the landscape offers for the proposed project. This issue is addressed as part of the 'site-selection analysis' (Chapter 7).

FIGURE 5.1 Hammershus Castle – a spatial view
How might a landscape analyst interpret this landscape on the island of Bornholm, Denmark, spatially? The linear feature running from an old castle to the visitor centre in the white building is clearly a *path* or *route*, which leads to the distinctive destination and *node* of the visitor centre. The bridge is a *landmark* along the way – together with the castle itself on a larger scale. The slope to the lower right, the forest edge in the background, and the wall all create spatial boundaries or *edges*, and the plot surrounded by a stone wall creates a distinctive bounded *district*. In this chapter we introduce a spatial language using symbols that enables a landscape analyst to get a better picture of the spatial pattern of a place, and to use a language that others can share to make spatial sense of the landscape in question.
Source: Photo by Stahlschmidt, P.

Main case: *The Image of the City*

In 1960 Kevin Lynch wrote *The Image of the City* because he was puzzled by people's ability to navigate their way around the huge grid-based cities that were expanding all across the USA. He asked residents in some of these cities to each draw a mental map of their city, and based on analysis of these maps he created a notation system to record the shared 'image' of the city, using five symbols explained in Figure 5.3. This work provides a continuing basis for urban landscape analysis, and even though the 'image' deals exclusively with urban landscapes, the method has also proved useful for the rural landscape, and has influenced the language of landscape ecology (see note regarding Steinitz in Chapter 1). An application of the approach in a rural landscape context is demonstrated by Lynch in his study of an island called Martha's Vineyard in the USA (Banerjee and Southworth 1990, pp. 316–337).

The *purpose* of a 'Lynch' analysis is to highlight those elements and features in the city's spatial structure that enable people to 'navigate' their way through the urban landscape. The 1960 book describes how the method was created and refined and offers examples of practical applications. In the following sections in this text, the emphasis will be on modifications of the method for specific practical purposes related to landscape analysis.

The method is particularly powerful because it is useful at any scale, from the coarse scale of a region to the fine scale of a garden, as the symbols simply take on different meanings, depending on the context. For example, London will be marked as a 'node' on a map of England, while Trafalgar Square will be a node on a map of London, and the Nelson's Column will be a node in Trafalgar Square. In other words, the spatial language developed by Lynch refers to the fundamental architecture of experienced space.

With regard to *type*, a 'Lynch' analysis is a qualitative analysis (as opposed to quantitative). However, the analysis does not evaluate the comparative quality of the landscape, as the perceptual experience of the objects is not assessed as positive or negative. It is therefore similar to landscape character assessment (see Chapter 6) which analyses what makes a landscape distinctive, not what makes it good or bad.

The *object* of a 'Lynch' analysis is the three-dimensional physical configuration of the landscape: its patterns and elements, areas and districts, boundaries and edges, features and landmarks, routes and nodes that give the landscape its spatial structure, which are represented by the five symbols featured in Figure 5.3. Depending on the situation, it may be necessary to modify the symbols and to add new ones to represent essential features in the landscape under investigation – this is shown in Figure 5.5, for example, where symbols are created to represent partial barriers. Kevin Lynch himself was flexible and pragmatic in his use of symbols when he carried out landscape analyses. They are a means of representing the object under investigation, a vocabulary used for spatial analysis, not the object itself.

The original *source* of information for the 'Lynch' analysis was the people he interviewed, who created maps of their own interpretation of their city, which Lynch then analysed to create his typology. It is possible to undertake spatial analysis in this way – by asking residents or other users to share their spatial understandings – and this can provide rich insights into particular landscapes. However, it can also be time consuming. More typically spatial analysis using the Lynch approach is undertaken by professionals, who use the 'Lynch' spatial language to undertake an analysis of a landscape based upon their expert interpretation of maps, aerial photos, and their own field reconnaissance.

There is a considerable element of personal judgement and professional interpretation in a Lynch analysis. The symbols such as edge or node are relative to the study area, and not defined by the absolute size of landscape elements, but by the analyst's perception of their importance. Therefore it is vital to have a clear under-standing of the purpose, the assumptions made, and the limitations in the situation given. A common pitfall is to confuse your 'map' of the study area with an objective reality, and to overlook other types of spatial structure – for example, to overlook a child's experience.

The *procedure* therefore begins with decisions on what spatial qualities of the landscape are relevant to the study, and at what scale, and therefore should be included in the analysis. That in turn suggests what symbols to use, and a work-ing vocabulary can be prepared, to ensure consistency in analysis. This is similar to the way in which countryside character assessment may use check sheets to help ensure consistency in analysis across different areas and by different people. A site reconnaissance is very helpful at this early stage – to gain a preliminary first-hand

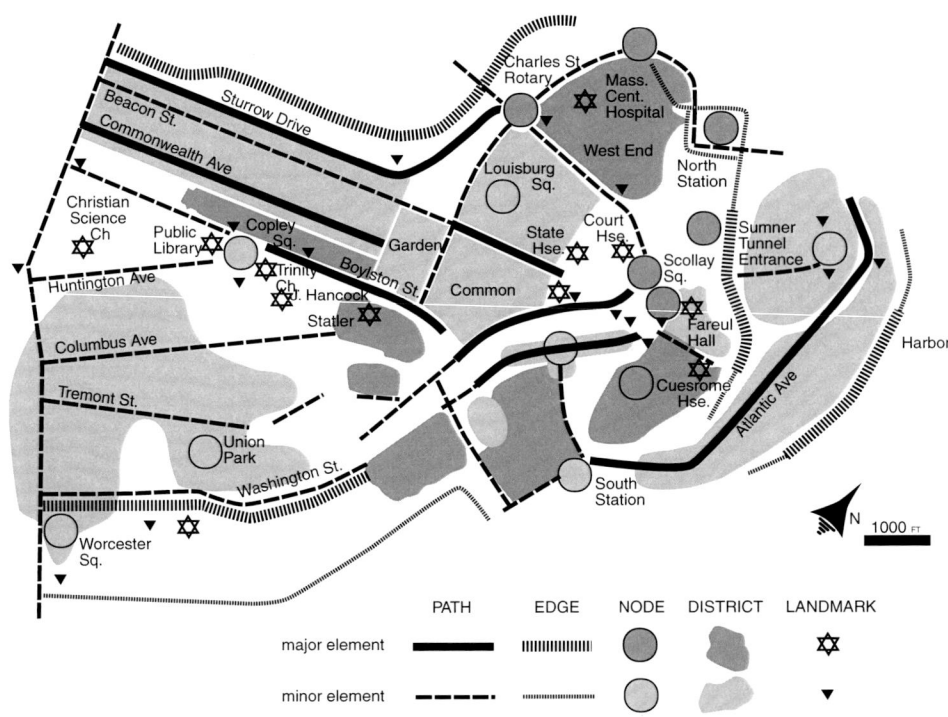

FIGURE 5.2 Kevin Lynch analysis, Boston
The map shows how the structure of Boston, USA, has been interpreted by the use of five different symbols. As each symbol represents two levels of significance – major and minor – ten symbols are available. There are significant edges at Charles River to the north and at the harbour to the east. Most paths point towards the city centre where the greatest concentration of edges and landmarks are also found. One of the charac-teristic districts is the dark-grey rectangular area along the river to the north. This is a distinctive area with blocks of residential houses, all built in red bricks.
Source: Lynch (1960): *The Image of the City*. Two figures from p. 19. ©1960 Massachusetts Institute of Technology, by permission of the MIT Press.

experience of the study area and its characteristics, and to test the symbolic vocabulary. A professional or expert analysis will then use the symbols to prepare a basic draft analytical map, based upon other types of maps such as topography and figure ground (see page 88), which helps develop an overview of the overall spatial structure, regardless of one's familiarity with the landscape.

When adding the selected symbols, it may be helpful to begin with the one that is clearest and most important. There is no pre-determined 'minimum level of importance', as long as the clarity of the map is not compromised. Even small landscape elements might be relevant; for example, a closely woven network of

Paths: Channels along which the observers move. Depending on scale they can be railroads, roads or trails, etc.

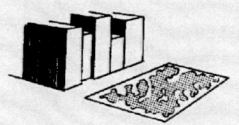

Edges: Linear elements not used as paths. They are boundaries, visual barriers, or linear breaks such as shores or walls. They may be more or less penetrable.

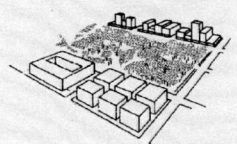

Districts: Medium- to large-size patches which have special meanings or functional significance to the observer; areas with identifying character.

Nodes: Point elements which can be entered and which have strategic significance to the observers – places where people meet, concentrations of events, transportation centres, crossing points, etc.

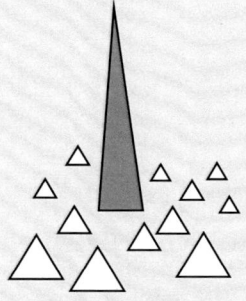

Landmarks: Point references which are not entered such as a tall distinctive building, a special tree, a special façade or, on a larger scale, a mountain. Landmarks are important orientation points for the observer moving in the landscape.

FIGURE 5.3 Five symbols to characterise the spatial pattern of a place or a landscape
Source: Lynch, K. (1960): *The Image of the City*. 5 marginal images pp. 47–48. ©1960 Massachusetts Institute of Technology, by permission of the MIT Press.

hedgerows may be an important spatial aspect in part of the study area. Leaving them out would help simplify the map and increase clarity but also risks leaving out a distinctive feature of that landscape. In the map of Boston, Figure 5.2, the five symbols appear in two grades to reflect their relative importance. When relevant, the symbols can be graded into three or more steps. The grading reflects the extent to which the landscape features a hierarchy of scale that may be a key characteristic of an area.

The next step is to go into the landscape and undertake a detailed field analysis, testing, correcting and revising the preliminary draft map. The aim for the final map is that it expresses and clarifies the spatial structure of the landscape in a way that is most useful and relevant to the purpose of the study. This is where professional judgement becomes important. In many contemporary studies the working drafts from professional experts may also be shared with key informants in the community, to validate the interpretations that have been made.

There is a range of possible *presentation techniques.* In a Lynch analysis this is typically the map itself, possibly in colour and with supplementary cross sections to explain the symbols. However, a range of different types of representation can be helpful: combining diagrams, sections, maps, 3D perspectives with multiple overlays, or animated videos. Again, the critical issue is the purpose of the study, and presentations should be designed to combine accuracy and validity with relevance and utility.

Variations

There are many variations on the basic 'Lynch' approach (e.g. Gosling (1996), Steenbergen and Reh (1996) and Steenbergen (2008)).The selected variations shown in the illustrations here are examples of analyses from different types of sites:

City: Boston, Figure 5.2; Rome, Figure 5.8; Holbaek, Figure 5.10; and Middelfart, Figure 5.11
Urban space: Hypothetical mountain village, Figure 5.7
Park: Hellerup Beach Park, Figure 5.5
Countryside: Randers Fjord, Figure 5.4; mountain landscape, Japan, Figure 5.9; Vaeth, Figure 5.12

As already noted, the purpose of the study and the scale of analysis determines which topics it is relevant to examine in the given project, but the same methodological principles apply from the micro-level of a garden to the macro-level of a region or district.

Furthermore, on a given geographical level it is often possible to transfer an analytical approach between different types of landscapes – for example, from the city to the rural landscape. However, a warning is needed at this stage. As the purpose of this type of analysis is to selectively interpret many spatial dimensions of the landscape through relatively few symbols, there must be some degree of complexity to be captured. If the landscape is extremely homogeneous and/or at a very fine scale – part of a backyard, for example – a formal spatial analysis may not add anything substantial to understanding. 'Analysis' in such trivial situations is not needed and should be avoided, as noted in Chapter 1. A simple photo or verbal description may be enough.

Spatial analysis can be organised in different ways: point by point, linear or areal (that is, covering an entire area). A point-by-point analysis (Randers Fjord, Figure 5.4) examines the visual experience of or from a given point in the landscape. A hypothetical mountain town (Figure 5.7) is an example of a linear analysis, where the experience is viewed from a line of movement. In his spatial analysis of motorways, Michael Varming (1970) distinguishes between *the road seen from the road*, *the landscape seen from the road*, and *the road seen from the landscape*. The other examples discussed here are all areal – that is synthetic analyses of an area.

Three further variations are shown later in the chapter: SAVE structural analysis, SAVE urban-edge analysis, and LCA spatial-visual analysis (SAVE means Survey of Achitectural Values in the Environment). These stand out by also being parts of larger analytical systems.

Visibility analysis

Analysis of visibility is a special form of spatial analysis dealing with visual catchments and zones of visual influence. A *visual catchment* means the total area that is visible for a person situated in a certain viewpoint, and the *zone of visual influence* means the total area from which a building or other object, existing or intended, is visible. Figure 5.4 is a study comparing the visual consequences by alternative locations of an intended new farm building. The resulting statements did not tell anything about visual quality, or whether assessment of the intended farm building will be positive or negative. However, they informed the analyst about future consequences for the extent of the zone of visual influence from two alternative locations, and thereby formed a basis for the sensitivity and site-selection analyses, and for the following scenarios for the relocation of farm buildings in the Randers Fjord area in Denmark (see more in the LCA analysis for site selection in Figure 7.20, Chapter 7).

Visibility analysis can be carried out as a digital analysis based on a terrain model supplemented with selected vertical elements such as forests, hedges and built developments, all of which are assigned a given standard height. A subsequent field survey can be used to verify the findings of the digital desk analysis and supplement it with a value assessment concerning the landscape experience. This value assessment of the visual consequences of a planned development is discussed in Chapter 8 on impact assessments.

Eye-level analysis

The visual catchment depends on the elevation of the viewpoint, and in finer scale analyses the height of a person becomes a significant factor. The purpose of an

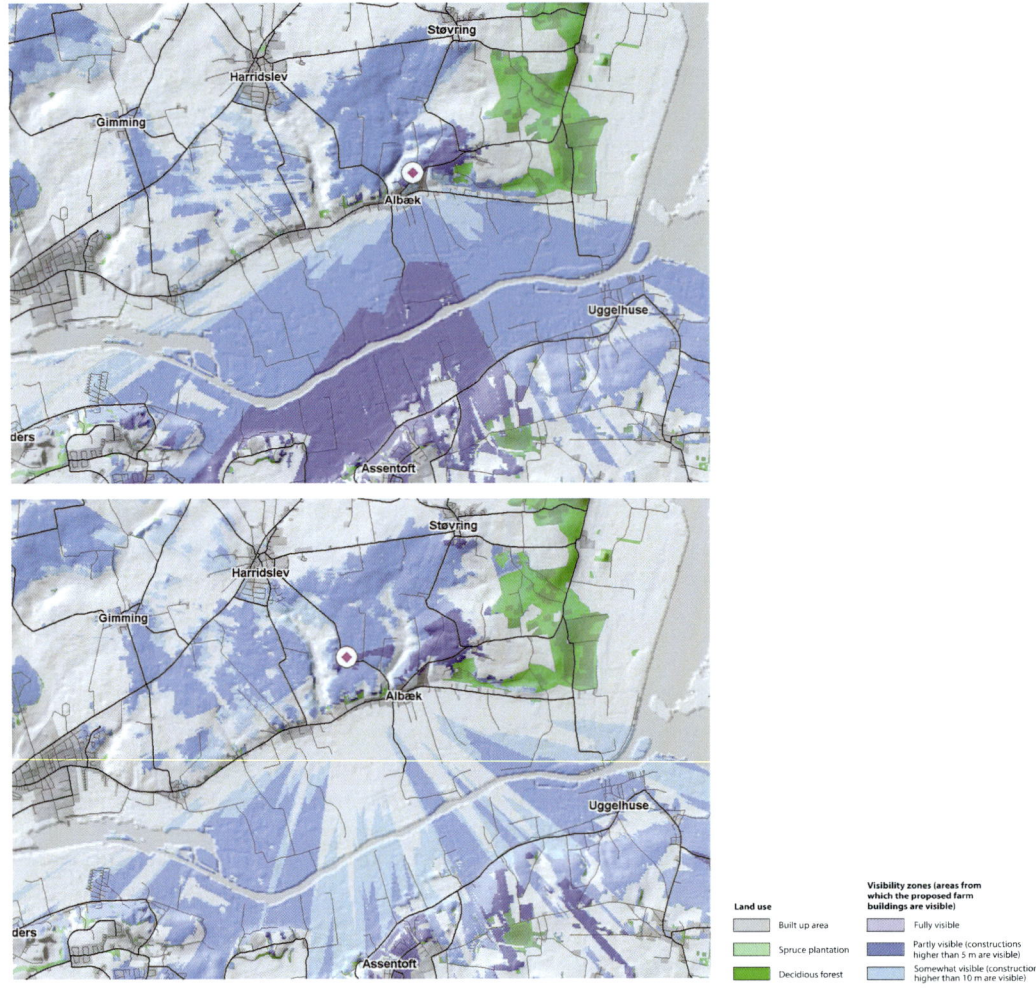

FIGURE 5.4 Digital visibility analysis, Randers Fjord

Zones of visual influence for a proposed new large farm to be relocated from the village of Albaek are shown for two alternative locations marked by red dots on the two maps. The village is located on marine foreland at the foot of a former coastal bluff, in the valley of the Gudenaa River near the mouth in Randers Fjord. On the top map the new buildings are located at the top edge of the bluff, which means they can be seen over a large area, since the zone of visual influence covers a large part of the valley floor. On the alternative shown below, the farm buildings are moved approximately 400 metres backwards from the top edge of the bluff. This relatively small change in location has a great effect on the zone of visual influence, reducing the zone significantly. The digital analysis could be supplemented by a field survey which takes into account specific conditions not included in the digital analysis, such as screening vegetation, for example.

Source: Kristensen, Denmark's Agricultural Research (2004): Digital visibility analysis. In Nellemann et al., *Landbrugsbygninger, landskab og lokal omraadeplanlaegning – metoder til landskabskaraktervurdering og oekonomivurdering*. By- og Landsplanserien no. 23, p. 57 (Figures 14 and 15). Forest & Landscape, Hoersholm, DK.

eye-level analysis is to focus on what happens at eye level, that is, in the horizontal visual field at eye level in the given situation – whether the person is seated, standing, riding a bicycle, travelling by car, an adult or a child, etc. Thus, the eye-level analysis can supplement the three-dimensional illustration forms (perspective plan, etc.) and vertical projections (cross sections and sectional elevations) by augmenting the horizontal plane with symbols that depict spatial barriers defined by visual perception. In other words, the eye-level analysis is a horizontal cross section – or a cross section that follows the movements of the terrain – at eye level (Figure 5.5).

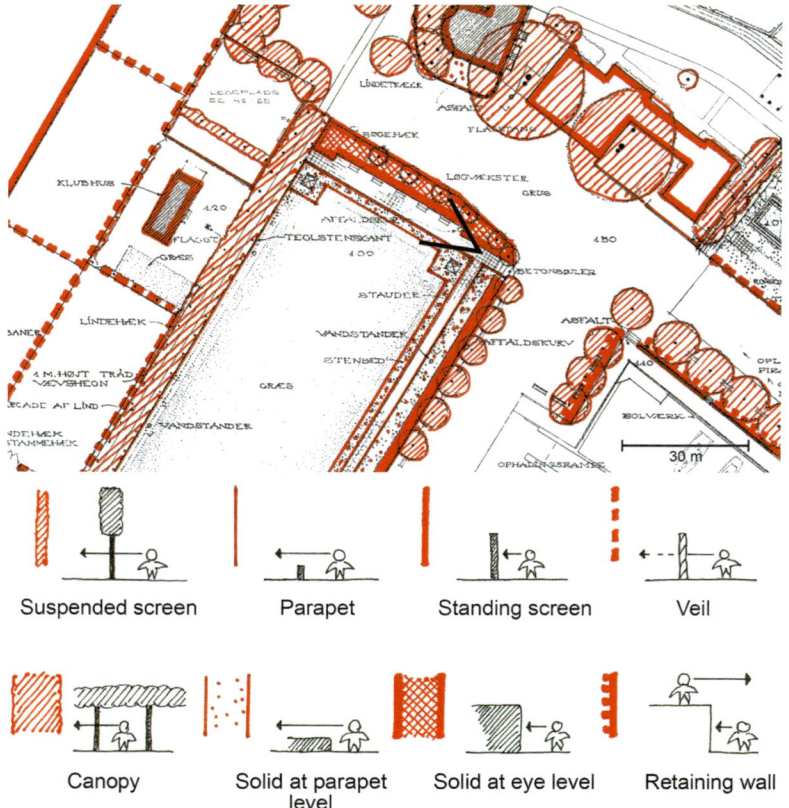

FIGURE 5.5 Eye-level analysis, Hellerup Beach Park
In this fine-scale study symbols for the character of spatial boundaries for a standing adult are shown in red. A bold line indicates no transparency and a dashed line some transparency. In the case of the retaining wall the symbol indicates there is no physical access and from the low side forms a visual barrier, while from the high side it is an open view.

The sophisticated spatial boundaries in Hellerup Beach Park in Copenhagen mean that the apparently sharply separated areas shown on the plan in reality provide complex experiences. The result is that the individual parts of the park are separated functionally and spatially, but visually integrated.

Source: Processed by Stahlschmidt, P. (2001).

FIGURE 5.6 Hellerup Beach Park
On your right the view is stopped visually by a standing screen of a trimmed beech hedge. In front of you – towards the tennis courts – the edge is more complex. The two tennis players can be seen faintly under the clipped canopy of lime trees and above a parapet of a beech hedge.
Source: Photo by Stahlschmidt, P. (2001).

The information offered by an eye-level analysis is similar to the information one can gain heuristically from looking horizontally into a cardboard model. An analogue model of this type (that is, a physical rather than digital model) is user-friendly in the sense that it can be experienced and understood directly, and by someone without specialist knowledge. A formal eye-level analysis is more abstract to decode but quicker to produce. An eye-level analysis adds nuance to the category of *edge* in a Kevin Lynch analysis.

Figure ground

Figure-ground analysis is a very long-established spatial analysis technique that simplifies the vertical dimension of a plan into two layers. The *figure* layer shows the presence of the phenomenon that the analysis intends to highlight. In an urban figure-ground analysis this is typically buildings, or in a park figure-ground analysis it may be tree canopies or dense vegetation. The *ground* layer is the background where the highlighted features are absent – typically this is the surface terrain. A figure-ground analysis of buildings in an urban neighbourhood is therefore a spatial analysis of building footprints and the ground shows areas where there are no buildings. It is therefore also an analysis of outside and inside, and it is widely used in analysis of dense urban settings where buildings create much of the spatial structure. The Cullen analysis of serial vision of a townscape shown in Figure 5.7 is mapped on a figure-ground diagram. In Nolli's map (Figure 5.8) the figure is private space – whether inside or out – and the ground shows the public space. One of the powerful aspects of figure ground is that the two layers can be graphically reversed (positive and negative) to highlight the spatial relationships that are of most interest.

Serial vision

Gordon Cullen, an English architect and urban-planning theorist, was interested in imbuing new cities and towns with experiential quality. In his classic book, 'Townscape' (1961), he uses photos and drawings to define urban aesthetic concepts. Figure 5.7 is reprinted from this book. Cullen was an important source of inspiration for the SAVE system, which was developed by the Danish Ministry of the Environment (see page 93).

Cullen's work highlights that movement is a critical variable in knowing and experiencing the spatial structure of a landscape. In conventional spatial analysis such as figure ground it is assumed that all parts of the 'open' landscape are of equal significance. In reality, however, we create a line of viewpoints when we move through the city. Serial vision is a technique in spatial analysis that involves providing a point-by-point depiction of a route through the landscape by means of photos, CAD drawings or free-hand drawings. A subsequent reading of the images can offer an impression of sequential spatial experience, and enable analysts to interpret the quality of movement through a city, in terms of its coherence and rhythm, with pauses that are decision points and places where we are drawn forward. The images represent a particular route and they should be uniform with regard to format and illustration technique. Normally, the distance between the points illustrated in the drawings or photos should not be fixed; instead the motifs should be selected with a view to telling the story of the varying spatial experiences, as in Figure 5.7. Selecting the route and the positions of images is clearly a matter of choice, depending on the purpose of the study. The serial vision technique is relevant when planning paths and roads, but as illustrated in Figure 5.7, the technique is also useful for characterising the sequence of spaces in a city, a park or a building.

A particular form of serial vision was described by Michael Varming in *Motorveje i landskabet* (1970) ("Motorways in the landscape"). This procedure involves plotting or modelling the major features of the landscape and the route of the future road, and then either creating images at evenly spaced points along the intended line for the road, or preparing continuous 'drive-through' virtual reality to provide an impression of the driver's experience of the road and the surrounding landscape. Thus, the serial vision is used as an input to impact assessment, where alternative route proposals can be evaluated and compared. The experience can be made more realistic if the drawings or digital model includes road equipment such as signs, road barriers and lighting, but this also adds considerably to the

FIGURE 5.7 Cullen's serial vision of a hypothetical mountain village
On the map of a hypothetical mountain town the eight arrows indicate the location and direction of the views shown on the eight drawings. The series shows the spatial rhythm experienced during a walk at a uniform pace through the town (in/out, dark/light, close/distant, enclosed/open). Furthermore, the drawings overlap, reinforcing the experience of movement. Such a serial vision can be done with drawings, photos or 3D-CAD.
Source: Cullen (1961): *The Concise Townscape*. Formerly published by The Architectural Press. London (paperback edition 1971, reprinted 1985), p. 17: Series of 8 + 1 small drawings from a hypothetical mountain village. Present publisher Taylor & Francis Group, UK.

production task. Modern animation and film technology allows seamless integration of digital models and representations of people and objects, and much effort is devoted to refining virtual reality techniques.

The question remains, however, of how to use and evaluate the results of such analyses. 'Fly-through' videos are exciting and provide an overview, but do not make the evaluation phase any easier – indeed in some ways the sheer volume of visual data they contain can make it harder to use. This highlights a paradox of spatial analysis. As noted in the introduction, analysis involves teasing apart in order to better understand. The 'Lynch' vocabulary is intended to simplify the rich experience of the city into a limited number of important elements. Recreating the complexity of the world in virtual reality models makes it possible to reproduce the 'real world' in controlled experimental settings, but this does not provide increased understanding until and unless some subsequent analysis is undertaken.

Nolli's analysis

Space is not neutral. As geographers have shown, space is also territory, controlled by different people or organisations. A very basic spatial analysis of territory is a map of political administration. Another is a map of ownership. Giambattista Nolli's map of Rome, Figure 5.8, exemplifies a brilliant thematic analysis of space as urban territory. Instead of distinguishing between 'inside' and 'outside', Nolli distinguished between 'public' and 'private' space. Hence the map records space that is open to all citizens, and space where access is restricted by property rights. It offers an impression of the city's spatial structure that is an immediately comprehensible indicator of shared space, where the public space of the church is presented on the same terms as streets and squares.

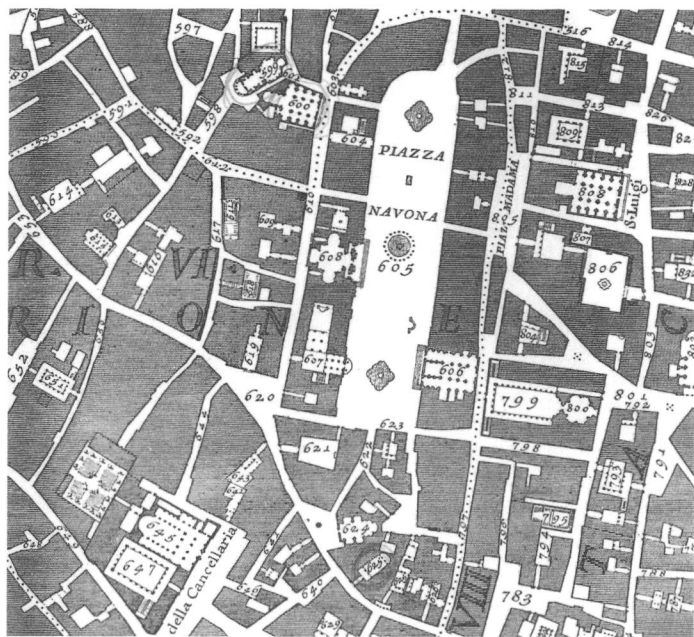

FIGURE 5.8 Nolli's map of Rome, 1748
Public spaces – both inside and outdoor spaces – are white in this section of Giambattista Nolli's map of Rome, while private spaces are shaded. Through these simple techniques the map provides a representation of the social character of space in the city by differentiating public space from restricted private space. Such a map is also an example of the interaction between 'analysis' and simple recording.
Source: Ehrle (1932): *Roma al tempo di Benedetto XIV; la Pianta di Roma di G.B. Nolli del 1748*, Città del Vaticano.

Higuchi analysis

Tadahiko Higuchi, a Japanese environmental engineer who studied with Kevin Lynch, illustrates how analysis can distil complex situations into essential experience. He has refined Lynch's analysis to characterise archetypes for site locations of Japanese temples (Higuchi 1983). As illustrated by the example with the Japanese mountain landscape in Figure 5.9, the symbols for *spatial barrier, landmark, path* and *district* have other designations and shapes than in Kevin Lynch's original version. There is no symbol for *node*, and *direction* has been added as a new symbol. Often, a landscape will give the impression that space has a motion energy that flows from a higher to a lower elevation in the terrain, in which case Higuchi's analysis may be directly applicable. However, Higuchi's approach may also be seen on a more general level as an example of how a Kevin Lynch analysis can be modified to match a given task.

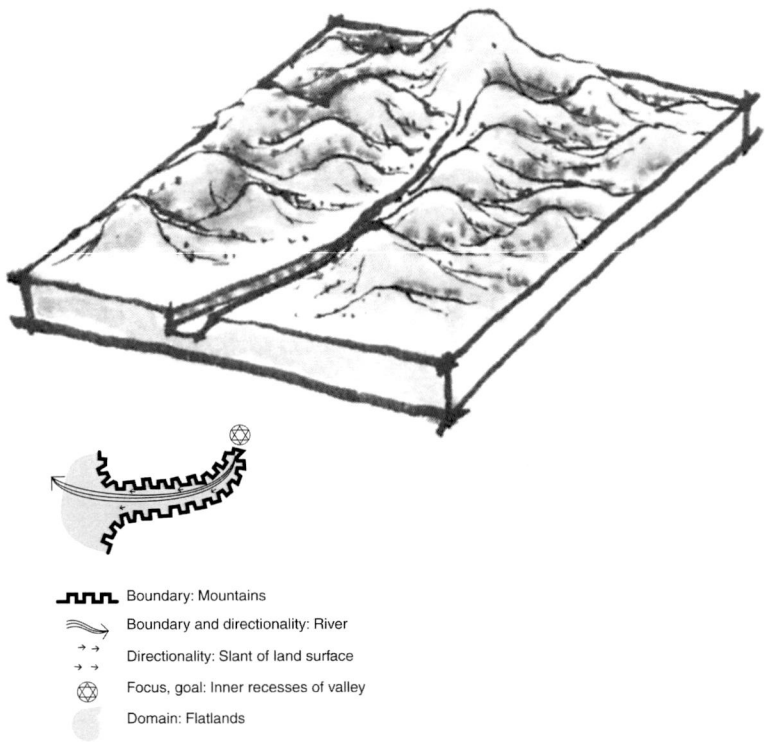

J─ΓLΓL Boundary: Mountains

Boundary and directionality: River

→ →
→ →   Directionality: Slant of land surface

✡ Focus, goal: Inner recesses of valley

Domain: Flatlands

FIGURE 5.9 Higuchi-analysis of Japanese mountain landscape
Block diagram and plan diagram of a Japanese mountain landscape where a river valley falls into a plain. The mountain top is a focus point from which the landscape gets direction towards the plain. The 'moving energy' in this landscape is caused by the river, the drop of the valley, and the wedge form of the valley. The valley sides are 'edges' and the plain a 'district'.

Source: Higuchi (1983): *Visual and Spatial Structure of Landscapes*. Two small drawings from p. 144. ©1983 Massachusetts Institute of Technology, by permission of the MIT Press.

SAVE structural analysis

The SAVE structural analysis can be seen as a further development of the *district analysis* in a Kevin Lynch analysis. The system was developed by the Danish Ministry of the Environment (1992) in order to understand and in planning decisions be aware of the history and quality of the townscape in Danish cities and villages. Figure 5.10 is a quick sketch giving the spatial image of Holbaek. The sketch focuses on districts under the theme of 'green wedges', which are shown with their position in relation to each other and in relation to the city core and the bay. The structural content of the large wedges is illustrated in a highly simplified form. The place names make it possible to gain a concrete understanding from the diagrammatic plan.

SAVE urban edge analysis

The SAVE urban edge analysis employs a further development of the 'edge' category in a Kevin Lynch analysis. In a Kevin Lynch analysis for the Danish city of Middelfart (Danish Ministry of Environment 1993c), the buildings on the slope along the harbour would be indicated as an edge. The SAVE urban edge analysis instead zooms in on the character of the buildings on the slope and their relationship to the water, the city and the terrain forms. In the cross section in Figure 5.11, the height of the terrain has been exaggerated by approximately 50 per cent in relation to the length. The buildings and the trees are less exaggerated to avoid distorting their proportions. In other words, the manipulation of scale in a 'perceived cross section' is based on the analyst's judgement. The goal is that the drawing should offer an understandable impression of the perceived reality rather than a precise rendition.

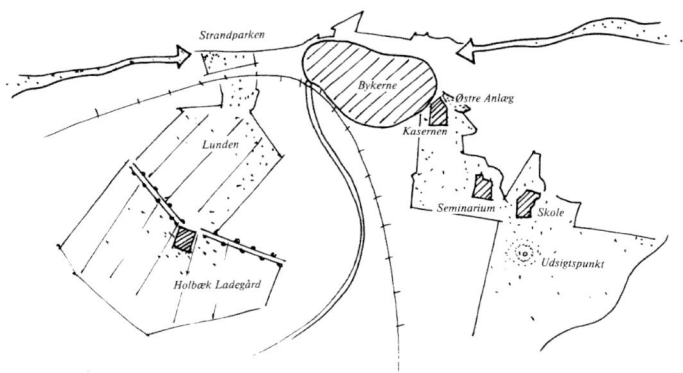

FIGURE 5.10 Structural analysis of city
Rough diagram of the spatial structure of Holbaek City in Denmark. Three characteristic districts are emphasised: the city centre, the former estate Holbaek Ladegaard (now an open space) and a green wedge with institutions. Along the fjord, north of the city centre ('Bykerne'), is a small green wedge connecting the countryside with the city. The road and the railroad touching the centre are shown.
Source: Danish Ministry of the Environment (1993b): *Kommuneatlas Holbaek*, p. 19.

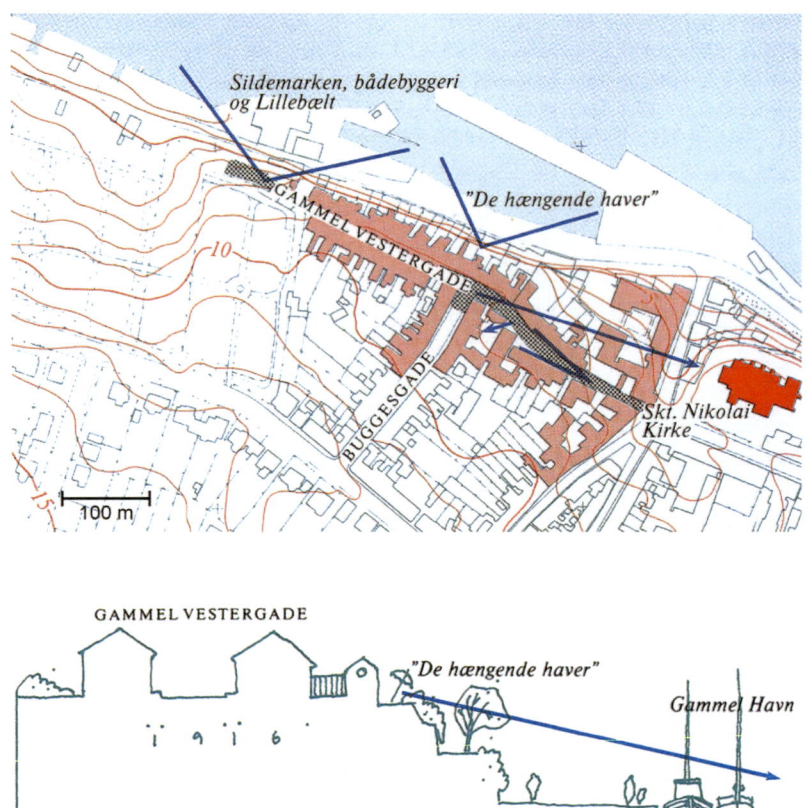

FIGURE 5.11 City-edge analysis
The waterfront of Middelfart City in Denmark is shown in two complementary ways: a rather abstract plan and a more realistic cross section. On the plan the dominant church is shown in red whereas the characteristic town houses are shown in pink. The line of sight towards the church is indicated by an arrow whereas the views to the fjord are shown as 'v's. 'De haengende haver' means 'The terrace gardens'. The terrain contours at 1m intervals are added to the map. The cross section is made with the vertical plan exaggerated.
Source: Danish Ministry of the Environment (1993c): *Kommuneatlas Middelfart*, p. 19.

LCA (DK) spatial-visual analysis

Spatial-visual analysis is included as a particular component of the Danish version of an LCA (LCA = landscape character assessment, see Chapter 6) focusing on the spatial and visual characteristics of a landscape character area. The purpose is to understand the appearance of the specific landscape and how it is perceived by people. This analysis identifies the characteristic elements and spatial-visual features of the landscape as well as any particular qualities of visual experiences and incongruent elements. The analysis is illustrated with a map using Kevin

Lynch-inspired symbols (Figure 5.13) and a digital survey form. The map and the form are completed in the field for each of the landscape character areas. In addition, reference photos are taken from representative survey points mapped by means of GPS.

The example in Figure 5.13 refers to the agricultural landscape character area of Vaeth. The area around the village is an undulating moraine plateau east of the river Gudenaa in Central Jutland. The plateau is an open, homogeneous agricultural landscape with fertile soil and thus a high proportion of arable land. Forests enclose the landscape visually towards the south and west, while a partially wooded hillside forms a wall toward the east *(edges)*. In the north, however, there is an open view of the Gudenaa River valley. A high-elevation sub area here with a church, a manor house and wooded ravines offers special visual experiences, *(contrasting sub area with special visual qualities)*.

The digital survey form provides a place for mapping and describing the following themes included in the spatial-visual analysis in LCA (DK):

1. *Characteristic landscape elements* include both the natural and the man-made elements and their form, patterns and interrelationships.
2. *Characteristic spatial-visual features* include the scale of the landscape, enclosure, complexity, structure and any connections with the coast.
3. *Special visual experiences* include sub areas and specific elements that offer rich visual qualities by virtue of the terrain, natural or cultural content, distinct landscape spaces and edges, landmarks and important visibility conditions (zones of visual influence, view sheds, etc.). These sub areas and elements may either express the particular character of the landscape or contrast with it. 'Sub areas' is synonymous with 'district' in the Kevin Lynch analysis.

Infrastructure analysis

Kevin Lynch focused his analysis upon the conventional type of city that was common in the USA in the mid-20th century, but we noted earlier that it can be applied at a range of scales. Over the past 20 years landscape theorists and designers have highlighted the way in which conventional distinctions between urban and rural are breaking down, and that infrastructure networks such as highways, water supply and drainage systems, waste management systems, power, wind turbines and digital communication networks, etc. now extend well beyond the cities they serve and structure the landscapes of whole regions or even small countries. Strang (1996) focused attention upon the way that infrastructure networks can be understood as landscapes, while Corner (1999) and others have reconceptualised landscape as

FIGURE 5.12 Vaeth farming plain
The farming plain is characterised by the slightly undulating plateau with extensive open fields and scattered farm buildings, such as for instance this dairy farm combined with a biogas plant that appears as a landmark in the area. The farming plain is surrounded by partly wooded hills and valley sides which create a spatial enclosure of the area to the adjacent landscapes/character areas to the east and west.
Source: Photo by Andersen, H.K.

the infrastructure of urban regions. Spatial landscape analysis can therefore also focus upon the role of infrastructure networks in shaping landscape.

Steenbergen (2008) includes a number of examples of how systematic analysis of the different layers and networks of infrastructure provide a powerful but very different perspective of how an urban landscape is organised. These networks may not be directly experienced as networks – we only ever directly experience fragments or sections – but the process of mapping reveals their spatial characteristics. The combination of rapidly increasing power and availability of remote-sensing data with digital models of the many components of a city region enable landscape architects and planners to experience the city in a new way which in turn creates new awareness of spatial relationships and spatial possibilities. The challenge this creates for landscape analysis is not new in essence – landscape analysis always requires interpretation, and the choice of representation influences how this is undertaken. Nor is the role of infrastructure new – cities have

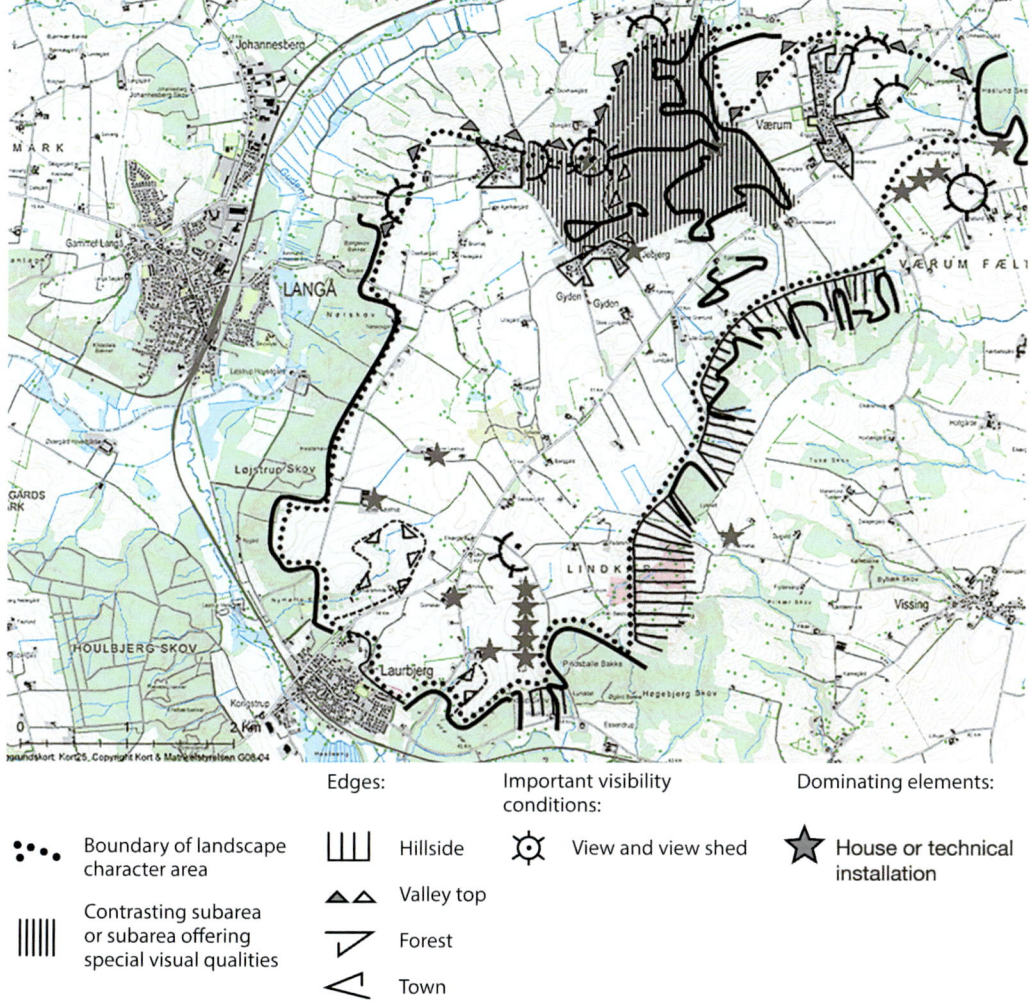

Edges:		Important visibility conditions:		Dominating elements:	
••••	Boundary of landscape character area	⊡	View and view shed	★	House or technical installation
‖‖‖	Contrasting subarea or subarea offering special visual qualities				
⊔⊔⊔	Hillside				
▲▲	Valley top				
▽	Forest				
◁	Town				

FIGURE 5.13 Spatial-visual analysis, Vaeth
The spatial-visual analysis is made on a topographic map in 1:25,000 at the field survey, guided by a digital survey form. The farming plain is surrounded by valley sides, to the east of wooded hills. The area creates a spatial enclosure to the adjacent landscape character areas. The analysis was used to identify agricultural areas suited for large new agricultural buildings.

Source: Nellemann et al. (2008): *Kommuneplanlaegning for fremtidens landbrugsbyggeri: Favrskov og Randers kommuner.* Copenhagen, Realdania. Available at: http://sl.ku.dk/rapporter/boeger-haefter >2008 / Annex 5. Bilag 1: Rumlig visuel analyse, Vaeth landbrugsflade (accessed 19 January 2016).

always depended upon infrastructure systems. However, the scale and extent of new digital technologies and the dramatic expansion of infrastructure networks in major industrialised city regions worldwide highlight the importance of making careful choices in spatial analysis, with a clear sense of purpose and a critical awareness of the factors and perspectives being considered and those being overlooked. The technologies blur the boundaries between what exists, how that is perceived and experienced, and what possibilities might be made and experienced in different ways, and for this reason we have focused upon basic processes using traditional mapping technologies, in order to highlight the process, rather than the output.

6

REGIONALISATION AND LANDSCAPE CHARACTER ASSESSMENT

Introduction

Regionalisation, a main subject of this chapter, represents an analytical tool widely used in landscape analysis, and ranges from suitability studies in regional planning to agricultural development potential assessments. It involves analytical classification of landscape into areas that display a significant degree of homogeneity in attributes, patterns and overall character. In recent decades an important method of regionalisation called *landscape character assessment (LCA)* has been developed and become widely used in landscape architecture. These LCA analyses are aimed at identification, classification and characterisation of homogeneous landscape areas, and enable judgements about their state and potentials, and represent an approach to landscape analysis that supports more integrated and collaborative forms of landscape planning. We have chosen two methodologically different examples of LCAs as the main cases in the chapter, and to introduce them we explain regionalisation as a methodical approach to landscape analysis and briefly outline the pioneering approach to mapping landscape character areas developed in the UK in the 1990s (Swanwick 2004).

Regionalisation and land classification

The classification of a landscape into homogeneous areas aims to provide an overview of the composition of the landscape in question and of the specific character of the individual areas identified. A *homogeneous region* means an area with homogeneity in its biophysical and cultural character, as opposed to a *functional region*, by which particular human activities are organised, e.g. a school district. 'Region' means 'an area, especially part of a country or the world having definable characteristics but not always fixed boundaries' (www.oxforddictionaries.com). In a regionalisation context, however, a region will usually be delineated with fixed boundaries. *Character* means a distinct, recognisable and consistent pattern of elements in the landscape that makes one landscape area different from another. *Characteristics* means elements, or combinations of elements, which make a particular contribution to distinctive character. Particular combinations of landform, soils, hydrology, vegetation and land use like field patterns and human settlements create the character. While historical and spatial analyses provide an overview of a theme within the larger project area, the classification into landscape character areas addresses the identity of each of the smaller homogeneous areas. The questions addressed by the classification into landscape character areas are "How are the interactions among the landscape's elements – cultural as well as natural – expressed in the character and potentials of the individual homogeneous area?" and "how does the individual area differ from the surrounding ones?"

The identification of distinctive landscape areas is a landscape analysis technique used in several European countries, including Great Britain (Mücher and Wascher 2007; Swanwick 2004; Jensen 2006), Denmark (Caspersen and Nellemann 2009; Caspersen 2009), and Belgium (Van Eetvelde and Antrop 2009). Within the UK tradition of landscape assessment, this process is termed 'landscape characterisation'. In some contexts this is coupled with evaluation or judgement of landscape qualities and potentials. In others the characterisation is strictly descriptive, and judgement about values and possibilities is a discrete step in the analysis process. For the purpose of consistency we term the whole body of work involving landscape characterisation, judgement and strategy as *landscape character assessment* (LCA in the following).

Many articles on landscape analysis, including Selman (2006) and Primdahl and Kristensen (2016), highlight the capacity of LCA to incorporate local conditions and the character dimension of landscape into the public and municipal planning process. An important question here is "to what degree and in what ways are local citizens and their perception of the landscape character included in LCA?" In a critical analysis of a number of LCA studies Butler (2016) argued that LCA as a general rule represents an outsider expert's (objective) view of the landscape as a visual surface, rather than 'lived experience' by those who live in the landscape, although there are approaches being developed which involve citizens in different ways.

Classification into homogeneous areas involves a 'regionalisation' or areal delineations of the landscape, which can be done based on single or multiple variables or characteristics (Claval 1998). The characteristics can either represent biophysical and cultural aspects of the landscape (undulating terrain form or field patterns, for example) or a functional dimension (a school district, for example). In this chapter we understand regionalisation in the specific way this concept is used in landscape character assessment (LCA), focused on identifying areas of distinctive landscape patterns and qualities.

The classification of landscape into homogeneous areas can serve as an important supplement to a thematic analysis, because the focus is on the spatial whole and upon how interacting landscape elements and processes have formed this particular area as a coherent area of distinctive character. By contrast, thematic analysis is concerned with a specific issue (noise, for example – see Figure 1.6) and how this issue varies across different landscapes and areas.

The regionalisation of a landscape can offer a systematic way of familiarising oneself with the landscape under investigation, serving as a form of *situation analysis* (for example, Kevin Lynch analysis Boston, Figure 5.2). Regionalisation may also, however, be part of an *action-oriented approach*, as the basis for other types of analysis. In a Danish LCA, for example, classification into landscape areas is used in the *Characterisation phase* (see Figure 6.10). The landscape character areas that are defined in this phase subsequently form the basis of the *judgement phase* (Figure 6.15) and the *strategy phase* (Figure 6.16).

An underlying idea behind regionalisation is that there will often be a certain degree of similarity between the distribution patterns of various landscape themes, as attributes such as land cover are partially dependent on natural factors and thus not randomly distributed. An example might be a sloping forest that blends into a horizontal meadow area, which are managed together. A classification into

FIGURE 6.1 Detailed level of landscape character areas
Smallholder farms on regular parcels are distinct from the large scale fields on the right and the area of small woodlands in the background. The red building between wood and lake is Spøttrup Manor House, Western Salling in Skive Municipality (Figure 6.9). An inventory would reveal that changes in landscape character are sometimes caused by natural factors, and sometimes mainly by cultural factors. In the area of woodlands the soil type is sandy in contrast to the surrounding fields and wetlands, whereas the natural conditions are the same for the smallholder area and the area of large fields, and the different patterns are cultural in origin.
Source: Photo by Primdahl, J.

homogeneous areas views each area as the result of an interaction between the natural factors of the site and the present land cover seen in a historical perspective of land-use practices. This makes it possible to describe a homogeneous area as a coherent whole and to judge the area's condition and its potential in relation to future changes.

Equivalent or nested hierarchical classification

An LCA may take either an *equivalent* or a *nested hierarchical* approach. In an *equivalent area classification*, the classification into homogeneous areas takes place on one level of generality, and each area constitutes a geographical unit. All areas are treated on the same scale. The grid cells and thus the degree of detailing in the classification may be large or small. The Svendborg case is an example of equivalent area classification at the municipal planning level. In a *nested hierarchical area classification* the classification into homogeneous areas takes place on two or more levels, so that each of the general areas is divided into smaller areas on a more detailed level. In other words, the coarser grid incorporates a finer grid. The English version of landscape character assessment (Swanwick 2002) which assigns landscape character areas/types on national/regional, county/municipal and local levels (Figures 6.4–6.5), and the classification into landscape areas in the Skive case (Figures 6.6–6.9) are both examples of nested hierarchical classifications.

   The analysis may take place in a *bottom-up* process, which goes from a fine to a coarser scale as small areas in the finer scale are combined into larger areas in the coarser scale (as LCA Scotland). In principle, however, the sequence might also be *top-down*, beginning on the coarser level and moving down to the more detailed level (as LCA England (LUC 1999; Swanwick 2002)).

Landscape ecological classification

Various landscape ecological concepts have been applied to classify landscapes. Forman and Godron (1986, p. 11–12) and others (Zonneveld 1995; Vos and Stortelder 1992) term the smallest landscape unit that is still a holistic ecological unit an *ecotope* or, more simply, a landscape element. Following Forman and Godron's (1986) terminology, a landscape element can be further divided up into *tesserae* (the original Roman meaning comes from a part of a stone mosaic), which are the smallest, homogeneous areas visible at the landscape scale. An example of tesserae could be small ponds in a field. Above the landscape scale is the region, which according to Forman and Godron is 'an extensive continuous part of land'.

   The purpose of ecological classification is to provide a basis not only for ecological analysis but also for landscape planning and management. This raises a general question in relation to classification into landscape areas: "To what extent can an analysis that rests on a classification based on one set of criteria be used for purposes related to a different set of criteria?" This criterion shift is evident in all the cases discussed in this chapter. For example, the classification criteria in the Skive case are based on the present landscape character, but different criteria are relevant if the purpose is to evaluate the area's capacity for a new wind turbine park. Primdahl and Kristensen (2016) have found in a few experimental planning cases that, although existing classifications were useful, additional classifications adapted to the situational purpose may be needed. Whether the issue at hand is best addressed using an existing classification into homogeneous areas as reference, or whether it is better to use a classification that is tailored to the given purpose, must be determined on a case-by-case basis.

Procedure for regionalisation

Classification of a region or a landscape includes both *delineation* into homogeneous *areas,* and *area descriptions*. A classification into homogeneous areas involves dividing the project area into smaller areas on a map. In an LCA context the areas must be homogeneous with regard to their characteristic (key) elements and visual appearance, based on their particular combination of terrain form, water, vegetation, pattern of built structures, etc., as well as special spatial and visual aspects. Relevant visual aspects could be *size* (from small to big elements), *enclosure* (from enclosed to open) and *complexity* (from uniform to complex, i.e. many different

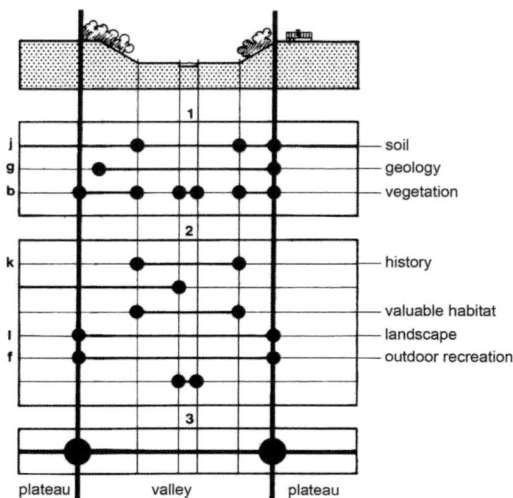

FIGURE 6.2 Regionalisation of a valley
The diagram illustrates that regionalisation depends on the purpose. Plateaus intersected by valleys represent a common overall pattern in glacial landscapes and also in many other landscapes of different geological formation. On this cross section area boundaries are shown for two categories: (1) biophysical basis (soil, geology and vegetation); (2) land use related to nature conservation (history, valuable habitat, scenic quality, outdoor recreation). In the bottom diagram the finally defined boundary is delineated at the valley top for the purpose of land-use planning, as the plateau will form a homogeneous agricultural management entity, whereas the valley sides, bottom and water course form various combinations of nature conservation interests.
Source: Danish Ministry of the Environment (1982): *Vejledning i fredningsplanlaegning* no. 2, p. 57.

elements). The classification should aim to achieve maximum homogeneity within each area and maximum distinction between areas. Homogeneity does not mean a lack of complexity. A homogeneous area may well have a high degree of detailed or fine-scale variation, in the sense that the landscape may contain many different elements, but all combine to create an overall distinctive character, such as Disney World. Or it may have a uniform fine-scale character throughout, such as a field of wheat. Both can be examples of homogeneous areas considered at a landscape scale.

The first step in a classification into homogeneous areas is the choice of classification criteria and level; this choice depends on the purpose of the analysis. The criteria chosen must be relevant to the way in which the classification will be used. For example, if part of the purpose is to develop biodiversity enhancement strategies, then habitat as a land cover will be important. The level or scale of the classification also depends on the purpose of the analysis, e.g. the county/district scale for municipal land-use planning, or the local scale for impact assessments of development projects or community-based landscape strategies (Figure 6.2). A classification into homogeneous areas may be either thematic or topographic, and in the next section we deal with each in turn.

Thematic approach

In a *thematic approach*, the classification is based on themes that are relevant in the given situation; in geographical terminology, the project area is divided into a series of formal single-factor areas. One theme could be terrain form (Figure 6.3), another the pattern of built structures, a third based on the presence of hedges and woodland, and a fourth based on the presence of wetlands and streams. Next, the four layers (or sheets) are placed on top of the basic map and a new, composite classification map is drawn up.

The aim of the analysis is to develop a classification that is relevant in its content, logical in its structure, and legible and easy to understand. These are not always easy to align. A good place to start is to begin the composite classification by outlining areas with congruent boundaries, that is, areas where boundaries based upon several different themes are congruent and thus reinforce each other and are not in doubt. From here, the next step is to identify the more definite and obvious individual thematic boundaries that are most relevant to the purpose of the study. This leaves the most difficult and ambiguous choices till last, which is where the expert's experience and judgement become most significant. However, it is also where individual interpretations become most influential, and so is often a phase where dialogue and discussion is particularly valuable.

In the Danish LCA, the classification of character areas is based on the identity of the landscape given by the characteristic elements, patterns and spatial-visual aspects, starting with the geomorphology, soils and terrain, and supplying the first-draft classification with land cover and spatial-visual layers. If the characteristic elements and spatial-visual aspects are composed of steep terrain and clearly enclosed fields, next to an open agricultural plain and woodlands, for example,

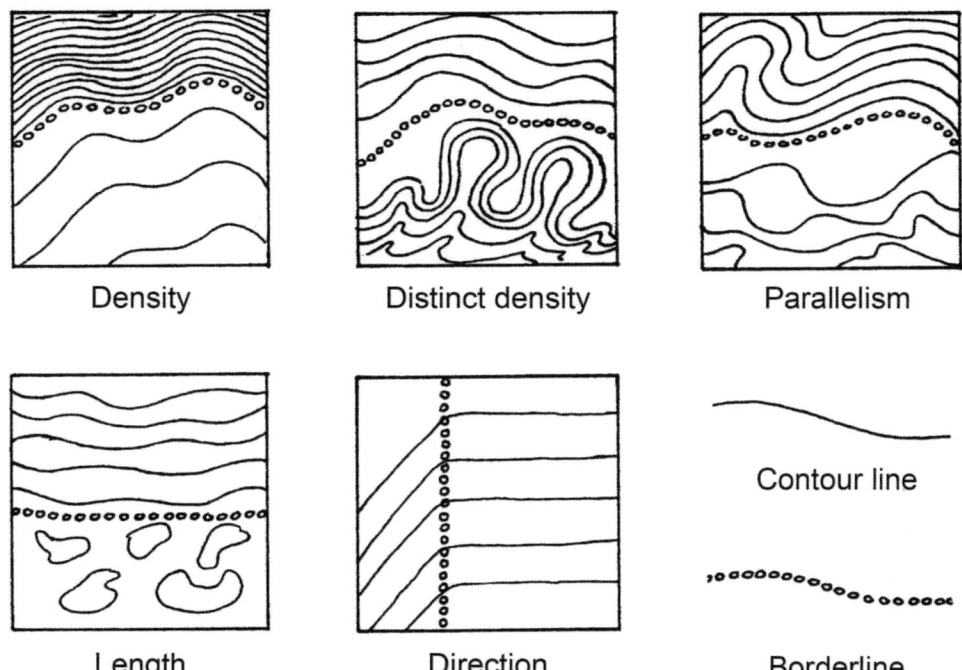

| Density | Distinct density | Parallelism |

| Length | Direction | Contour line |
| | | Borderline |

FIGURE 6.3 Delineation based on contour lines
Contour lines may be characterised through five pattern-making attributes: density, distinct density, parallelism, length and direction. The *density* describes how relatively close together the contour lines are at the given scale, and this indicates how steep the terrain is – its amplitude. *Distinct density* indicates that the terrain is changing vertically in different directions over short distances. *Parallelism* indicates where the terrain is changing in uniform ways. Short *contour length* indicates that there are many small humps and hollows. *Direction* indicates in what way the terrain is oriented (north, east, etc.). Each of the five patterns may vary and therefore determine the delineation of an area, but more often the delineation will be based on the relationship between two or more of the patterns. For example, a combination or juxtaposition of distinct density and short contours indicate a complex land surface, although it may have only low amplitude. On the other hand distinct density combined with density but long contours might indicate steep slopes and high bluffs.
Source: Moderated from Jensen and Kuhlman (1971): *Danmarks Geografi. Kort oevelsesvejledning.*

the terrain transitions from hill to plain and the edge of the forest will form the basis for delineation of the character areas. In the case shown in Figure 6.12 (LCA, Svendborg), a first step might be to draw the obvious boundary between the farmland in Area 1 and the town of Svendborg, and to conclude by drawing a boundary between the general farmland and the farmland belonging to the Hvidkilde Estate to the north (between Areas 1 and 2), where the criteria for the boundary are less obvious. The difference between the latter two areas consists of a change from small-scale farming, with many small individual farms and villages, to an estate landscape characterised by large undulating fields without buildings, except for the manor house, and scattered wooded areas. Hence, the boundary is drawn along the property line that divides the small farms from the estate, showing how boundaries can be derived from a range of different natural and cultural factors.

Topographic approach

In the *topographic approach*, the analyst begins with the final, topographic and composite classification – establishing formal multiple-factor homogeneous areas, to use the geographical terminology. In this case the process also begins with the simplest and most obvious boundaries and moves gradually to increasingly ambiguous boundaries. However, in contrast to the thematic approach, all relevant criteria are considered simultaneously and weighed against each other throughout the process.

Whether the approach is thematic or topographic, an experienced analyst will be able to ascertain from the finished draft whether the classification was successful. If the classification has resulted in area enclaves that have been singled out for their character and are surrounded by 'residual areas' then the classification is incomplete. The classification is also incomplete if boundaries can be shifted without reducing the clarity of the classification. In a successful classification the whole of the study area should be included in the typology, and the different areas broadly equivalent in scale and degree of homogeneity. Once the draft appears successful on the drawing table it should normally be validated and refined in the field. On-site studies will usually uncover factors that call for modifications.

With growing experience and knowledge about the landscape in question, delineating boundaries becomes gradually quicker and less ambiguous. However, since the study purpose, grid size (small or large areas), designation of characteristics (key elements and key spatial-visual factors) and personal judgement all affect the process, there is no one right way to carry out a classification of landscape areas. In character assessment, the ultimate success depends upon the plausibility and subsequent use of the classification. Furthermore, a classification into landscape areas should not be confused with the highlighting of 'districts' in a Kevin Lynch analysis, which are sub areas that offer particular visual experiences (Figure 5.2).

Regionalisation of a landscape into homogeneous areas may therefore be done in different ways and scales. Below we illustrate this through three cases. Two Danish cases are described in relative detail, and are introduced by a brief outline of the English landscape character assessment which has functioned as an inspiration for many European LCAs.

Nested hierarchical classification into landscape areas/types, England

Landscape character assessment (LCA) is a system of analysis based on landscape character that was developed in England, and which is used in modified versions for landscape planning and management in several European countries, including Denmark. The system is applicable on every geographical level, from the whole of Europe to the local level (Swanwick 2002). The original English version has a three-tiered nested hierarchy: national/regional level with a scale of 1:250,000, county/

district level with a scale of 1:50,000 and 1:25,000, and local level with scales down to 1:10,000. On all three levels, areas are classified both as landscape character areas and as landscape character types (Figure 6.5).

The English approach has been top-down with a classification into homogeneous areas that begins on the national level (Figure 6.4), primarily based on characteristic natural factors (geology and terrain forms) supplemented with general patterns in land use and land cover (woodlands, agricultural landscapes and major urban concentrations). The national level is expanded with a classification into homogeneous areas on the county/district level and, in some cases, on the local level. In Scotland a bottom-up approach has been applied, where the LCA begins with analyses on a scale of 1:50,000 or 1:25,000, carried out by private consultancy firms. The local landscape character areas are subsequently gathered and aggregated to higher levels. Many variations in the application of the LCA system have been produced and the variety has sometimes created difficulties in comparative analysis.

FIGURE 6.4 Landscape character areas at national scale, England
The 159 character areas in England mapped out give an indication of the diversity of landscape character at national scale. Note that area number 36 in yellow is on the top of Figure 6.5.

Source: *The Character of England map*. © Countryside Agency copyright. Based on the Ordnance Survey map © Crown copyright. In Swanwick (2002): *Landscape Character Assessment – Guidance for England and Scotland*.

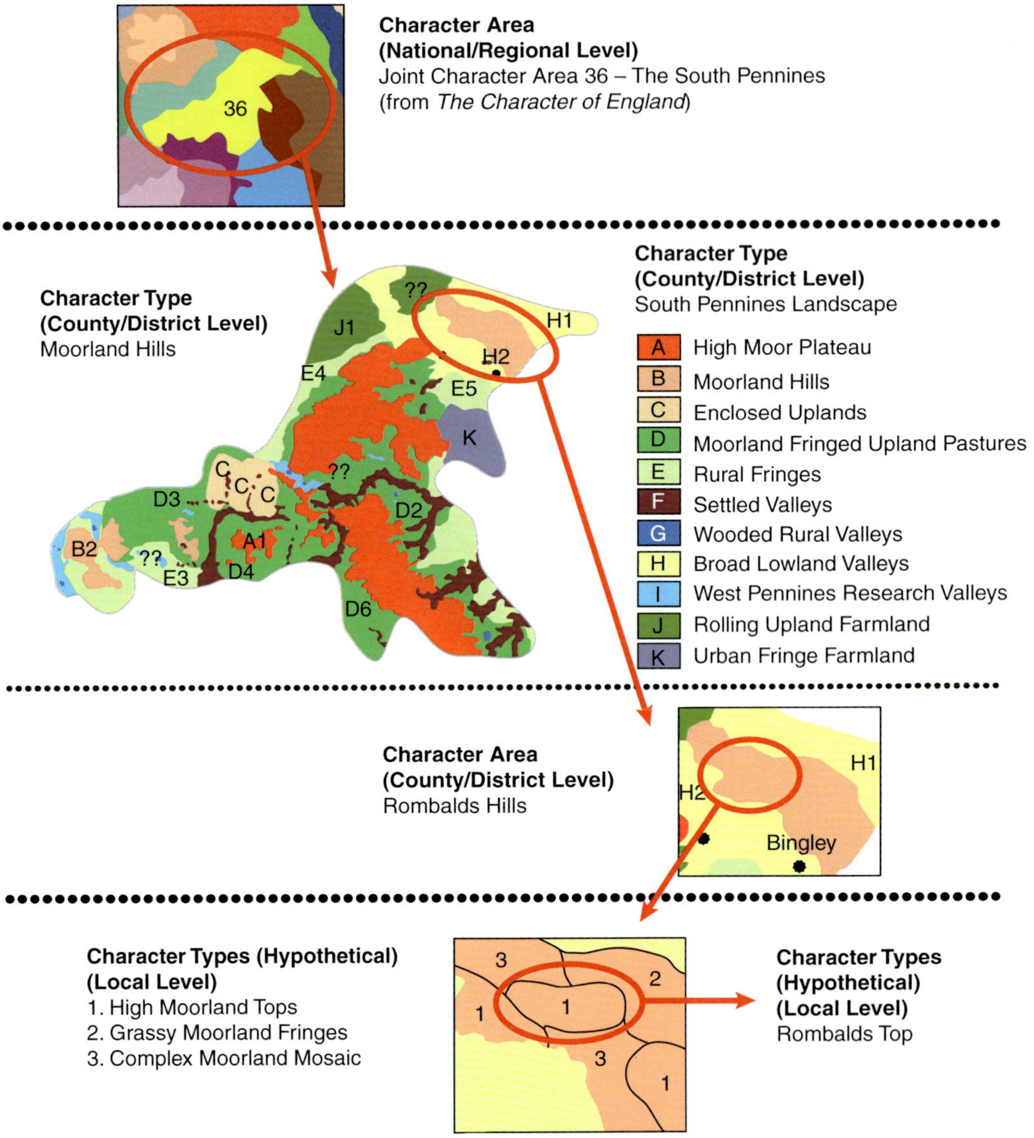

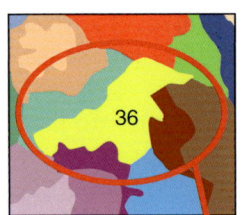

**Character Area
(National/Regional Level)**
Joint Character Area 36 – The South Pennines
(from *The Character of England*)

**Character Type
(County/District Level)**
Moorland Hills

**Character Type
(County/District Level)**
South Pennines Landscape

A	High Moor Plateau
B	Moorland Hills
C	Enclosed Uplands
D	Moorland Fringed Upland Pastures
E	Rural Fringes
F	Settled Valleys
G	Wooded Rural Valleys
H	Broad Lowland Valleys
I	West Pennines Research Valleys
J	Rolling Upland Farmland
K	Urban Fringe Farmland

**Character Area
(County/District Level)**
Rombalds Hills

**Character Types (Hypothetical)
(Local Level)**
1. High Moorland Tops
2. Grassy Moorland Fringes
3. Complex Moorland Mosaic

**Character Types
(Hypothetical)
(Local Level)**
Rombalds Top

FIGURE 6.5 Hierarchic landscape character mapping, England
The example shows the different levels of landscape character types and areas. The landscape character types are types of landscapes occurring in different places within larger areas, such as 'settled valleys' and 'rural fringes'. Landscape character areas on the other hand are unique and occur only in one location, where they represent one specific type. For example, the local character 'area' of the Rombalds Hills is a 'moorland hill type' at the county /district level which is in turn included in the South Pennines Character Area 36 on the national/regional level.

Source: Derived from LUC (1999): *South Pennines Landscape Character Assessment*. For SCOSPA, Bradford. In Swanwick (2002): *Landscape Character Assessment – Guidance for England and Scotland*. © Countryside Agency and Scottish Natural Heritage copyright.

Main case A: nested hierarchical landscape analysis Skive

This analysis was carried out in spring 2009 for the Municipality of Skive, Northern Jutland in Denmark (Linnet et al. 2009). The *purpose* was to incorporate landscape considerations in municipal planning, by using the homogeneous areas as reference areas internally in the municipal administration and in the dialogue between the municipality and the citizens. In a municipal-development project including the five case areas (as part of an experimental planning project), the classification into landscape areas proved very useful as a dialogue tool, and the classification served as an eye-opener that made people aware of areas and characteristics in the local environment that they were not familiar with. The process gave the citizens a better understanding of their own landscape, and the classification has been used as a reference point in work by local citizens groups (Primdahl and Kristensen 2016). The Municipality of Skive also wanted to use the classification of landscape areas to explain the basis of planning decisions, by improving the dialogue on rural zone management with the Ministry of Environment, for example. Based on these observations, the classification into landscape areas was expanded to include the entire municipality, except for the urban area of Skive.

The general *procedure* was to go from the desk to the field and back again to the desk. The draft for the delineation was prepared at the desk based on current, topographic print maps on a scale of 1:25,000 with clear terrain contours (2.5m intervals). The map was of the same type as the basic map shown in Figure 6.6. To support the classification into homogeneous areas, the analysis also included same-scale topographic maps from 1900–1920, sub-soil maps, landform maps, and a regional landscape analysis carried out in 1974 (Viborg County 1974). In the final draft map, each area was assigned a code for landscape type (for example, 'wet' for wetland).

In the field, the boundaries of each area were checked and modified and the draft classification of landscape types was validated. Where the boundaries had been easy to draw at the desk – for example, in the landscape surrounding Hoejslev (Figure 6.6), modifications were rarely needed. But where the delineation process had been more challenging – for example, in the vast areas of intensive farming in Middle Salling – the boundaries were often modified as a result of the field studies. To complete the analysis of an area, keywords were noted for the description (Figure 6.7). In an average work day, two people were able to cover 30–40 areas, and it took ten days to complete the field studies for the 331 homogeneous areas into which the municipality was divided.

In the area descriptions, the concept of *stability* played a role and deserves an explanation. In this context, 'stable' means that under the current conditions – in terms of use, society and nature – the landscape area appears to have found a harmonious form. In a stable area, there will typically be a legible link between form and function. If new functions are introduced into a stable area, the area becomes unstable and evolves and adapts until a new stable condition is reached and the landscape expression is once again in accordance with the functions of the area. For example, as an area begins to grow back after grazing has been abandoned or major new plantings have been carried out, it appears as a dynamic and potentially unstable landscape, until it matures into a new woodland character.

A settlement of smallholdings, where farming has been pushed out and replaced by a mix of horticulture, hobby farming, storage yards, etc. is another example of a landscape area which appears unstable, due to changing land uses. On the other hand, an estate that has recently switched from cattle to cash crops and then become intensively mechanised may appear quite stable, even though the underlying systems may remain vulnerable to changing conditions which may emerge at a future time. The stability of these types of landscape will normally be related to other types of stability – for example, economic or ecological conditions. However, this evaluation only addresses the appearance of the landscape. In the Skive study, four degrees of stability were defined: stable, fairly stable, fairly unstable, and unstable.

Following field studies, the boundaries were digitised in a GIS program. The 331 landscape areas were combined into seven *landscape regions*, each with its own distinctive character (Figure 6.9). For the island of Fur and the peninsula of Northern Fjends east of Skive Bay, the regional classification and delineation was obvious. The same applied to the Flyndersoe area south of Salling, a moorland plain with a character typical of western Jutland. In Salling, the narrow eastern foreshore with its slopes, ravines, uplands and fertile deciduous forests forms a sharp contrast to the hinterland which is the open lands of Middle Salling and consists of fully cultivated clay soil with wind turbines and cattle and pig farms. Northern Salling consists of equal parts low-lying plains and flattened moraine country, predominantly with sandy soil. With its wavy shores, sandy soil, great density of low windbreaks and many smallholding farms, Western Salling is quite distinct from Northern Salling and Middle Salling (see description of the landscape regions in Figure 6.9).

The *product of the analysis* is a delineation and description of 331 landscape areas grouped into 11 landscape types and seven landscape regions. Landscape types and landscape regions are defined and explained with photos and text. The photo in Figure 6.8 displays four landscape types.

Six landscape character types are shown on Figures 6.6 and 6.7:

- W = wetlands
- S = slopes and ravines
- B = built-up areas
- H = dense patterns of hedgerows and windbreaks
- SM = Smallholder subdivisions
- M = mosaics of forest and arable fields.

Other landscape character types identified in Skive Municipality:

- arable fields without farm buildings
- farms scattered on level terrain

- farms scattered in hilly areas
- forest areas
- heathlands.

Each of the delineated areas are characterised by short descriptions as shown in the two examples below taken from areas shown on Figures 6.6 and 6.7. Examples:

S7. Svenstrup-Ramsdal. Valley landscape with steep gullies and rich in natural and semi-natural habitats. Mainly occupied by lifestyle farmers.
H8. Frederiksberg. Westerly hillside with undulating terrain and dense pattern of hedgerows.

FIGURE 6.6 Regionalisation of Hoejslev, map
The code letters indicate the landscape type of the area (W for wetland, for example), while the figures indicate the serial number within the map section. Areas W2 and W3 represent raised seabed formed since the Neolithic Age. Areas M1 and H4 are sandy 'islands' surrounded by lowlands without buildings. The village Hoejslev (area B5) is located at the foot of a terminal moraine (area H8) which is penetrated by gullies (S7). The photo in Figure 6.8 is taken from a hilltop as shown on the eastern part of the map.
Source: Stahlschmidt and Nellemann (2009): *Metoder til landskabsanalyse*.

FIGURE 6.7 Regionalisation of Hoejslev, air photo
An orthophoto of the area shown in Figure 6.6. The highly diverse land use in area S7 with wood patches intermixed with semi-natural grasslands and arable fields contrasts with the linear hedgerow landscape in area H8. In other places the transition is less clear. Each of the homogeneous landscape areas has been characterised by a place name and a short description of the terrain form, land use and possible special features.
Source: Stahlschmidt and Nellemann (2009): *Metoder til landskabsanalyse*.

The intended *application of the analysis* is both to serve as a basis for dialogue with the citizens about the development of the municipality and as an internal management tool. Internally, the usefulness of the analysis relies on its integration of the GIS maps with the GIS tools that local authorities use for other landscape-planning and management purposes. The classification into homogeneous areas – that is, the definition of area boundaries – becomes a GIS layer that can be accessed and combined with other layers – for example, protection listings and conservation lines.

If the objective of the planning process is to guide development – for example, the selection of a site for a wind turbine farm in the Municipality of Skive – then perhaps four of the seven landscape regions can be ruled out immediately, and within the three remaining landscape regions it may be possible to rule out six landscape types. This initial filtering narrows the field down to five landscape

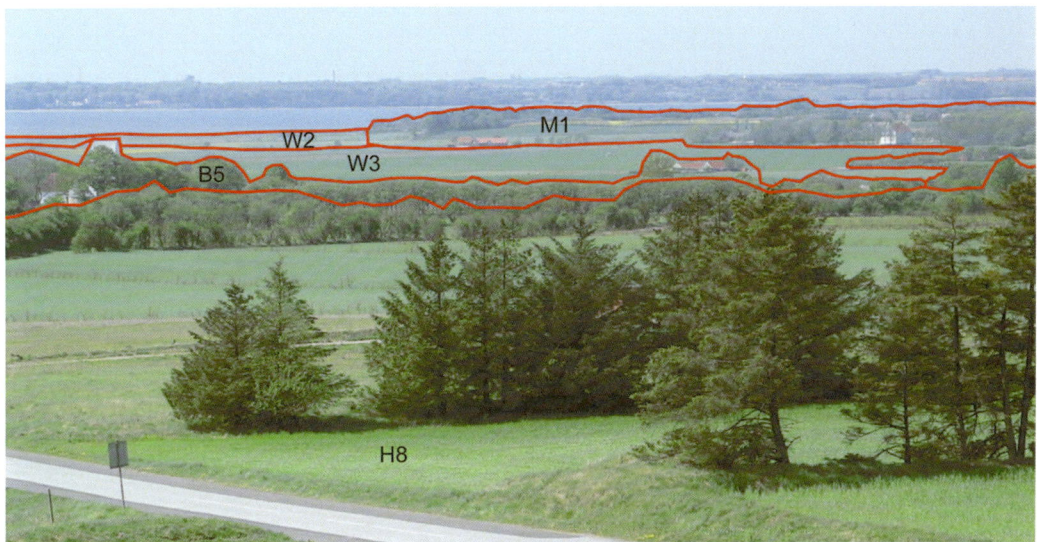

FIGURE 6.8 Regionalisation of Hoejslev, ground photo
The area in the foreground (area 8) represents the landscape character type 'dense hedgerows'. The old spruce trees are slowly dying out. Further down the hill new deciduous hedgerows can be seen faintly. The village of Hoejslev (area B5) is hidden by trees; only the church can be seen to the left. The wetlands (W2 and W3) are almost without woody vegetation. The white building to the right in the mosaic landscape (area M1) is the Staarup Estate. The photo point is shown on Figures 6.6 and 6.7.
Source: Stahlschmidt and Nellemann (2009): *Metoder til landskabsanalyse*.

types in three landscape regions. Once the potential landscape areas are highlighted on the computer screen, the next step in the sorting process is to call up other, relevant GIS layers. Later in the process it may be relevant to classify a selected landscape area into homogeneous sub areas to clarify the subtle differences within the area.

Alternatively if the landscape management issue is about approving the construction of new residential areas in the rural zone, the case can be addressed by examining the topographic map and the aerial photo of the landscape area by clicking on the description of the landscape area for the landscape type and region in question. The understanding of the site that is achieved by classifying it into landscape areas cannot replace field studies, where the landscape planner/ administrator surveys the real world first-hand, but it makes it possible to target the analysis and make it more efficient.

In the management of rural zones and the dialogue with the Ministry of Environment, the digitisation of the classification into landscape areas helps provide a quicker overview of the degree of coverage that the given landscape type has in the municipality. In the GIS program, the landscape type in question and its locations in the municipality are activated, providing a quicker overview of the degree of coverage. In this way the landscape areas represent an alternative to the existing sector-based approach to decision-making where all areas are treated

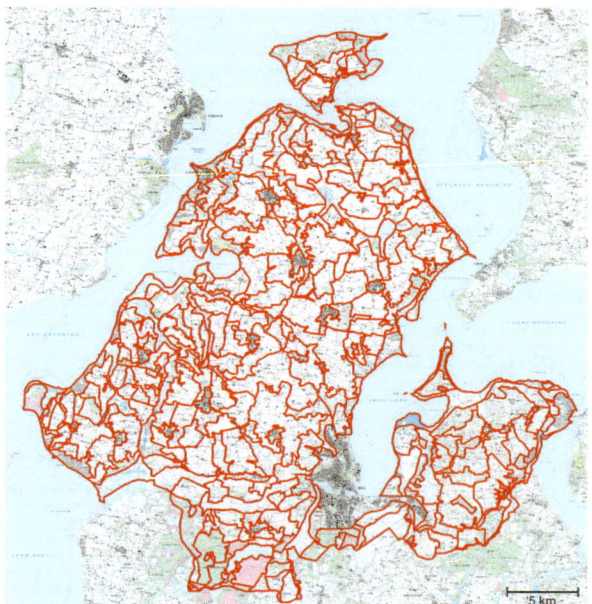

FIGURE 6.9 Regionalisation of Skive Municipality

Except for the city of Skive, the whole municipality is delineated into 331 landscape character areas. The landscape character areas are grouped according to the main characteristics into seven regional landscapes. The town of Skive is mapped as a separate eighth region. A standard topographic map at the scale of 1:100,000 and with emphasised contour lines is used as the basic map. The contour patterns differ across the regions. The village of Hoejslev (Figures 6.6–6.8) is located left of the 'N' in 'Northern Fjends'. Each of the regions has been characterised with references to each other.

Source: Skive municipality (2009): www.skive.dk/media/4703/landskabsanalyse2009.pdf.

the same, regardless of the degree of coverage of landscape type. The classification into landscape areas offers an accessible tool for considering the landscape type and the character of the individual area. The choice can then be made to maintain the use of the landscape in its current state or to alter it.

THE SEVEN LANDSCAPE REGIONS (FROM NORTH)

Fur. The island of Fur has a great landscape heterogeneity and a strong character. The northern part of the island consists of a hill crest with ravines, open moler clay pits, and mixed land uses. The southern part is dominated by smallholder agriculture, a few farms, and industrial farms. Curved beach ridges are found in the eastern part.

Northern Salling. In northern Salling, patches of wetlands alternate with levelled-out moraine hills. Most former wetlands are drained arable fields, while others are wet pastures or unused bogs. Sandy soils, hedgerows and peasant farms dominate the moraine hills.

Eastern Salling. The eastern coastal zone of Salling is characterised by hills, bluffs and ravines. All types of building structures are found from large estates to second-home developments. The landscape is rich both in land use and visual qualities, including views of the inlet.

Western Salling. Along the west coast of Salling the bluffs alternate with low shorelines. The cove is rich in shoreline form. A great proportion of the second homes in Salling are located in this western part. In several places wetlands stretch for several kilometres from the coast to the hinterland. The region is influenced by western wind, sandy soils and hedgerows planted as windbreaks. Agriculture is characterised by a mixture of lifestyle farms and large-scale industrial farms.

Middle Salling. Middle Salling has a landscape of open plains, intensive husbandry farms, and wind turbines. Agricultural conditions are favourable with fertile loamy soils and level plateaus. Overall the landscape is homogeneous with scattered villages and rural towns and long-distance views of churches.

Flyndersoe. The Flynder Lake area is characterised by a large-scale plain forming a clear contrast to the moraine landscape of Salling. The western part is a former inlet, now a freshwater lake with surrounding wetland. The two-kilometre wide river valley is located in the eastern part with mosaics of arable fields, pastures, plantations and networks of ditches. The area around Flynder Lake consists of outwash plain and kettle areas covered by heathlands and spruce plantations.

Northern Fjends. In the Northern Fjends Peninsula moraine hills alternate with raised former shore lands, patches of outwash plains, and ravines. Soils are mainly sandy and there are dense patterns of windbreaks and small forest thickets in most of the area. The landscape is heterogeneous with diverse terrain forms and scenic views.

115

The homogeneous areas are categorised as landscape types and grouped into landscape regions. Thus, the hierarchical procedure is a bottom-up process similar to a Scottish LCA and different to the English LCA described above which represents a top-down approach. The mapping into relatively detailed landscape types turned out to be useful for local collaborative processes. However, in another experimental planning process aiming at a landscape strategy for part of the Flyndersoe region, these types were too detailed. In this case a new, coarser classification of types was produced. The new classification then became the basis for discussion and to structure the recommended developments of the different areas (Primdahl and Kristensen 2016).

Main case B: the Danish LCA approach Svendborg

The Danish approach to LCA is a system of analysis and planning that was initiated by the Danish Ministry of the Environment, and from 2007 has been recommended by the ministry as a tool for municipal countryside planning and management (Danish Ministry of the Environment 2007a; Caspersen and Nellemann 2009). The Danish approach was inspired by the UK method of landscape character assessment (Swanwick 2002) and by an approach to landscape assessment that was developed for regional-planning purposes in Roskilde County (Nellemann and Wainoe 1992). In the following, LCA (DK) means the Danish approach to LCA.

The *purpose* in Svendborg, on the Island of Fyn in Denmark, was to create a commonly recognised method to identify and describe local landscape character and visual qualities, as a basis for an action-oriented procedure to assist in managing development and change in the landscape in respect of the character of the local landscape, and to prioritise the municipalities' landscape planning and management. It was an important requirement that the method should be systematic, well documented and transparent, and to a large extent based on GIS in order to allow the assessment to be updated, and to coordinate with other planning themes (Danish Ministry of Environment 2007a).

LCA (DK) has the *landscape character area* as basic unit of analysis and planning. Landscape character refers to the particular interaction between the natural factors and the land cover in a landscape area as well as the particular spatial and visual factors that characterise the area and make it different from the surrounding landscapes. The point of departure is the character of the existing landscape, but the analysis also includes the origins and development of the landscape. Unlike several previous methods for landscape analysis in planning, the emphasis in LCA (DK) is on characterising and developing landscape strategies for the countryside in its entirety, that is, not only the particular parts of the landscape that have been deemed worthy of preservation in an amenity evaluation but also *everyday land-scapes* and their development. LCA (DK) is based on extensive use of GIS, and thus the outcomes of the individual phases can be updated with relative ease to reflect subsequent developments in landscape and society. The assessments are carried

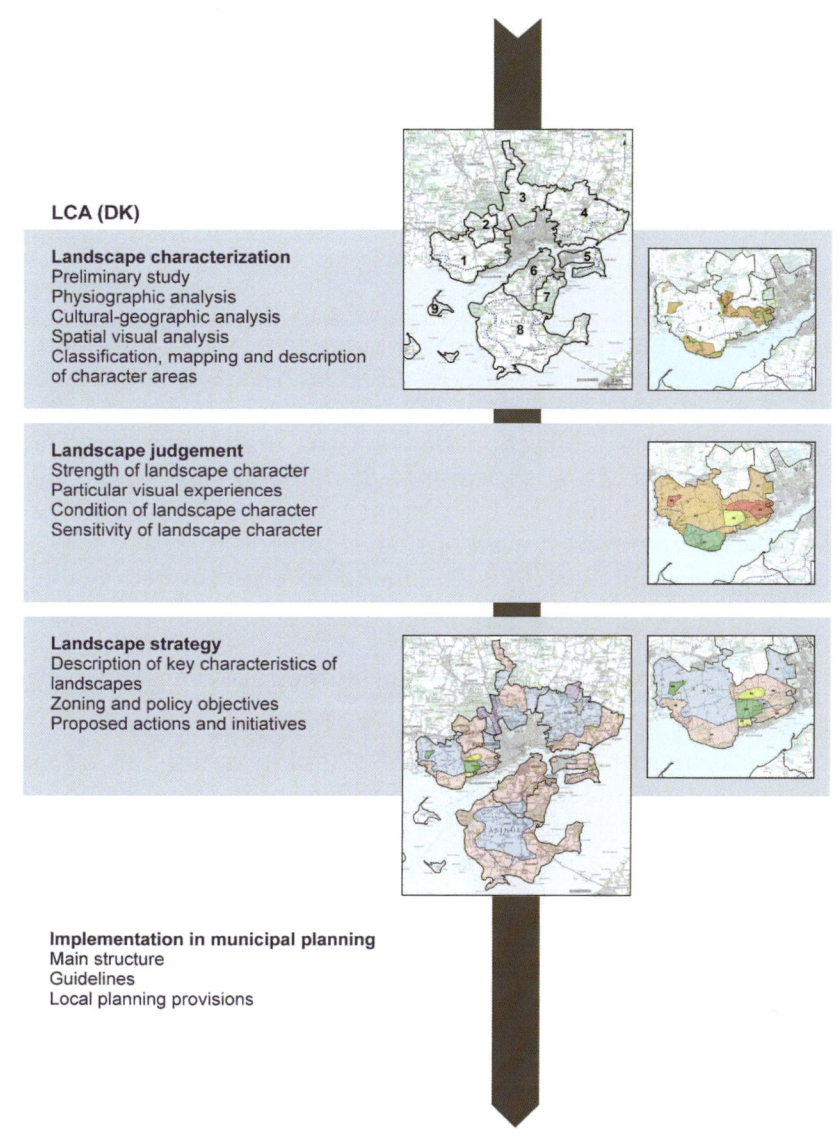

FIGURE 6.10 Phases in landscape character assessment LCA (DK)
The four phases in the Danish LCA as designed for supporting municipal planning: (A) landscape characterisation, (B) landscape judgement, (C) landscape strategy and (D) implementation. The area shown in the figure is from Svendborg Municipality, DK. For Area 1, Egense west of Svendborg city, examples of partial analysis are shown and areas identified during the first three of the four phases. In the fourth phase, implementation of the strategy is converted into planning provisions in the municipal plan in the form of its main structure, guidelines for planning for landscape and other themes, as well as framework for local planning and management.

Source: Moderated from Danish Ministry of Environment (2007a): *Vejledning om landskabet i kommuneplanlaegningen*.

out in scales of 1:25,000 and 1:50,000. In the following section the different phases of the assessment are described in more detail.

The LCA (DK) *procedure* in municipal planning includes the following four phases: phase A – landscape characterisation, phase B – landscape judgement, phase C – landscape strategy, and phase D – implementation – see Figure 6.10 and the more specific description below.

Landscape characterisation / phase A

The characterisation phase includes a regionalisation of the municipality based on identification of areas of distinctive homogeneous character – landscape character areas – and an analysis and description of each area, focusing on the characteristic ('key') elements and the interaction between natural factors and land cover, and on the characteristic visual appearance of the landscape (Figures 6.11–6.14). Although the analysis is based on the current landscape, it also incorporates the origins of the landscape character and its development in a backward-looking as well as forward-looking perspective. The mapping is performed at the desk and verified in the field. See also the main case Kaloe in Chapter 3 (Figures 3.4–3.10) and the Vaeth example in Chapter 5 (Figure 5.13).

The landscape characterisation phase involves the following sequential steps:

1. *Preliminary study* of existing maps and planning data, such as the municipal master plan and any legal restrictions (e.g. protection status and ownership), statistical data about the development of the area, and national and local priorities (such as areas of national geological interest, cultural heritage areas, etc.).
2. *Physiographic GIS analysis* includes a delineation of *physiographic regions in the municipality.* The point of departure is patterns and connections in geomorphology, terrain form and soil (Figure 6.11).
3. *Cultural-geographic GIS analysis* and a delineation of *preliminary landscape character areas.* Based on main features in the man-made landscape elements – in the form of vegetation as hedgerows and woods, cultivated areas, built constructions and settlements, historical factors and technical installations, and their interactions with the natural factors – the boundary outlines in step 1 are modified. The historical origins and the time-depth of the landscape character are identified along with the key functions that are important for preserving the landscape character.
4. *Spatial-visual analysis.* This is the final identification of key characteristics for each character area in the form of characteristic landscape elements and spatial-visual features (scale, enclosure, complexity, etc.) as well as area boundaries. In addition, outstanding sub areas and individual elements that offer particular visual experiences and any dominating technical installations are identified, including parts of the character area that have a visual

connection with the sea and the opposite shore (Figures 6.13–6.14). The spatial-visual LCA (DK) analysis shown on Figure 5.13 represents an example of a visual analysis carried out for a single character area (and mapped with a slightly different legend).

5. *Classification/mapping and description of all character areas in the municipality* is the final mapping of all the landscape character areas of Svendborg Municipality with the exception of Svendborg city (Figure 6.12).

FIGURE 6.11 Physiographic regions, Svendborg Municipality
The municipality is divided into 9 regions based on geomorphology, terrain form and soil.

1. Moraine plain, undulating plateau and clay soils
2. Tunnel valley, bluffs, stream and clay soils
3. Dead-ice formations, undulating and clay soils
4. Moraine plain with gradually sloping plain and clay soils
5. Marine foreland, plain with sandy/clay soils
6. Moraine hill, gradually sloping terrain and clay soils
7. Moraine plain, plain with clay soils
8. Marine foreland, plain with sandy/clay soils
9. The archipelago of southern Funen, islands with moraine plains and clay soils

Source: Danish Ministry of the Environment (2007a): *Vejledning om landskabet i kommuneplanlaegningen.*

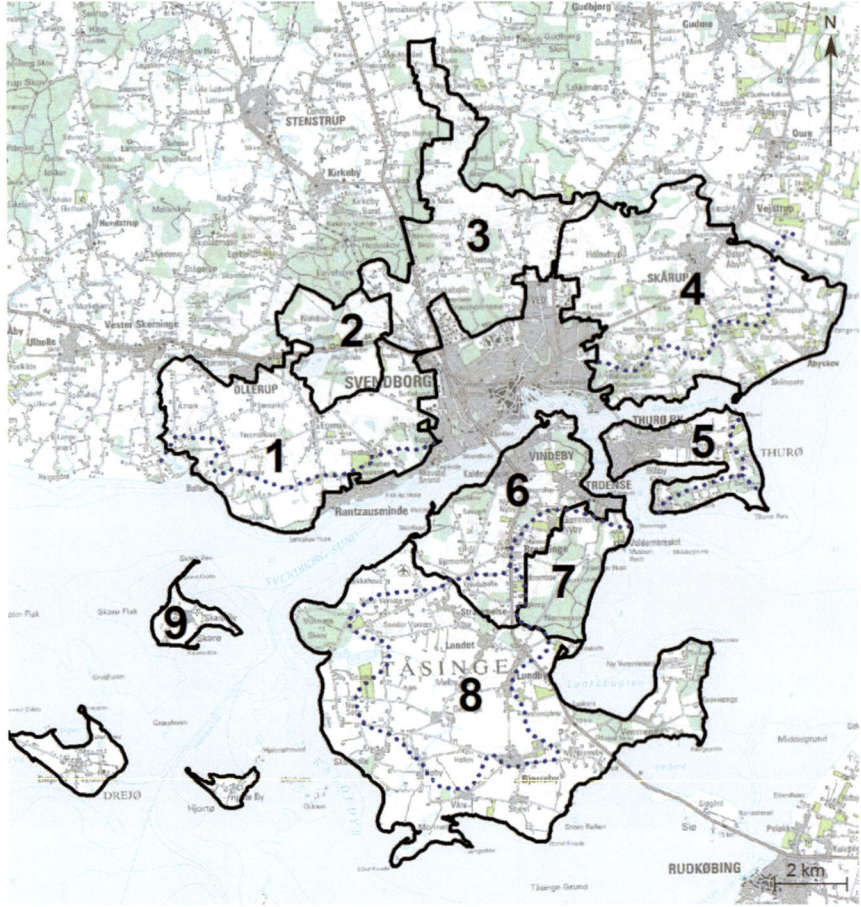

FIGURE 6.12 Landscape character areas, Svendborg Municipality

In the cultural-geographic and the spatial-visual analyses the focus is on the countryside; Svendborg city is not included. The moraine plateau therefore becomes divided into areas 1 and 4 characterised as 'hedgerow agricultural plains with scattered villages and farms'. Another example of alterations to the *physiographic delineation* is landscape character area 2, an estate where the manor house in the valley is surrounded by large open fields and small woodlands. Finally, landscape character area 3 is adjusted following the edges between forests and undulating farming plains.

1. The agricultural plain of Egense (Figure 6.13)
2. The estate landscape of Hvidkilde
3. The hilly landscape of Heldager
4. The agricultural plain of Skaarup
5. The island of Thuroe
6. Bregninge hills
7. The etstate landscape of Valdemar Castle
8. The agricultural plain of Taasinge
9. The archipelago of southern Funen

Source: Danish Ministry of the Environment (2007a): *Vejledning om landskabet i kommuneplanlaegningen*.

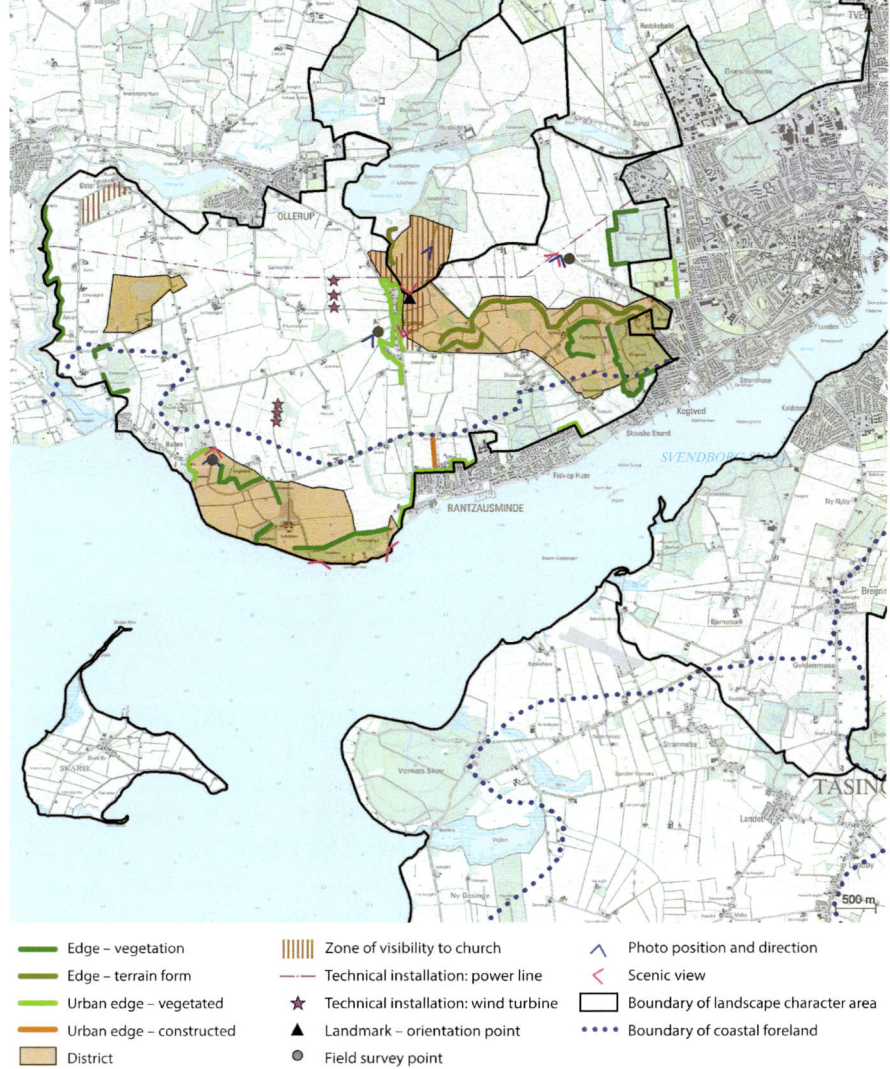

━━ Edge – vegetation	▐▐▐▐▐ Zone of visibility to church	∧ Photo position and direction
━━ Edge – terrain form	—·—· Technical installation: power line	⟨ Scenic view
━━ Urban edge – vegetated	★ Technical installation: wind turbine	☐ Boundary of landscape character area
━━ Urban edge – constructed	▲ Landmark – orientation point	···· Boundary of coastal foreland
▨ District	⦿ Field survey point	

FIGURE 6.13 Spatial-visual analysis, Egense

The analytical map shows significant spatial and visual characteristics of the character area 1 - Egense. The following distinctive sub areas have been identified:

- Egense esker
- the fringe of Egense village with views to the church
- the coastal area at Lehnskov
- an area in the western part dominated by gravel extraction.

The esker, some wood edges and urban edges are identified as significant elements. Egense church is an important landmark. Infrastructure such as power lines and wind turbines dominate the surroundings. The 'boundary of coastal foreland' shows the areas in visual contact with the sea and facing coastlines. Finally, the most important viewpoints and photo points used by the field survey are indicated.

Source: Danish Ministry of the Environment (2007a): *Vejledning om landskabet i kommuneplanlaegningen.*

FIGURE 6.14 Characterisation, Egense
The undulating agricultural plain (area 1 in Figure 6.12) has middle-size fields intersected by hedgerows and banks partly overgrown by a rich variety of woody species.
The farms (small- to middle-size) located along the roads and scattered ponds surrounded by woody vegetation also contribute to the character. Together these elements make up a semi-transparent landscape of medium scale. Towards the north the
area is bounded by forests and hills. Key functions for managing the landscape include
arable farming and management of hedgerows and banks.

Photo: The area is characterised by an undulating agricultural plain intersected by long hedgerows. The
photo is from the boundary of the coastal foreland (Figure 6.13); the archipelago of southern Funen is
visible in the background. Source: Photo by Mortensen, B.

The landscape character areas, and sub areas within them, make up the framework for the judgement and landscape strategy in the subsequent phases of
the LCA for the municipality, and provide a basis for other planning themes in
the municipal-planning process. One example is the southern elevated part of the
Egense agricultural plain, which is characterised by particular visual experiences
and sensitivity due to the close visual connection with the coastal landscape.
This classification indicates the need to treat this area with particularly careful
planning and management in the subsequent judgement and strategy phases –
for example, it is not suitable for afforestation or urban development. Furthermore, the landscape characterisation forms a basis for planning and impact
assessments on other levels – see main case Frederikssund Motorway in Chapter 8
(Figure 8.4).

Landscape judgement / phase B

The *purpose* of the judgement phase is to make an overall assessment of the qualities,
condition and sensitivity of the different landscape character areas, and to determine
priorities in relation to ongoing developments and planned or foreseen changes.

The four themes of the judgement phase

Before the process begins, clear criteria have been established to make the judgement process as transparent and uniform as possible. The four criteria that are
considered in the individual landscape character areas are:

1. *Strength of character* (Figure 6.15a): the presence and clarity of the essential landscape elements and spatial-visual factors, that is, key characteristics in the various parts of the area. The interaction between the natural factors and the land cover/land use and the clarity of the origins of the landscape character are also important for assessing the strength of the character. Sub areas with a contrasting character are assessed specifically in relation to their importance in the character area.
2. *Particular visual qualities* (Figure 6.15b): These two sub areas offer particularly rich experiences by virtue of their terrain or their natural or cultural content, as well as distinctive spatial and visual factors).
3. *Condition* (Figure 6.15c): The intactness of the landscape character is judged in relation to its historical origins, state of maintenance and influence of major technical installations, urban areas, etc. The assessment of the overall condition serves as a sort of diagnosis of the current condition of the character and the need for interventions.
4. *Sensitivity* (Figure 6.15d): The potential impact on the landscape character is judged. Sensitivity depends on types and degrees of possible changes. It is primarily assessed in relation to ongoing developments and any planned or foreseen changes. The evaluation of sensitivity will influence the proposals for landscape management that are put forth in the landscape strategy.

Judgement of landscape character strength (Figure 6.15a)

Very characteristic: Key characteristics are clearly represented, and the relationships between the fertile, open coastal plain and the intensive arable farming gives the sub area a strong character.
Characteristic: In most of this sub area the landscape character has an intermediate strength as the historic origin is somewhat blurred due to changes in the original structure of hedgerows that has partly erased the traces from the former farming system. New developments in the southern part of the village Egense have also blurred the original structure of the village.
Weak character: Tall poplars and a plant nursery combined with a complex and somewhat extensive arable farming system give this sub area an indistinct character that is hard to read and interpret.
Contrasting character: A large esker in the eastern part of the character area with its distinctive terrain form, small wood thickets and extensive farmed fields gives a distinct character which stands out in contrast to the surrounding sub areas. A gravel pit in the western part also stands out as a distinctive and contrasting area.
Source: Danish Ministry of the Environment (2007a): *Vejledning om landskabet i kommuneplanlaegningen*.

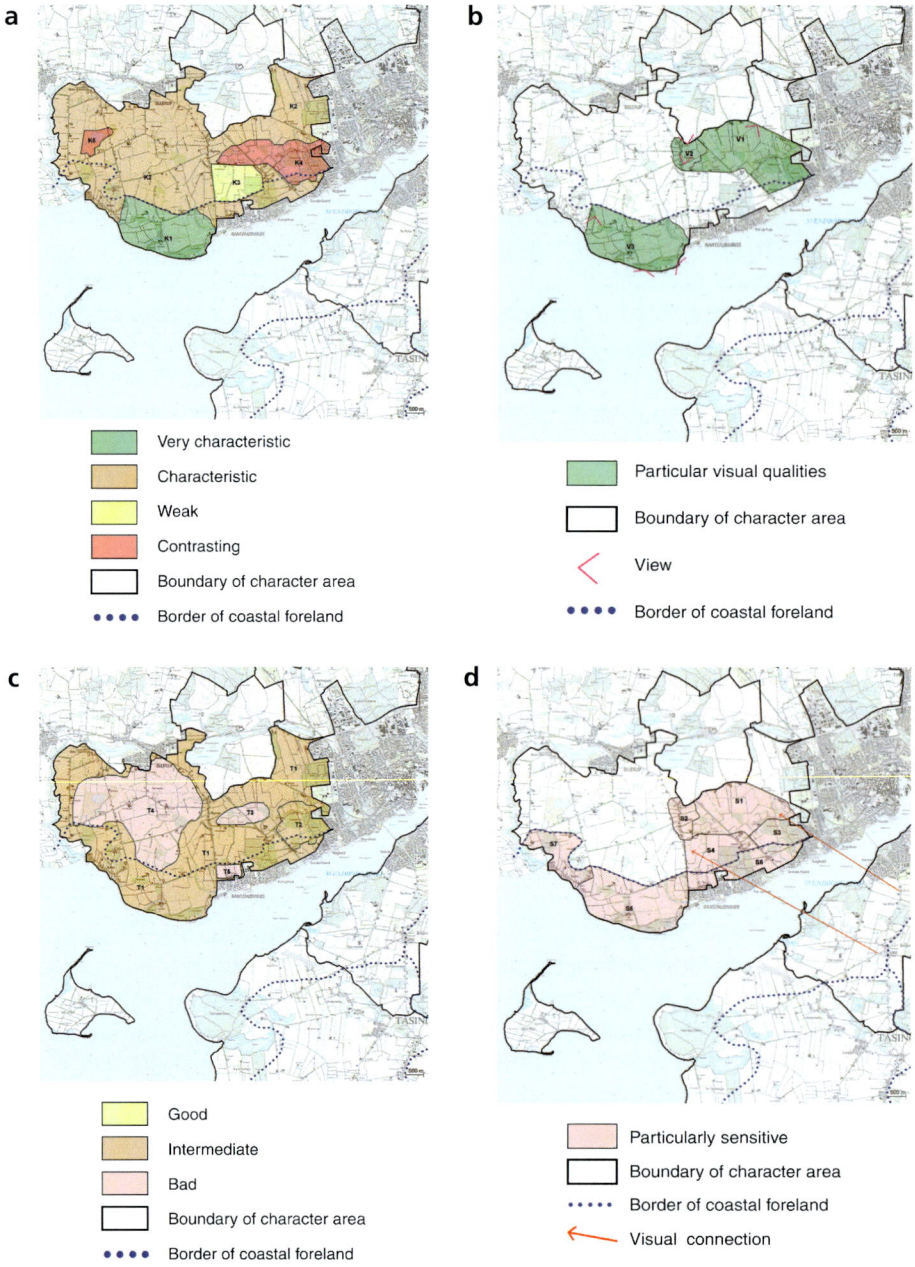

a

Very characteristic

Characteristic

Weak

Contrasting

Boundary of character area

•••• Border of coastal foreland

b

Particular visual qualities

Boundary of character area

< View

•••• Border of coastal foreland

c

Good

Intermediate

Bad

Boundary of character area

•••• Border of coastal foreland

d

Particularly sensitive

Boundary of character area

••••• Border of coastal foreland

← Visual connection

FIGURE 6.15 Judgement, Egense
a. **Strength of character**
b. **Particular visual qualities**
c. **Condition**
d. **Sensitivity**

Source: Danish Ministry of the Environment (2007a): *Vejledning om landskabet i kommuneplanlaeg-ningen.*

The landscape judgement is carried out as a combination of field and desk studies that identify and value elements within each landscape character area, thus it does not involve a comparison with other landscape character areas (i.e. evaluation). The field judgement, which can take place in connection with the spatial-visual analysis, uses a draft map (scale 1:25,000 on paper or in GIS) and a form for noting the rationale for the individual evaluations. Subsequently, four thematic maps are drawn up at the desk. In each thematic map, sub areas are identified with related descriptions of the reasons for the designation (Figure 6.15). Apart from creating a basis for the next phase of the LCA (the Landscape Strategy), the outcome of the judgement phase provides knowledge of potentials and possible weaknesses as to future development and projects at a local level, e.g. estimating the best location of a new biogas plant. The judgement phase is also suited to involvement of citizens in deciding landscape priorities.

Landscape strategy / phase C

The *purpose* of the strategy phase is to create a basis for specific policy objectives for the different character areas, as well as specific proposals for planning and management of their landscape qualities, potentials and problems. Based on the judgement of each of the landscape character areas and thus the entire municipality, the areas are *divided into zones with specific policy objectives*. The method involves combining the strength of the landscape character and any special visual qualities with the condition and sensitivity of the landscape character by layering the thematic maps (Figure 6.15).

Product: The partitioning results in the strategic objectives for respectively *protecting* (and possibly *enhancing*), *maintaining* (and possibly *restoring* and *enhancing*), or *creating* the landscape character. In sub areas that offer particular visual qualities (Figure 6.15b) the qualities should be protected, regardless of the strength of the landscape character. In addition, the assignment of strategic objectives should incorporate regional and national concerns that may necessitate particular management interventions.

Once the whole municipality has been analysed, planners will have a comprehensive understanding of areas with proposals for specific *policy objectives* in the municipality. Figure 6.16 shows an overall map of these target areas in the municipality of Svendborg. Furthermore the proposals for policy objectives are suited for involvement of politicians and citizens in determining landscape priorities. The *specific interventions and initiatives* that are needed to achieve the policy objectives depend on the character of the landscape and the particular visual qualities it offers, as well as its condition and sensitivity. Each target area is associated with specific proposals for the future management of the area – for example, the regular clearing of new shrubs and trees in a wetland, the promotion of ecological corridors, and the consideration of characteristic and structurally important hedgerows and important scenic viewpoints in future local plans for new residential areas, etc.

LCA and the results of the strategy phase can therefore inform the planning process and priorities for landscape as well as other themes in the municipal plan, such

TABLE 6.1 Strategic options future management. Principles for the choice of policy objectives for future management and planning are based on the interplay between the strength and the condition of the landscape character of sub areas. There is an imperative to improve areas with poor conditions and weak character, but there is no great need or demand for changes to areas with good conditions and strong character. Here the main need is to conserve existing qualities.

The principles formulated by Warnock and Brown (1998) have been an important inspiration for LCA (DK). Some terms in the Danish model are slightly changed. On Figure 6.16 'maintain' is parallel to 'restore' in this figure, and 'protect' parallel to 'conserve'.

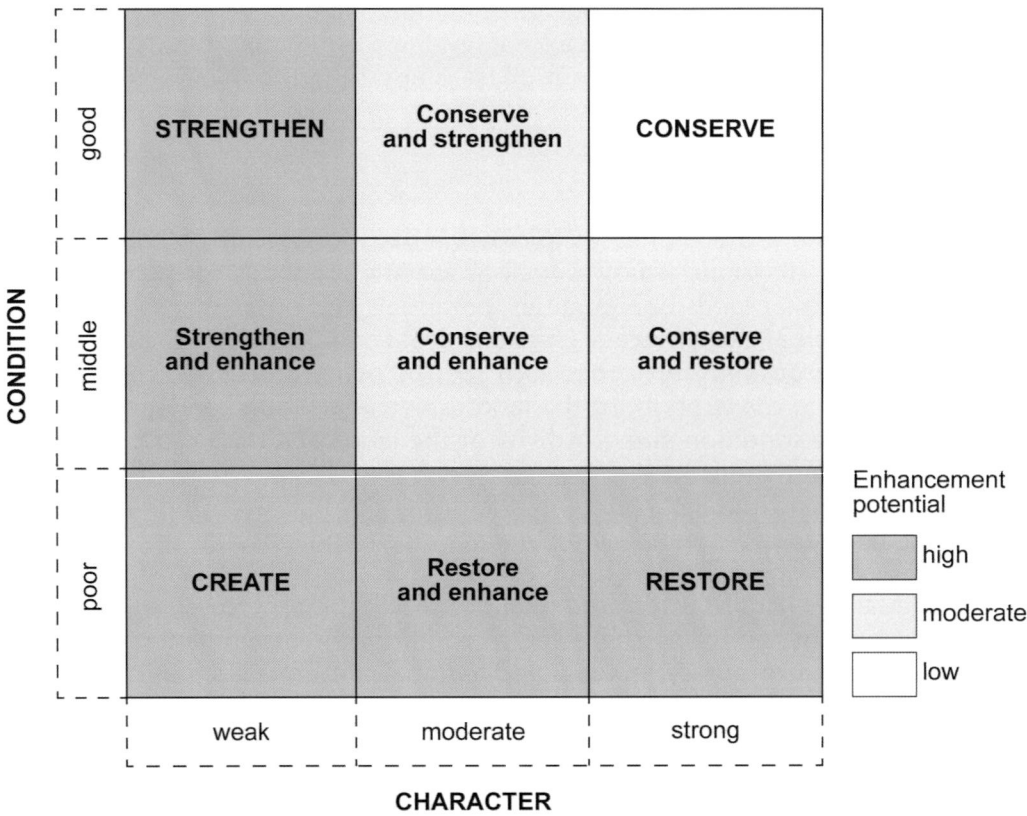

Source: Moderated from Warnock and Brown (1998): EA and visual assessment: A vision for the countryside. *Landscape Design*, p. 24.

as urban development, recreation, new wind turbines, afforestation and nature management. Furthermore, it can form the basis for planning and management at local and project level.

Implementation / phase D

The purpose of the implementation of the landscape strategy into the municipal plan is to assure coordination of the strategy with other planning themes, such

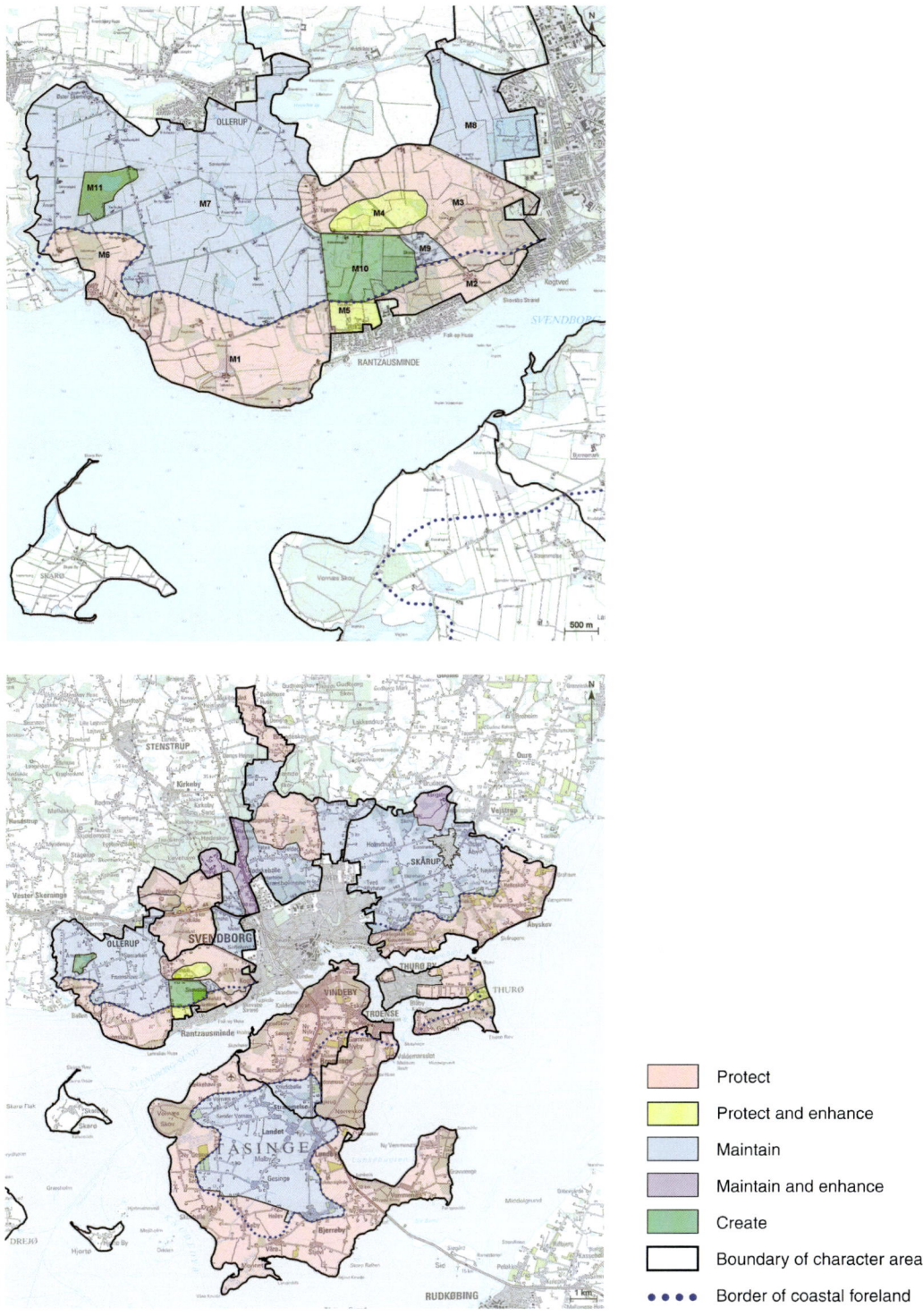

FIGURE 6.16 Policy objectives, Svendborg Municipality and Egense

Source: Danish Ministry of Environment (2007a): *Vejledning om landskabet i kommuneplanlaegningen.*

FIGURE 6.17 Egense agricultural plain
The undulating agricultural plain in the foreground represents a characteristic element of character area 1. The Egense esker in the background forms a contrast to the surroundings. The esker represents a sub area with particular visual qualities, and should be protected.
Source: Photo by Mortensen, B.

as the sectoral plans for urban development, nature protection, afforestation, etc. After due political process and consideration of other interests, the landscape issues can be incorporated into the municipal plan with guidelines (such as guidelines for 'valuable landscapes') and provisions for local planning and rural-zone management.

The LCA (DK) has been applied in different ways and for different purposes. An investigation (Danish Ministry of Environment 2013) performed five years after publication and recommendation of the method, showed that about two-thirds of the countryside municipalities outside the capital area had performed (18 per cent) or were performing (47 per cent) an LCA (DK), which indicates its utility for planning.

7

SITE SELECTION AND LANDSCAPE POTENTIAL

Introduction

We use the term site-selection analysis to mean a systematic search for and selection of possible sites for an intended development. The question that is addressed in a site-selection analysis is "Where in the landscape do we find the best potential site(s) for the proposed development?" A landscape-based site-selection analysis provides a response to the question based upon landscape factors.

Oxford Dictionaries (2011) defines *site* as 'an area of ground on which a town, building, or monument is constructed', and Meyer (2005) argued that site is a fundamental basis for landscape architecture. *Selection* is defined by the Oxford Dictionaries as 'the action or fact of carefully choosing someone or something as being the best or most suitable'. Hence site selection in the context of this text is the process of identifying the best or most suitable site upon which to implement a project within a landscape.

Site-selection analyses can be used on every level of landscape design and planning, from the national level of planning for major infrastructure such as motorways or power lines, to the neighbourhood level of selecting a site for a new house. Site-selection analysis can therefore involve large tracts of land and address complex conditions that require considerable amounts of data and skilful data processing. For example, a municipality may decide that it needs to establish a new rubbish dump, but where? Or a power company may seek a location for a new wind farm, or a transmission line. There are likely to be many factors in these kinds of complex site selections that require technical understanding that landscape planners do not possess, and so in large-scale projects the landscape-based site-selection analysis may be part of a larger task involving several different disciplines, professional teams and assignments. On the other hand, in a landscape-design project the landscape planner may be the lead analyst. The scope of the brief to the landscape planner is therefore a critical starting point for the landscape analysis, and

FIGURE 7.1 Feeling of being well situated in the landscape
A common aim of landscape analysis is to locate a new construction in the right place. Good location is not only a question of aesthetics but also a condition which may be biologically rooted (Appleton 1996). The instinctive feeling of the right location for a sleeping child may be expanded to a conscious evaluation of the location of a house, for example, or the best site for Robinson Crusoe's camp (Chapter 1).
Source: Photo by Stahlschmidt, P.

landscape planners may be involved in more than one scale and type of analysis, as choices for a project location narrow down from a national or regional search to more specific site searches in a particular landscape.

A traditional approach to site-selection analysis involves identification of site-selection factors based on the development requirements and the different types of landscape impact that must be considered. This means delineating areas on a map that offer different landscape-based potentials and constraints in relation to the intended development (Figure 7.2). This technique is simple and fast to use, and will often be useful in an initial scoping of possible sites. Subsequently, other techniques can be included in the analysis process.

The purpose for defining site-selection factors is to identify sites in the landscape where there are strong arguments in favour of or against a prospective develop-ment, and also areas where there is flexibility in response. Thus, site-selection fac-tors should be seen as landscape conditions which can be mapped, and which guide

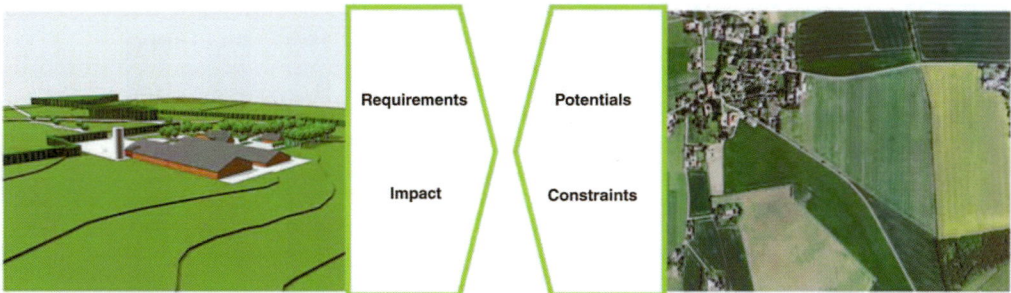

New development
The proposed project/land-use change

The existing landscape

FIGURE 7.2 The relationship between new development and existing landscape
The development imposes certain requirements for the site, which are compared with
the potentials offered by the landscape. Similarly, the landscape imposes certain constraints on the development, which are compared with the likely impacts of the development on the site. For example, in selecting the optimal site for a clothes line in the
garden, the *development* requires a site with sun and wind, which may potentially be
found on the lawn south of the house. The *landscape* constraint is that the line should
not impact upon the view of the garden from the living room window. The task is to
identify a site that satisfies both sets of considerations. Or, as seen in the illustration,
a new large-scale pig farm would require proximity to the road and a relatively flat
area with stable ground. The landscape constraints include that the impact of the farm
will not be too dominant in relation to a valuable existing cultural environment around
a village, or lead to problems with noise or bad smells for the local residents.
Source: Dansk Landbrugsraadgivning, Landscentret (2008): Visualisation. In Stahlschmidt and
Nellemann (2009), p. 86. Forlaget Groent Miljoe, Copenhagen.

where a given development should be located. Site-selection factors may include
landscape elements (for example, a lake is an attractive feature when selecting a
site for a summer house), landscape attributes (for example, noise makes an area
less appealing as the site of a park), and landscape functions (for example, a land
use such as a waste-recycling depot would not be a good neighbour for a children's playground). When several site-selection factors are combined, the result is
a *composite classification map*. This so-called *overlay technique* is explained in the
procedural section below.

Figure 7.3 illustrates a typical planning process involving a site-selection and
landscape potentials analysis. The suggested site is based on combining site-
selection factor analysis based on project requirements with analysis of landscape
potentials and constraints. A good synthesis requires a well-defined relationship
between the proposed development and the landscape including the points in
favour, both from the perspective of the development (for example, "where would
a new house enjoy fine views?") and from the perspective of the landscape setting
(for example, "how visible is the site to neighbours?").

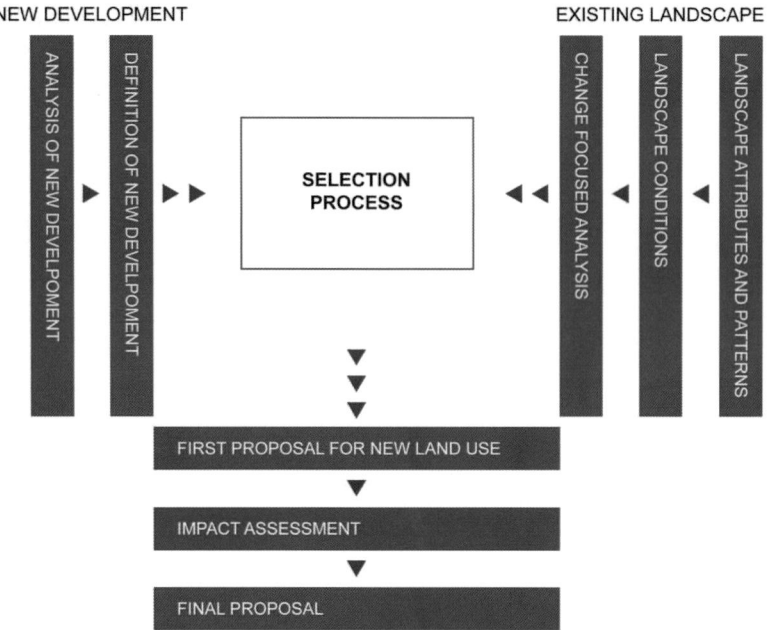

FIGURE 7.3 The process of site-selection analysis
From the left, the new development is defined. From the right, the assessment of the landscape becomes increasingly focused on the goal. To allow the two processes to influence each other, there will, in practice, be a number of interactions going back and forth. The draft of a new land use is the synthesis of development and landscape, which is subjected to an impact assessment (Chapter 8) before the final proposal is drawn up.
Source: Stahlschmidt, P. (1992).

In this context, the term *development* (meaning project) should be understood in a broad sense. A development is not necessarily a new *element* or a new *object*, such as a building, a road, a windmill or a power cable. It may also be a new *primary land use*, such as residential areas, parks, agriculture. It may be a new *secondary land use*, such as recreational hiking. Finally, it may be a new *area designation* that reflects the goals of the public administration, such as a nature conversation reserve, or a ground-water protection area.

Such a broad definition of development means that site selection may include a wide range of possible project types, with different degrees of certainty and specification, from construction projects that have an exact size and shape from the outset, to feasibility studies where a final design is still very flexible and open to change. A road safety sign is an example of an inflexible development. Regardless of the setting in which it is placed, the sign must remain in its specified form, size and colour. Afforestation, by contrast, is an example of flexible development which can be shaped in a range of ways, creating different forms, patterns and colours in a landscape. Roads and buildings lie in between these extremes, as the design can usually be modified to adapt to the landscape setting to some extent. When the development does not represent a specific element but a land use or area designation, the selection issue is more abstract and intangible – for example, seeking an area suitable for biodiversity enhancement. Correspondingly, visualising a concrete development, such as a wind turbine, is less open to ambiguity than visualising a more abstract development such as habitat restoration.

Both site-selection and landscape-potentials studies belong in the category of action-oriented analyses discussed in Chapter 1. The aim is different, but in both cases the synthesis reflects an examination of the relationship between development and landscape.

Procedure

In a site-selection analysis, the development for which a site is needed is already well defined. The question addressed by the analysis is where the development could best be sited. In a potentials study, the situation is the reverse; the location is given and the analysis question is for what functions is the landscape best suited. Typical questions concerning the potentials of an area include, for example: (1) What could an abandoned quarry be used for in the future? Is it best for recreational purposes, or agriculture, or for habitat restoration? (2) What could an obsolescent industrial site be converted into: a park, a residential area, or commercial offices, or some combination? (3) What are the potentials of the landscape setting, and what opportunities can be realised?

Finding potential uses for a given landscape requires an analysis of the uses or purposes that are relevant to the situation – for example, activities that are in demand in that locality. It then involves undertaking an outline impact assessment to assess their potential relationship with the landscape, and compare the findings to identify the range of possible land uses. The critical underlying idea in a potentials study is that the attributes of a landscape should be an important influence on its future use. This approach is also found in so-called land classification (German: 'standortskartierung') in forestry, where a key principle is that the local site conditions for tree growth (including soil and drainage) should guide the choice of tree species and the methods used in establishment/operations. This contrasts with a more interventionist approach where there is considerable investment in changing the site conditions to suit a pre-determined choice of species.

The Skovbo case presented in Figures 7.16–7.18 is categorised as both a potentials study and a site-selection analysis. It is a potentials analysis because each of the homogeneous areas is assessed in respect to the most appropriate future use(s) (development(s)) for the area. The Skovbo case is also a site-selection analysis, as it seeks to determine the best site for each of five selected developments. In this particular example, in other words, the way the analysis is described depends on whether the point of departure is the site or the development.

FIGURE 7.4 Building integrated in the existing landscape pattern
Comwell Campus Klarskovgaard south of Korsoer, DK, is an example of a development that adapts to the landscape structure. The belt between the sea and a plain of arable fields consists of abandoned orchards and woodlands. The residential wings follow the pattern of the windbreaks, standing at right angles to the coastline, while the restaurants and conference rooms are clustered near the access road, matching the pattern of former orchard work buildings. The open space abutting the wood and the beach are laid out as an uninterrupted green. Built 1968–70 by architects Viggo Moeller-Jensen and Thyge Arnfred and landscape architect Sven Ingvar Andersson.
Source: Photo by Comwell Hotels, Campus Klarskovgaard.

The first step in a site-selection analysis is to define the 'development' proposal that prompts the analysis. What are the underlying needs or drivers for a new development in this landscape? What type of development is relevant? How big is the development? What development requirements are involved, and what is the brief for the development and its technical requirements (described in site planning as the site programme)? What are the landscape potentials in relation to the development, that is, what does the landscape offer in respect to the proposed development and where in the landscape are the needs of the development best met? The impact of the development (Chapter 8) should also be analysed and compared to the constraints to be found in the landscape. For example, site-selection factors for a new pig farm would include good access roads, stable ground and no neighbours who would be bothered by smell or noise. The various types of site-selection factors will be discussed below.

When defining site-selection factors, the landscape analyst also needs to select analytical symbols, scales, maps, and map sections that lead to the clearest overview of the factors that affect the site selection. This may involve some experimentation in the scoping stage of the analysis. A well-established technique is to combine a number of site-selection factors in an overlay technique to form a composite classification map. Overlay maps have a long history in landscape analysis, starting with the use of transparent maps (Steinitz et al. 1976). Today physical overlays will normally be replaced by digital layers in a GIS program involving a specific layer produced for each of the chosen site-selection factors. This involves first preparing a map (or layer) for each of the selection factors, which must have the same general type of significance for the site selection – for example, they all serve as constraints for the given project. Each map/layer shows the distribution of the constraints – for example, in a grey raster. To avoid counting a given phenomenon twice in the composite classification map, each factor must be distinct from the others, with no (or very limited) overlap. For example, in a broad multi-factor analysis a specific factor such as bird protection will be counted twice if one layer is 'Ramsar area' and another is 'Area of high ornithological interest', and so to avoid this only one indicator of bird protection needs would be included.

When all the thematic maps/layers are prepared and combined, a *composite classification map* forms the conclusion to the analysis. The individual maps/layers may be the result of other types of analysis or assessment presented elsewhere in this book. Such analyses could include historical analyses, spatial analyses or value assessments as site-selection factors on equal terms with the thematic surveys. In some cases, the site-selection factors can be plotted on a single map/layer; in other cases it is preferable to use several maps/layers in the same or different scales. In a site-selection and landscape potentials analysis, the characterisation of site-selection factors can be combined with a classification into landscape character areas, as in the Skovbo case (Figures 7.16–7.18) and the Randers Fjord case (Figure 7.19).

Identifying and grouping selection factors

Site-selection factors can be ordered and grouped in different ways. In any given assignment, one must determine which factors and categories are most appropriate. The following list is intended as a prompt for organising possible map layers of site-selection factors. Choosing the most appropriate combination and arrangement of factors depends on the task at hand.

1. Development requirements and landscape potentials or constraints
2. Definitive or relative site constraints
3. Reciprocity of potentials and constraints
4. Zones of influence around sensitive locations
5. Future site possibilities
6. Scale.

An additional distinction is that of site-selection factors stemming from outside sources versus those that were identified in one's own studies – for example, a classification into landscape character areas or a value assessment. Official information sources and policy guidance and regulation from planning authorities may be vital considerations and ensure the site-selection analysis is relevant, authoritative and objective. On the other hand factors based on an expert's experience may also be relevant if their rationale and assumptions are explained.

Development requirements and landscape potentials or constraints

The interactions between the intended development and the existing landscape are illustrated in Figure 7.2. Development requirements are matched against the potentials and constraints of the landscape; similarly, the attributes of the landscape are matched against the impact of the development. As a metaphor for the site-selection process, the development may be viewed as a piece of iron, which is attracted by a positive magnetic force in some places but repelled in others. Based on both the requirements of the development and the landscape conditions, it is possible to identify the landscape attributes that attract (potentials) and repel (constraints).

This can be illustrated with an everyday example. On a picnic, one wants to find the best place to spread out the blanket and enjoy one's lunch. The development requirements in this site-selection analysis involve dry ground without sharp branches, a nice view, sun and no noise. Once a site has been identified that offers these possibilities, the development requirements are satisfied. But that is not the end to the site-selection process. One must also consider the landscape requirements, which means the impact of the picnic on the site and the surroundings, which might involve not destroying crops, or not blocking a path or someone else's view. A good site satisfies both development and landscape factors (Figure 7.5).

Development requirements concern what is appropriate from the perspective of the development. Landscape potentials and constraints, on the other hand, concern what is good or bad, seen from the perspective of the landscape (the existing landscape values including those of the people who already live in or use the location as well as the biophysical and historical values). In other words, a site with no landscape constraints is an area where the development can be established without conflicting with either landscape values or the current users. In practice the introduction of a new development will often supersede the existing use. In a site-selection analysis, therefore, the task is more about assessing the relative

	Good site selection	Poor site selection
Development Requirements (Change interest)	The landscape complies with the requirements	The landscape conflicts with the requirements
Landscape potentials (protection and conservation interests)	The change has an overall positive effect on the landscape	The change has a negative effect on the landscape

FIGURE 7.5 Good and poor site selection for landscape development
Ideally, the site selection for new developments leads to outcomes that are beneficial for both the new function and the existing landscape.
Source: Stahlschmidt, P. (1992).

strength of the landscape constraints and identifying potentials for combining different uses on the same site.

Distinguishing between the different types of impact on the surroundings can add more nuance to the assessment. For example, a distinction can be drawn between the noise impact of a wind farm, which can be limited by placing the wind turbines at a good distance from homes, and its visual impact, which may extend well beyond the zone of noise impact alone and change the appearance of an extensive tract of landscape.

The impetus to establish a new development does not always come from outside agents. It may be initiated by local land owners or communities – for example, the development in question may arise from a farmer's plan to expand his production by adding a new piggery, or the desire of local villagers to establish a new foot-path leading to a beach or recreational area.

Assessing landscape potentials and constraints should also be more than a zero sum game. Warnock and Brown (1998) and Wood and Handley (2001) identify four possible landscape management strategies – conserve, restore, strengthen or create (Table 6.1) – and the ambition should be to ensure that the development at the focus of the analysis has a *positive* effect on the landscape. Healey (1998) argued that a focus on conflict resolution – a *neutral* impact or *minimum harm approach* to land-use conflicts – may represent an unduly modest level of ambition, and she has promoted constructive and collaborative place-making in which the end result is an improvement over current circumstances.

Site selection also sets up a tension between finding sites that maximise the benefits for the development, and finding a site that creates benefit for the land-scape as well as the development. The first approach involves finding the 'sweet spot' for the development that draws on the existing landscape qualities – perhaps even at their cost – while the other would be finding the 'healthy spot', where the development can lead to a qualitative improvement for the landscape as a whole. Alexander et al. (1977, p. 511) argue in favour of the latter in the so-called 'Site Repair pattern' which is based on the principle that 'On no account place buildings in the places which are most beautiful. In fact do the opposite. Consider the site and its buildings as a single living eco-system. Leave those areas that are the most precious, beautiful, comfortable, and healthy as they are, and build new structures in those parts of the site which are least pleasant now.' In this case, development is also used as a positive public initiative, hence establishing a camping ground in an abandoned quarry may involve a clean-up and restoration effort and thus enhance the site as whole. At a larger scale, one of the location factors for major developments such as the London Olympic site has been that the infrastructure required for the event should also have a long-term benefit for the surrounding area.

The balance between these two possible approaches may depend upon the nature of the development client; public authorities, for example, are typically more likely and willing to seek multiple benefits from a development than private developers. But this is not always the case, and creative landscape analysis can inform and shape opinions and willingness to consider more widely beneficial site choice. The distinction between development requirements and landscape potentials and constraints serves to remind the landscape analyst to keep both in mind throughout the process to avoid arriving at a solution that only considers either construction or protection interests.

Definitive or relative site constraints

A site-selection factor poses a *definitive* constraint to a given development if it logically or absolutely precludes the given development. That is the case, for example, if it would be physically impossible or illegal to place the development in a given location – for example, locating housing in a site that is regularly flooded under two metres of water, or in a prohibited conservation area. On the other hand, a site-selection factor poses a *relative* constraint if it detracts from the options without actually precluding them. For example, urban expansion into fertile farmland may be undesirable in terms of sustainability and food security, but the good soil does not pose an absolute obstacle to construction.

Definitive constraints represent a quick and effective filter in the first screening of possible sites; a single definitive constraint for a given development is a de facto veto against selecting the site. For example, if the development is a holiday village, a definitive constraint might be the presence of an internationally designated and protected habitat. In that case, even the (otherwise) best site would be ruled out as a site for the development. This means that there is no need to collect additional information about the habitat area, and time-consuming field studies are superfluous. The site can be quickly and effectively eliminated from the search.

Definitive constraints must meet strict conditions with regard to site specification and rationale if they are to be included in a site-selection process, as the exclusion should not be open to be called into doubt at a later stage in the process. Hence, the delimitation must be exact (for example, a legal boundary). On the other hand, relative constraints can be a gradually diminishing factor where the weight given to the constraint is open to discussion and the exact location of boundaries is uncertain. In selecting a site for a given development, therefore, one may decide and justify that flood-protection zones and protected nature areas should be treated as definitive constraints, while a noise zone should be treated as a relative constraint.

FIGURE 7.6 New farm buildings out of scale of existing landscape
Technological changes are major drivers of change in cultural landscapes. In this image new large-scale barns and stables contrast with the small-scale terrain form and with the original farm buildings which are now outdated. The functional requirements of large horizontal floors in modern barns may result in earthworks and modification of levels, which reinforce the contrast between new and old. Careful site selection and earthworks, building design, choice of materials, and plantings can integrate old and new in better ways.
Source: Photo by Primdahl, J.

Reciprocity in potentials and constraints

In preparing the composite map it might seem most obvious to represent attractions (for example, a good bathing beach) as landscape potentials (positive), and nuisances (for example, noise) as landscape constraints (negative). However, the designation can be switched from a plus to a minus and vice versa, like converting a black/white photo from negative to positive or vice versa. If the designation is switched, the area category becomes *not suitable* for bathing rather than *suitable* for bathing, and *noise-free* replaces *noise-affected*. Methodologically it makes no difference whether the focus is on site-selection factors defined as landscape potentials or constraints (see Figure 7.7), as the two are each other's mirror images. The reversal may assist in focusing choices more quickly.

If a development requirement for a factory is level ground (for example, a slope of less than 5 per cent), this can be illustrated in the map as a development potential or as a development constraint. In the latter case, the symbol would indicate 'slope of more than 5 per cent' (Figure 7.7). It may be convenient to choose the solution that covers the smallest area: Figure 7.7a rather than 7.7b. However, the most important factor to consider in defining designations is the site-selection analysis process. In principle, there is nothing wrong with categorising positive requirements as definitive site-selection factors, but in practice, definitive factors would normally be defined as negative, that is, as constraints. Figure 7.14 illustrates the overlay technique, which requires that all the site-selection factors are defined as constraints.

Zones of influence around sensitive locations

Development requirements also concern the surroundings of a project, which means areas adjacent to the project site as well as more distant locations, and may influence the site search in different ways. For example, a wetland may pose a constraint in relation to a proposed holiday village in relation to the site itself, but be a potential in relation to the surroundings because of scenic and wildlife qualities. The development potentials offered by the wetland can be clarified by plotting a surrounding zone of influence (Figure 7.8). Similarly, a surrounding zone of influence may be plotted around an access road, a shop, etc. The width of the zone is, of course, a matter of judgement.

The main impact of a development is on the site it occupies, but it will also have a more or less pronounced impact on the surroundings in the form of smell, noise, traffic, visual appearance, etc. A motorcycle track will expose the surroundings to noise, and a holiday village will increase wear on adjacent nature areas. In these cases, a protection zone is plotted to mark the existing interests of the sensitive area. In Figure 7.9, a protection zone has been placed around a meadow with interesting botanical features.

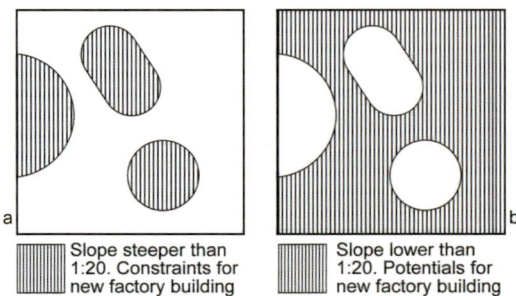

FIGURE 7.7 Positive or negative factors
The positive and negative site-selection factors may be each other's mirror images, so the plus or minus signs can be turned around to suit the purpose.
Source: Stahlschmidt, P. (1992).

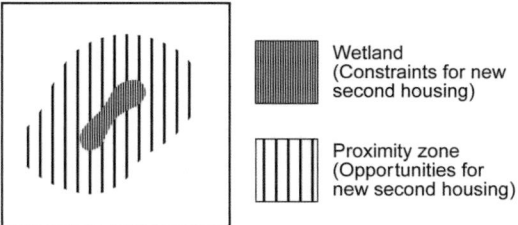

FIGURE 7.8 Surrounding zone for wetland
When distinguishing between site and surrounding zone, there is no inherent contra-diction in the conclusion that the wetland both attracts and excludes the siting of a new holiday village.
Source: Stahlschmidt, P. (1992).

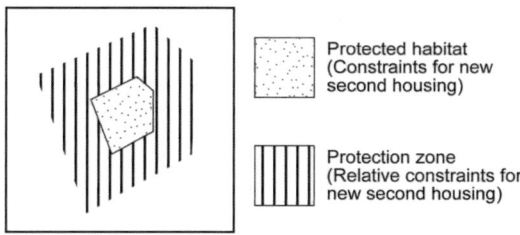

FIGURE 7.9 Protected zone around protected habitat
The habitat may offer a fine site for a holiday village, but the local area around it may impose a relative constraint.
Source: Stahlschmidt, P. (1992).

Future site possibilities

The landscape analyst may tend to focus on determining whether the planned devel-opment will be realised but, in many cases, no one can answer that, and in that case one has to deal with the uncertainty. Figure 7.10 not only includes the noise zone generated by the existing road but also the noise zone that would be generated by

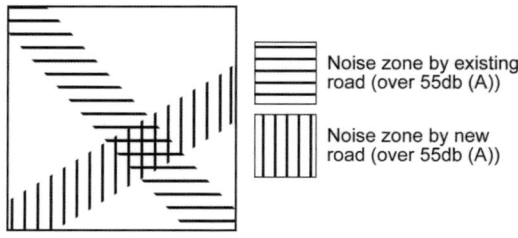

FIGURE 7.10 Existing and planned projected site-selection factors
Even if it is unknown whether the planned road is actually going to be built, it may be relevant to include it as a constraint in relation to new noise-sensitive developments – for example, residential buildings.
Source: Stahlschmidt, P. (1992).

a planned road, treating it as a development constraint. Perhaps the planned road will never be constructed, but the possibility alone may be reason enough to include the planned road in the site-selection analysis for housing for example.

Scale

Finally, we note that it is often helpful to use maps in a variety of scales in order to sort the site-selection factors according to the degree of detail that is relevant. Typically, site-selection factors such as wind shelter and shade will only be addressed in an analysis of selected areas in a fine-scale map (Figure 7.11), whereas topography may be relevant at a much coarser scale. In other words, the map scale helps the analyst distinguish relevant from irrelevant factors.

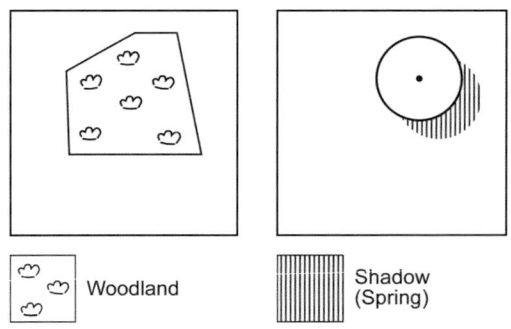

Woodland

Shadow
(Spring)

FIGURE 7.11 Scale as a determining factor
The site-selection factor 'shade' represents a relevant issue on a 1:500 map but is irrelevant on a 1:25,000 map.
Source: Stahlschmidt, P. (1992).

Main case: McHarg's overlay analysis

This example is taken from Ian McHarg's *Design with Nature* from 1969, a classic in the field of landscape analysis. The book argues that every site has intrinsic properties that can and should guide future land use. Thus, the landscape planner's job is to keep an open mind in identifying appropriate land uses in a given location. Landscape analysis uncovers the relevant landscape attributes and incorporates them into the planning process. McHarg also argued that the site may determine the specific future land use.

McHarg's book is a varied mix of essays and case examples and has a progressively increasing degree of complexity from one chapter to the next. The case example of Richmond Parkway (Figures 7.12–7.15) is discussed in the early part of the book. It illustrates the treatment of a relatively simple planning task, where the *purpose* is to select the route for a new stretch of motorway in a suburban area of New York. The originally proposed route for the new road was located inside a green belt. With his proposal for an alternative, McHarg wanted to demonstrate that if all the social costs were considered, the green belt solution was more costly than an alternative route located west of the belt. The original alignment proposal is illustrated with a dotted line in Figure 7.15.

The overlay technique can be used to uncover the site-selection possibilities but it is not helpful to a good outcome to include a large number of thematic maps as the basis of the composite classification map. The key requirement is that the analysis includes the most essential site-selection factors, and that the composite classification map is used as the basis for drafting possible solutions, not as a means to determine the actual site selection.

The *type of analysis* in the Richmond Parkway case is a site-selection analysis that characterises site-selection factors in an overlay technique, which represent the predominant analytical technique used in *Design with Nature*. In the case example, the overlay technique has a particularly intricate construction and stands alone, without being supplemented by a classification into landscape areas or a spatial analysis. The proposal for the new motorway alignment is plotted directly onto the composite classification map (Figure 7.15).

The *object* of this analysis is site selection, which includes landscape potentials and constraints as well as technical development requirements. However, it excludes scenic requirements, such as ensuring motorists a good visual experience.

SLOPE

FIGURE 7.12 Slope, Richmond Parkway
Slope is one of the layers in Figure 7.14. In light-grey areas the slope is 2.5–10 per cent, while dark-grey areas are slopes in excess of 10 per cent. The choice of level is essential for the result.

Source: McHarg (1969): *Design with nature*, Copyright ©1991 John Wiley and Sons.

143

SURFACE DRAINAGE

FIGURE 7.13 Surface drainage, Richmond Parkway
Surface drainage is another constraint for the new parkway. Light-grey areas mean natural drainage channels and areas of constricted drainage; dark grey means surface-water features.
Source: McHarg (1969): *Design with nature*, Copyright ©1991 John Wiley and Sons.

The solution resulting from the analysis is cheaper to construct and minimises harm to the existing landscape interests; however, if in addition it also proves to be a beautiful solution, that will not be due to the analysis.

The most important *sources* for the 16 thematic maps in the analysis are calculation (for example, of slope), field studies (for example, of ground and soil conditions), existing data (for example, real estate prices) and expert assessments (for example, of historical and recreational values).

The *procedure* applied in the Richmond Parkway case was to characterise six thematic layers of development requirements and ten thematic layers of landscape potentials and constraints. The indicator is the same for all the factors: a grey raster for each factor. Each thematic map has three ranked scales: a dark-grey raster for strong significance of the factor, a light-grey raster for medium significance and no raster when the factor has no significance in relation to the road project. All the transparent maps were combined in an overlay technique. The result is a composite classification map for development factors and one for landscape factors.

Figure 7.14 shows the composite classification map for development requirements. With its many shades between black and white, it resembles an X-ray photo. The development map and the map illustrating the values of the existing landscape (not included here) were then combined to form a final composite classification map. The darker the area in this composite classification map, the more *resistance* there is in the landscape to the new motorway development. The darkest areas are the sites that offer the smallest social benefits and savings and the largest social costs.

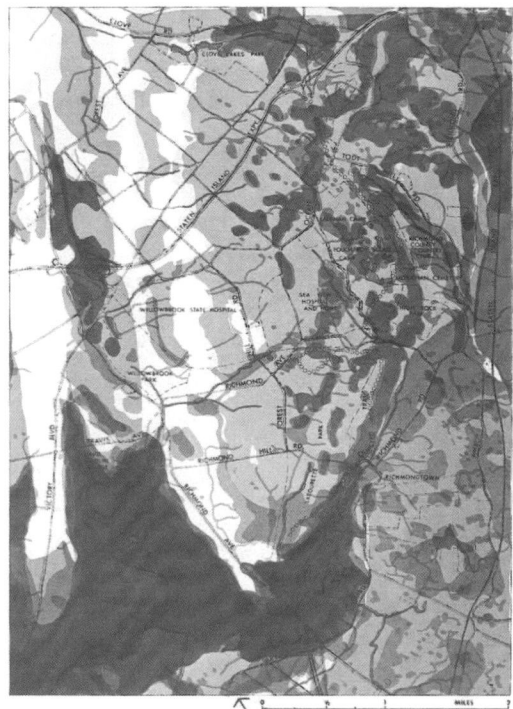

COMPOSITE: PHYSIOGRAPHIC OBSTRUCTIONS

FIGURE 7.14 Overlay techniques, Richmond Parkway
The composite classification map combines information from six maps, each depicting a specific set of requirements (slope, surface runoff, drainage conditions, rocky ground, soil and erosion risk). Each thematic map contains a ranked value assessment based on a three-zone breakdown. Zone 1, which involves the most severe requirements for the highway, is always marked with the darkest raster. Theoretically, the composite map would therefore have a scale of 6 x 3, that is, 18 steps, from white to black. As the signature is always either negative or positive, this produces a graphic illustration of the best site for a new road from a development point of view, which appears as the lighter areas.
Source: McHarg (1969): *Design with nature*, Copyright ©1991 John Wiley and Sons.

In the Richmond case, all the site-selection factors included in the composite classification map carry equal weight, which is problematic when some factors are causally linked, or when their value is not the same. GIS (geographic information system) was not available for McHarg when the Richmond Parkway was planned, but his approach lends itself perfectly to digital processing and there are many examples of this in the landscape-planning literature. With GIS the method can also be made more refined, so that each factor is weighted individually in a weighted overlay analysis.

The *representation technique* in the Richmond Parkway case gives a strong and rational impression due to the many thematic maps, and demonstrates the logic of the process. It suggests a road alignment proposal can be determined by careful

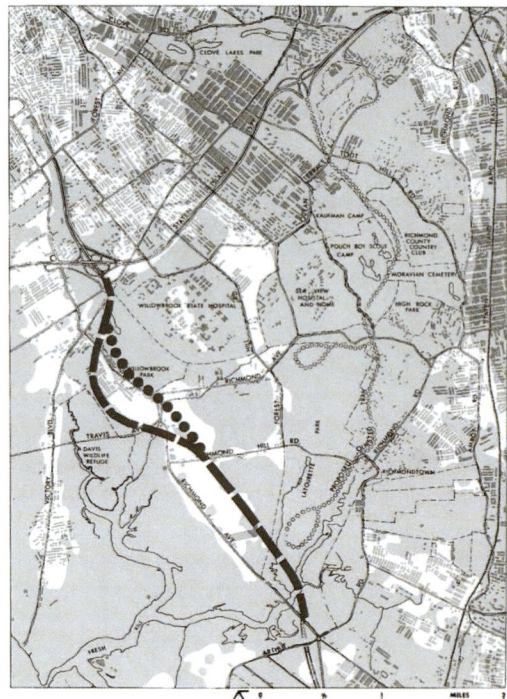

RECOMMENDED MINIMUM-SOCIAL-COST ALIGNMENT

FIGURE 7.15 Proposal for alignment, Richmond Parkway
Landscape requirements are shown in a similar composite map to the map depicting development requirements, Figure 7.14. The composite map of landscape constraints combines ten thematic maps, each depicting a value assessment of an interest (property value, tides, history, views, recreation, water, woodland, wildlife, housing and public institutions). Again, the two composite maps are merged into a single map depicting all the societal values. Figure 7.15 shows the summary map, simplified to two surface signatures: white for areas that are light on the composite map and a grey raster for all the darker areas. Fortunately, the highway alignment can be sited mainly within areas showing a positive balance of benefits and costs. The stretch marked with a chain of weaker empty circles in the right side of the image, from the interchange in the north and heading south, indicates the original proposal for the alignment of the road through a green belt.
Source: McHarg (1969): *Design with nature*, Copyright ©1991 John Wiley and Sons.

and systematic spatial analysis of landscape conditions, interpreted as potentials and constraints. Although the map in Figure 7.14 is derived from large data sets, the analysis is illustrated in an instructive and simple graphic form.

Variations

The multiple factors that influence site selection mean that a *site-selection analysis* has certain features in common with the *character assessment* that was discussed in Chapter 6. The difference is that a site-selection analysis aims to identify and select a site for a specific project, while a landscape character assessment represents a broader type of analysis that is more open in respect to possible future changes. However, they can be combined, and both the variations on site-selection analysis that are discussed below include identification of site-selection factors combined with landscape character areas.

Skovbo site-selection analysis

In this example, the classification into landscape character areas precedes the definition of site-selection factors, and site-selection potentials are only considered in landscape character areas that are already classified as suitable for the given development. In 1975 Skovbo was a municipality 40km SW of Copenhagen which expected a massive urban development, and therefore required a landscape analysis. The Skovbo analysis first identified homogeneous landscape areas. In the next step the potentials of individual character areas were judged for a number of land-use types, including urban development, industrial areas, main roads, parks and other recreational areas, and agriculture. This is done through an analysis of landscape constraints as indicated in Figure 7.16. The result is then a classification

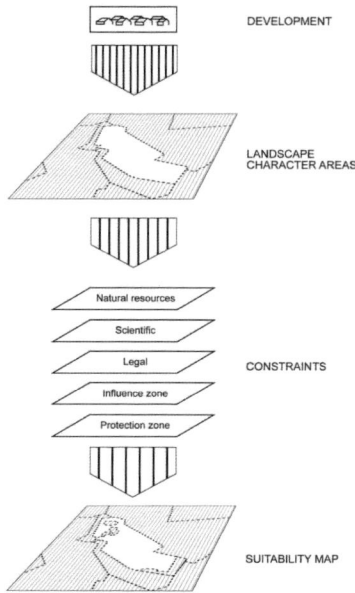

FIGURE 7.16 Landscape areas and site-selection factors, Skovbo
The Skovbo study first identified 115 landscape character areas, and for each of these the potentials of five different types of land use is judged. In the diagram only the central area is suited for residential development. For the suitable landscape character areas a series of filters has reduced the potential sites for urbanisation. The white area below represents a landscape area which has general potential for residential development, reduced by the landscape constraints.
Source: Olsen and Stahlschmidt (1975): Egnethedsanalyse for Skovbo Kommune. *Landskab* no. 6, p. 111.

of all the landscape areas into suitable, not-suitable and conditionally suitable categories in relation to each land-use type. This classification is, however, too rough to function in a site-selection context. For each of the land-use types the individual landscape areas were then included in the subsequent site-selection analysis if they had been classified as 'suitable' or 'conditionally suitable'. This was done by analysing landscape constraints.

Figure 7.18 shows the detailed constraints that apply to 'urbanisation' in area 9 (indicated by hatched areas in Figure 7.17). As a result of this analysis the site suitable for urban development is indicated by the green colour in Figure 7.18, whereas the unsuitable parts are left in white. However, as this is done for a number of potential land uses, further adjustments can be expected before the chosen site for a residential area is finally selected.

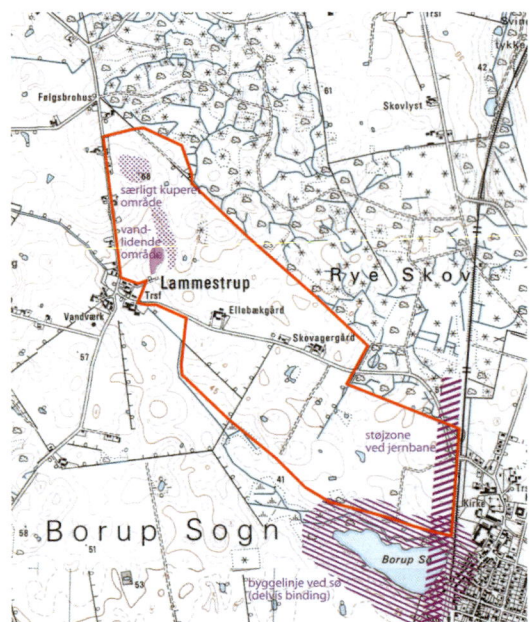

FIGURE 7.17 Characterisation of site-selection factors, Skovbo
The figure shows an extract with the four constraints that apply to 'urban development' in area 9. Earlier in the analytical process, area 9 was found suitable for new residential development. There is a 100-metre noise zone along the railway, a waterlogged area by Lammestrup and two small 'especially undulating areas' (slope above 16 per cent and at least five metres difference in elevation). These factors pose definitive constraints for a new urban area (development requirements). The 150-metre protection zone by Borup Lake is considered a relative constraint (landscape requirements).
Source: Olsen and Stahlschmidt (1975): Egnethedsanalyse for Skovbo Kommune. *Landskab* no. 6, p. 111. Here depicted on map sheet 1513 III NE. Surveyed: 1969. Corrected: 1970.

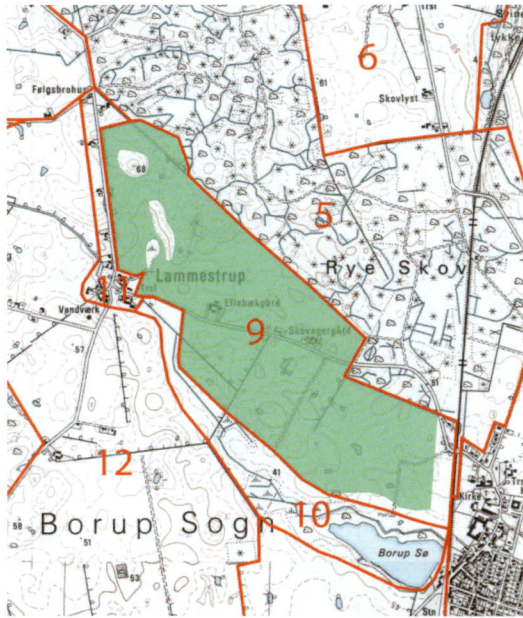

FIGURE 7.18 Adjustment of classification into landscape areas, Skovbo
The conclusion is that the green areas have potential for urban development, while the white areas inside area 9 reflect constraints (shown in figure 7.17), which definitively preclude site selection.
Source: Olsen and Stahlschmidt (1975): Egnethedsanalyse for Skovbo Kommune. *Landskab* no. 6, p. 111. Here depicted in map sheet 1513 III NE. Surveyed: 1969. Corrected: 1970.

Danish LCA site-selection analysis Randers Bay

This example illustrates how a site-selection analysis can be carried out based on a landscape characterisation as described in case B in Chapter 6. The area is the same area as shown in the visibility analysis in Chapter 5 (Figure 5.4) and the purpose of the site-selection analysis is to establish a basis for afforestation and major new farm developments. Danish legislation requires that due to environmental impacts (noise, smell, pollution, etc.) new large farm buildings, including pig barns, must be moved away from villages.

The LCA site-selection analysis is based on the character areas that are the result of interactions among natural factors, land cover, land use and spatial-visual aspects. The site-selection analysis involves defining the development, analysing the sensitivity of the landscape and classifying constraints and site-selection potentials.

The *sensitivity analysis* (Figure 7.19) is based on the landscape characterisation and a visibility analysis (Figure 5.4). In addition to this GIS-based visibility analysis, the sensitivity analysis also includes a field study. The marine foreland by Randers Bay in Eastern Jutland has no buildings and is intensively cultivated and open. The

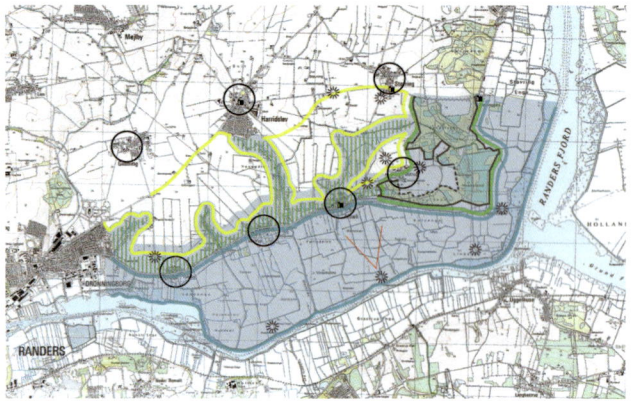

FIGURE 7.19 **Sensitivity study, Randers Bay**
The sensitivity study is based on character areas and the visibility analysis – see also Figure 5.4. The landscape character area indicated by a blue outline is cultivated marine foreland without built structures. Character areas with a yellow outline are moraine plateaux with intensive cultivation. The green outline marks scattered wood-lands. Finally, the green striping marks distinctive Stone-Age coastal bluffs and erosion ravines. The small 'suns' indicate key look-out points. The circles mark the villages where the expanding livestock farms were located. The red angle refers to the view-point of the photo in Figure 7.21. The grey areas are considered particularly sensitive with regard to both new agricultural buildings and afforestation.

Source: Nellemann et al. (2004): *Landbrugsbygninger, landskab og lokal omraadeplanlægning – metoder til landskabskaraktervurdering og oekonomivurdering.* By- og Landsplanserien no. 23, p. 58. Skov & Landskab, Hoersholm).

foreland has been judged as particularly sensitive to the new developments; the same applies to the distinctive cliffs and the ravines.

The *classification of constraints and potential sites* for farm expansion or relocation is illustrated in Figure 7.20. They include sensitive areas, distance zones to residences and wind turbines, and mapping of the individual farm properties. The map shows that there are few possible sites for the new farm developments, all with poor access conditions, when distance zones and sensitive landscape values are treated as definitive constraints. If the site-selection factor of 'good access roads' had also been treated as a definitive constraint, only one farm in Albaek would have a possible development site within existing property lines. Consequently, the site-selection analysis indicates the need for further land-use planning for the area combined with land consolidation.

Based on the site-selection analysis for the Randers Bay area, alternative *scenarios* for new farm developments and afforestation have been developed; potential solutions that consider the characteristic terrain forms of the landscape, vegetation and building patterns and the special visual qualities, as well as the road structure. One of these scenarios is illustrated in Figure 7.22. Futures analysis using scenarios is discussed further in Chapter 8.

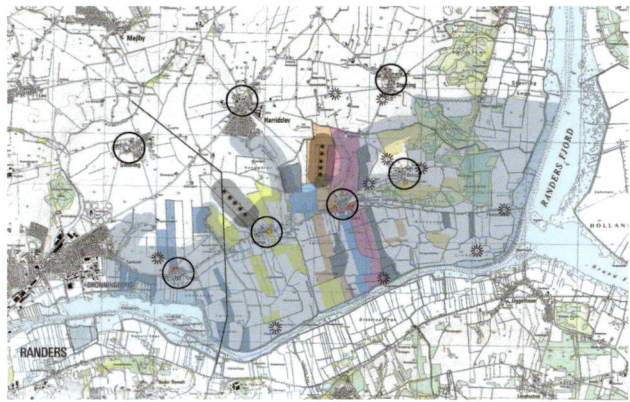

FIGURE 7.20 Mapping of constraints and site-selection options, Randers Bay
The sensitive areas and statutory distance zones in relation to residential structures are shown in grey, and distance zones to wind turbines (marked with 'stars') in dark grey. In the village Albæk there are four expanding farms (red circles). The land belonging to these farms is shown in ochre, pink, blue and dark blue. With the grey areas as definitive constraints, there are few remaining sites within each of the properties in Albæk that would be appropriate sites for new farm structures. Consequently, sites for three new large farm buildings are proposed outside the existing properties, on the moraine plateau east of the road from Albæk to Harridslev in the scenario shown in Figure 7.22.

Source: Nellemann et al. (2004): *Landbrugsbygninger, landskab og lokal omraadeplanlægning – metoder til landskabskaraktervurdering og oekonomivurdering.* By- og Landsplanserien no. 23, p. 59. Skov & Landskab, Hoersholm.

FIGURE 7.21 Albk Village
The village is clearly delineated in the border area at the foot of the former coastal bluff between the marine foreland and the higher moraine plateaux. There are four expanding livestock farms in Albæk. The purpose of the site-selection analysis is to identify potential areas in environmental as well as landscape terms for the intended relocation of these livestock farms.

Source: Photo by Nellemann, V. (2001).

FIGURE 7.22 Scenario of relocated farms, Randers Bay
3D visualisation of a proposal for the relocation of three livestock farms from Albæk. The farms are located along the road across the elevated farming plain between the villages of Albæk and Harridslev. An afforestation area forms a 'boundary' against the adjacent erosion ravine, anchoring the farms in the landscape, and furthermore supplies the schoolchildren in Harridslev with a recreational area. The scenario is based on the landscape characterisation and the site-selection analysis.
Source: Kristensen (2004): Photocollage. In Nellemann et al. (2004): *Landbrugsbygninger, landskab og lokal omraadeplanlaegning – metoder til landskabskaraktervurdering og oekonomivurdering*, p. 70. By- og Landsplanserien no. 23. Skov & Landskab, Hoersholm.

One of the critical features of site-selection analysis as described in this chapter is the focus on identifying the potentials and constraints of landscape in relation to development. This is based on the presumption that some types of development are poorly suited to particular sites because of the negative effect the development would have on the landscape. The process of selection therefore involves what is in effect an outline 'impact assessment' of the proposed development on all possible sites within the study area. In the next chapter we turn to the detailed process of impact assessment when a preferred site has been identified.

8

IMPACT ASSESSMENT AND FUTURES ANALYSIS

Introduction

As has been illustrated in many of the preceding chapters, landscape analysis involves thinking about the past, the present *and* the future. There are several types of analysis procedure that focus primarily upon the *future* consequences for the landscape of proposed actions, and a range of different words for what we have termed in this chapter *impact assessment* (IA) (Harrop and Nixon 1999) and *futures analysis* (Emmelin 1996). Impact Assessment is often used with a range of qualifying terms, such as environment, ecosystem, visual and landscape. Environmental assessment (EA) and environmental impact assessment (EIA) are two of the most common ways to describe processes that have been developed to assess the environmental consequences of 'proposed activities that are likely to have significant adverse impacts on the environment and are subject to a decision of a competent national authority' (United Nations 1992, Annex 1: Principle 17).

Impact assessment is typically focused upon the consequences of particular project proposals, but governments and planning agencies are increasingly undertaking analysis of the broad-scale and longer-term environmental effects of dynamics such as urbanisation, new technologies, changing markets, and climate change. This is termed *futures analysis*, and there is a growing suite of procedures and techniques that explore the environmental and landscape characteristics of possible future situations under a range of different assumptions. In this book we focus on assessment of impacts associated with site selection and project development within a landscape context, and consider IA as a form of landscape analysis. In this chapter we therefore highlight two interconnected roles of project-related IA – the assessment of landscape and visual impacts, and their design implications. However, we also introduce futures analysis as a variation of IA that is focused upon exploring alternative landscape futures.

FIGURE 8.1 Raippaluoto Bridge
Many aspects of impact assessment are involved in a bridge project. This bridge, the longest in Finland, is 1045 metres long, built in 1997. The bridge has – among other things – an impact on the natural aquatic and terrestrial environment, and it has visual and noise impacts for users of the area.
Source: Photo by Primdahl, J.

Impact assessment (IA)

IA has two critical dimensions. First and foremost, it involves the analysis of the impact or effects of a proposed change (such as a construction project, or a series of projects) upon a given site or location in a landscape. Second, an IA can also analyse the consequences of these impacts for the design of the proposed development. Figure 8.2 illustrates a generalised process of Impact Assessment. It shows how a proposed project changes the condition of a site and its relationship with the landscape, and how knowledge of the potential impacts of a project might in turn influence the design of the proposed solution. This feedback loop between assessment of predicted impacts of a project and its design is vital to the way projects are developed and adapted to their location, and impact assessment is often central to the professional involvement of a landscape architect or environmental planner in a major new project. In principle, many of the methods of assessment and analysis that are used to examine an existing landscape, and that have been described in previous chapters, can also be used to examine the impacts of a proposed project on a site and its landscape context.

As the previous quote from the United Nations (page 154) highlighted, impact assessment is focused upon influencing or informing decisions. The aim is to help decision-makers reach the best possible solution and prevent unforeseen and undesirable consequences. Once a project is built, it is often hard and usually expensive to reduce undesirable effects, and may be impossible, which makes it too late for regrets! IA has developed as a distinctive planning approach over the past 50 years, and was initially developed in response to concerns by environmentalists and others about the environmental consequences of the rapid economic growth experienced during the 1950s and 1960s. It has since become a legal requirement for a range of types of project in many countries (Jay et al. 2007).

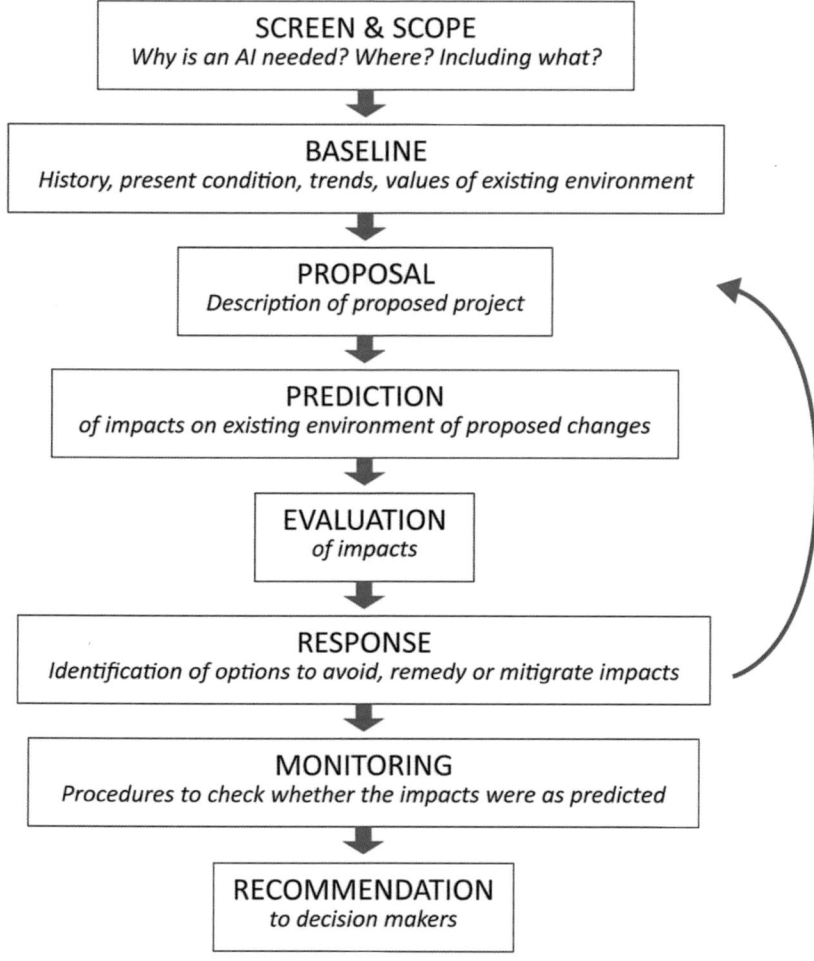

FIGURE 8.2 Generalised model of Impact Assessment (IA)

In 1969 the need for 'environmental impact assessment' of federal projects was a feature of the US National Environmental Policy Act, and from the mid-1980s similar requirements were introduced in European environmental policy (Wood 2003). Many other countries now have similar requirements, and various types of impact assessment are also promoted by global funding agencies such as the World Bank.

A conventional impact assessment is carried out when there is a specific proposal to examine, and hence an *impact* to assess, but different types and stages of assessment will often be carried out as part of the process leading up to a final proposal, and subsequently during its operation. Strategic impact assessment (Tetlow and Hanusch 2012), for example, has emerged as a 'family of tools' intended to assess the impacts of public policies, plans and programmes before particular projects have been formulated, so that environmental considerations can influence the nature and location of projects from their inception. Impact assessment may also be applied to the process of site selection, and in some applications (such as the Resource Management Act in New Zealand) it is mandatory to identify what alternatives have been considered as part of a project assessment. Adaptive environmental assessment (Holling 1978) on the other hand has developed with a primary focus upon the management of projects and ecosystems as a process of *continual adaption* in the light of increasing knowledge and changing circumstances.

Most fundamentally, impact assessment helps decision-makers decide between the two options presented in all planning situations: you either implement a proposed change or you don't. Planning authorities therefore use impact assessments as information in approval procedures, including public hearings, and this may extend to consideration of ways to avoid, remedy or mitigate adverse effects. In other words, to ask "What will be the likely impact on the landscape of undertaking a particular development at this site, and how can the design of the development be adapted to reduce or avoid unwanted impacts or effects?" The inclusion of the term 'effects' in this discussion draws upon New Zealand practice, where the term is neutral, in that the consequences of change can be either a positive or adverse 'effect', and so assessment of effects emphasises a weighing up of consequences. 'Impacts' can also be thought of as positive or adverse, but the term 'impact' is often more value-laden, reflecting its initial use in IA as part of the environmental revolution in the 1960s.

Environmental impact assessment (EIA) reporting

The output of an impact or effects assessment is typically known as an EIA *statement* or report, and both the process itself and its outputs (statements) have to meet certain formal standards with regard to content and procedure. Denmark provides an example of how EIA requirements are defined in planning law (Danish Ministry of Environment 2007b). Local authorities are required to incorporate guidelines into the municipal plan about the location and design of the types of development that require an EIA, along with a description and assessment of their environmental impact. The types of landscape-related projects and changes that are included in the Danish EIA regulations include:

- large polluting facilities such as power plants, refineries, incineration plants and manufacturing plants
- large transport installations, power lines and wind turbines
- major specific alterations or intensifications of agricultural land use and large livestock facilities
- certain types of afforestation as well as logging in forest reserve areas
- large quarries and gravel pits
- large shopping centres and hotels/resorts and other recreational facilities.

The EIA statement must provide information about the design, location and environmental impact of the proposed change, including potential impacts on habitats, environment, cultural heritage, people, the landscape itself, and its recreational accessibility. In addition, it must provide an overview of the most important alternatives and possible initiatives to mitigate any negative impact on the environment. The legal requirements are supported by a manual (Danish Ministry of Environment 2002) with directions for handling issues concerning the landscape throughout the phases of the EIA.

Another example of IA as a statutory requirement is found in the main planning legislation in New Zealand (The Resource Management Act). This law requires a type of impact assessment called an Assessment of Environmental Effects (AEE) (Ministry for Environment 2006). This must be provided as supporting information for an application for a resource consent (a consent to use a resource or undertake a new activity). The assessment documents may range from a short two- or three-page assessment for a minor project in an already well-developed area, to a major report involving many experts in the case of a large-infrastructure development. The AEE process places particular emphasis upon the possibilities to avoid, remedy or mitigate 'adverse' effects, as well as recognising the potential for positive effects. Hence IA becomes integrated with project design (see Figure 8.2 above).

Landscape visual and aesthetic assessment

EIA statements are often divided into different sections and may include a specific 'landscape' assessment that evaluates the impact on the landscape of the intended project or change, or a 'visual assessment' that is focused on the visual and scenic impacts, or an assessment of 'aesthetic' impacts – see the case example 'Aesthetic EIA assessment Frederikssund Motorway'. This raises the question of how landscape, visual and aesthetic assessments relate to each other.

Depending upon the way it is defined in particular countries, *landscape* assessment can include a wide range of environmental dimensions, from biophysical systems to transient sensory qualities of place. Visual may range from *objective* appearance,

FIGURE 8.3 Dynamic of vegetation succession
It is always hard to predict landscape change due to social and cultural factors. Naturally caused changes are not entirely predictable either, although vegetation succession can be projected. Left to natural processes, without management intervention, the open grazing hill in the foreground of the picture from Bornholm island, Denmark will develop into woodland. Impact assessments should be carried out as part of any habitat-management plan, both concerning the preservation of a specific environment or succession stage, and the dynamics following a change in management.
Source: Photo by Stahlschmidt, P.

to scenery, to individual perception. Aesthetics may be defined formally, as shape and pattern, or in a more transactional way – that is, as an experience rather than a quality of a setting. Each of these will lead to different techniques being adopted and even different processes – for example, in determining how to consult with communities.

Despite over 40 years of research and investigations, there is still no standard scientific model of landscape or visual assessment (National Cooperative Highway Research Program 2013) and there is also debate among researchers about how best to deal with the requirements of valid and effective assessment. It can be frustrating for decision-makers when different landscape experts offer different advice, because they adopted different assessment procedures, and in some countries there have been attempts to develop a recognised protocol for the components, stages, or activities in an IA. One useful model is provided by the UK Landscape Institute (2013) which includes a series of stages, each of which can prompt a question. These follow very closely the generic model of impact assessment described above:

1. Screening – is a landscape or visual assessment needed?
2. Scoping – what should it contain?
3. Project description – what is the nature of the proposal?
4. Baseline – what are the current conditions of the landscape?
5. Assessment – what are the predicted effects of the proposal?
6. Mitigation – how can the adverse effects be mitigated?
7. Presentation – how to communicate the results and to whom?
8. Monitoring – was the assessment accurate?

Landscape impact-assessment techniques may include different types of landscape analysis, but of particular relevance are value assessment (Chapter 2), spatial analysis (Chapter 5) and site-selection analysis (Chapter 7) (Turner 1998).

Finally, as we have noted previously, strategic environmental assessment (Short et al. 2005) applies environmental-assessment processes to assess the broad-scale implications of public policies and land-use plans for a regional or even national environment. However, in this chapter we focus upon project-based assessment, highlighting the processes that are most relevant to the assessment of a proposed project upon a particular landscape defined according to the European Landscape Convention as an area of land with particular character as perceived by people.

Main case: aesthetic EIA assessment Frederikssund Motorway

This example is part of an EIA of a new major road in the 'Frederikssund Finger' of the Copenhagen Finger Plan (Figure 8.4). According to the 'Finger Plan', Copenhagen is to develop along five 'fingers' centred on rail lines which extend from the 'palm' of the hand. The new road in this example is intended to link the Motor Ring 3 in the east – as an extension of Jyllingevej – to the town of Frederikssund in the west. It had not been determined at that stage whether the road should be a motorway or an A-road. The aesthetic assessment was carried out by landscape architects Thing & Wainoe for the Danish Road Directorate. The alternatives consisted of a visualisation of two main routes – a 'landscape solution' and an 'urban finger solution'. For each of the two main routes, alternative alignments were outlined for certain sections of the road (Thing and Wainoe 2002).

The *purpose* of the aesthetic assessment includes the inclusion of landscape considerations in the design of specific project proposals, and the assessment and visualisation of the alternative routes and alignments with regard to their impact on and interactions with the landscape. In addition, the aesthetic assessment forms the basis for recommendations for landscape and visual 'mitigation' of the negative effects of the proposed road system. The ultimate purpose is to choose the best route as seen from a holistic perspective.

159

a

Hilly, open landscape with new urban areas

Valley landscape around the river Vaerebro

Hilly, open landscape with villages

b

Frederikssund

Store Rørbæk

Lille Rørbæk

Udlejre

Ølstykke

Stenløse

Veksø

Måløv

Smørumnedre

Østrup

Smørumovre

Hove

Ballerup

Ledøje

Forest landscape 'Vestskoven'

Motorring 3

| ★ Village | —— Power line |
| Forest | ⌢ Terrain edge |

c

Frederikssund

Store Rørbæk

Lille Rørbæk

Udlejre

Ølstykke

Stenløse

The urban finger solution

The landscape solution

Veksø

Måløv

Smørumnedre

Østrup

Smørumovre

Hove

Ballerup

Ledøje

Motorring 3

| —— Examples of alternative alignments |
| —— Boundary of landscape character area |

FIGURE 8.4a–c Aesthetic assessment, Frederikssund Motorway
The three maps a–c are part of an EA process for a new road west of Copenhagen.

a. Landscape character areas. The road section being investigated runs between Ring 3 (approximately 20km west of Copenhagen) and further west in the direction of the town of Frederikssund. The heterogeneous and complex terrain has had an important influence on land-use developments over time, on the spatial pattern and visual qualities in the assessment area, as well as for the possible location and impacts of the new road. The aesthetic assessment is based on a digitised terrain model, in which the lowest areas are shown with a green colour and highest with yellow. The four landscape character areas including key characteristics are shown on the map, originally on the scale 1:25,000.

b. **The spatial and visual analysis** emphasises the main spatial patterns of importance for the present landscape character as well as for the route selection of the road.

c. **Alternative alignments**. The section between Ledoeje and Udlejre is the most sensitive, and alternative proposals have been produced. The alternatives include two overall proposals: 'The landscape solution' and the 'Urban finger solution'. Within these two main alternatives, detailed variations have been considered for specific sub-sections.

Source: Thing and Wainoe (2002): *Ny hoejklasset vej i Frederikssundfingeren – VVM-redegoerelse. Aestetisk vurdering og visualisering*, pp. 6–8. Danish Road Directorate.

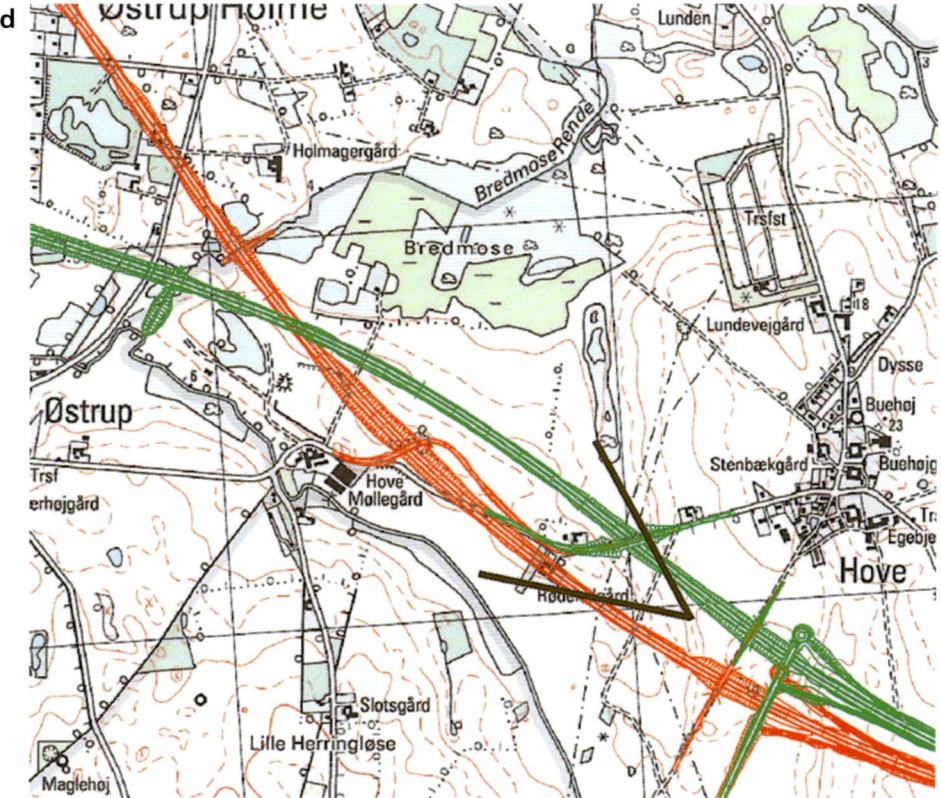

FIGURE 8.4d **Red and green alternatives at Hove**
Detailed assessment of the 'landscape solution'. On the sub-section south of Hove two alternative routes are shown. The valuable landscape with vulnerable habitats and cultural heritage make the detailed route choice and landscape adaptation a difficult task. The viewpoint in black shows the location and direction of the three air photos shown in Figures 8.4e–g.

Source: Thing and Wainoe (2002): *Ny hoejklasset vej i Frederikssundfingeren – VVM-redegoerelse. Aestetisk vurdering og visualisering*, p. 24. Danish Road Directorate.

As a basis for the aesthetic assessment, a landscape characterisation was carried out for the area (Figures 8.4a and 8.4b). Next, an impact assessment was prepared for the alternative alignments in certain sections of the road, both the 'landscape solution' and the 'urban finger solution'. The process is illustrated in the map detail of the area by Hove (Figures 8.4d–g).

The *key issue* in the aesthetic assessment of the routes is the proposed road system and its impact on the experience of the existing landscape values as well as the experience of the road system from the surroundings.

The *source* of information for the assessment is a landscape characterisation based on spatial analyses using GIS (geographic information system) of the area's biophysical factors (geomorphology, terrain and surface waters) and of the historically conditioned and current patterns in land use, combined with a field-based spatial-visual analysis, terrain cross sections, and aerial and ground photography.

The *procedure* involves dividing the assessment area into homogeneous units, each with their characteristic landscape elements and particular spatial and visual features and aesthetic values. These were assessed in order to identify and illustrate the potentials and problematic issues arising from adapting the landscape to accommodate the road, as well as considering possibilities for adapting the road to the landscape through alternative routes. A digital terrain model was produced in order to provide an overview of the relationship between the landforms and the road. Bridges, earthworks and approach ramps were also addressed in order to make the representation of a potential new road as realistic as possible. Based on these models, the expected visual impact of the road system was assessed, and proposals for mitigating features drawn up, such as placing the road system low in the terrain, adapting the route and earthworks to the terrain, planting screening vegetation, or clearing and preserving open areas – for example, around the villages.

The *presentation techniques* include GIS mapping, a digital terrain model, terrain cross sections, and before-and-after images in the form of photomontages. In the visualisations, the proposal was merged with existing conditions. The presentation covers the main proposal as well as alternative road alignments for the sections that require special attention. The visualisations consist of photos of the current landscape into which a representation of the proposed road and its infrastructure is added by means of computer montage. The visualisations use aerial photos from an oblique bird's-eye perspective representing longer sections of road (Figures 8.4e–g), as well as ground-level photos to represent the road layout in a specific area. This corresponds to the real-life experience where the road is not only experienced from within the adjacent landscape, but also seen from higher viewpoints due to the complex combination of valleys and hills in the area.

The photomontages offer a reasonably realistic representation of the current landscape with the addition of the envisaged development. However, Downes and Lange (2015) demonstrate that the choice of photographic point of view and angle can serve to emphasise or diminish the dominance of a proposed project

e

FIGURE 8.4e The current landscape at Hove
Bird's-eye view towards Frederiksund. A mosaic moraine landscape with crop farming intermixed with wetlands on organic soils and with different land uses. The road from Hove to Oestrup is seen in the centre of the image. To the left of the road is a heavily modified river. The river and the road intersect at Hove Moellegaard in the middle distance.

Source: Thing and Wainoe (2002): *Ny hoejklasset vej i Frederikssundfingeren – VVM-redegoerelse. Aestetisk vurdering og visualisering*, p. 25. Danish Road Directorate.

f

FIGURE 8.4f Photomontage, red alternative
Visualisation of the red alternative in which the new road runs through the undulating landscape along the Hove River and continues through the valley. At the site where the current road crosses the proposed road on a bridge in the middle distance there will be extensive removal of soil caused by lowering the road into a cutting in the terrain.

Source: Thing and Wainoe (2002): *Ny hoejklasset vej i Frederikssundfingeren – VVM-redegoerelse. Aestetisk vurdering og visualisering*, p. 24. Danish Road Directorate.

g

FIGURE 8.4g Photomontage, green alternative
This option leaves the vulnerable (biotope and cultural-heritage) landscape of the river valley and Hove Moellegaard unchanged. Notice the significant landfills and cuttings at the crossing of the old road and new road in the foreground. The new road is lowered in the terrain whereas the old road is lifted on landfill.

Source: Thing and Wainoe (2002): *Ny hoejklasset vej i Frederikssundfingeren – VVM-redegoerelse. Aestetisk vurdering og visualisering*, p. 25. Danish Road Directorate.

in the landscape, and so the creation of representations using photomontage and related digital techniques requires particularly careful consideration. Inclusion of views from areas where the impact of the road is high as well as views from a range of locations where it is less visible is needed to achieve a balanced approach.

This highlights the issue of sensitivity to visual impacts. It is now standard practice in landscape and visual assessment (Landscape Institute 2013) to prepare maps that show the zones of theoretical visibility of proposed development, which enable the analyst to identify where the proposed development could potentially be seen. The zone is described as *theoretical* visibility because it is generated from a terrain model and does not take into account the screening effects of minor, opaque and seasonal landscape elements such as trees. Then, locations that are particularly sensitive in visual or aesthetic terms are identified. This may be due to the number of people that live, or visit, or travel through the location, or due to the particular values of the viewpoint – for example, being a heritage site. Highly sensitive locations may require the road alignment to be revised to reduce the impacts, or may need additional mitigation measures, including actions such as mounding, fencing or tree planting along the road corridor. The measures may even be undertaken some distance from the road itself, in the case of a particularly sensitive view point. Analysis of visibility is illustrated in Figure 5.4.

Variations

Representing change

IA reports always contain text and usually also diagrams, cross sections and plans. In addition, when considering landscape, visual or aesthetic impacts there are typically visualisations of the intended installation or development and its impact or effects. These representations may be in the form of spatial presentations, aerial photographs, perspective photographs, before-and-after images, analogue (physical) models and model photos, or digital models. Regardless of the presentation mode, there is a choice between *abstract* and *realistic* representation, between representation of how a landscape *works* and how it *appears*, between *factual information* and *illustrative presentation,* and between *reliable* and *biased representation*. These choices, which are also discussed in 'The nature of landscape analysis' in Chapter 1, are particularly important in impact assessments, where the task is often to help decision-makers and non-professionals visualise what *might* happen, and where what is shown will affect the decisions that are made.

The most basic way of representing change in a landscape is *before-and-after images.* These have been used to illustrate proposed landscape developments ever since Humphry Repton (1976) prepared his 'Red Books' at the end of the 18th century, and they are an established and useful method for carrying out impact assessments and illustrating planning proposals. At their most basic, before-and-after illustrations consist of one drawing of the existing landscape and one drawing of the potential future landscape. Figures 3.26 and 3.27 are examples with two maps of this simple technique. Another common variation is when a drawing is added to a photograph, forming a representation of the future development superimposed on an image of the current state of affairs. Thus, the principle is analogous to the type of historic analysis referred to as a 'historic map series' (Figure 4.8).

Today, such visual modelling of projected change due to a proposed project is typically undertaken using more or less sophisticated digital models such as so-called ZTV maps showing the *zones of theoretical visibility* (Figure 5.4), photomon-tage (Figure 8.4) and GIS-generated 3D visualisations (Figure 7.22). Some of these models can also be used interactively in participatory processes. However sophis-ticated the techniques may be, the fundamental issues remain the same, namely to enable both an effective response to a specific intervention and a systematic (analytical) assessment of the visual and aesthetic consequences of the change (Sheppard et al. 2011). In a study of various techniques used to communicate visual impacts of a new wind farm (Berry et al. 2011), the influence and effectiveness of different visualisations in enabling public involvement were evaluated through a web-based survey. Among the different types shown, a relatively simple pho-tomontage technique was ranked highest by public users, compared to a terrain model with the wind turbines located upon it, and to maps showing ZTV maps (see Figure 5.4 as an example) and to various 3D visualisations concerning a number of dimensions (Figure 8.5).

In a practical situation the analysts have to decide how to simplify the com-plexity of landscape into a plausible and useful representation, how to represent the process of change, and how to provide clarity for decision-makers when many aspects of the future may be uncertain or unknown. The way that 'plausible' and 'useful' are defined in this context is no easy job and what may be 'useful' from the developers' point of view may be different from a local stakeholder's perspective.

Downes and Lange (2015) have analysed how visualisation of proposed con-struction compares to photos of the same location taken after construction, and have shown how and to what degree the representations may differ (Figure 8.6). This highlights the importance of careful validation of visualisations to ensure their accuracy. Visualisation can provide inaccurate images of the proposed changes for a range of reasons. These may include technical modelling prob-lems, or even errors or over-optimistic assumptions about a predicted action to remedy or mitigate impacts – for example, the growth of vegetation planted to screen development. It may also be distorted due to a deliberate or inadvertent choice of viewpoint or view angle which reduces the apparent visual impacts of new constructions. Another inaccuracy can come from omission of some tran-sient effects, such as traffic or seasonal effects, on vegetation screening. Valida-tion of visual modelling used in IA is now a critical part of professional practice, and validation studies are often included when reporting the results of IA to decision-makers.

FIGURE 8.5 Wind farm, Evanstown
The upper image shows a terrain skeleton illustration with the wind turbines located in South Wales – a so-called wireframe. The lower picture shows a photomontage of the proposed windmills. The photomontage was ranked higher than other visual techniques in a web survey (which included the terrain model).
Source: Berry et al. (2011): *Web-based GIS Approaches to Enhance Public Participation in Wind Farm Planning. Transactions in GIS*, 15(2), 155. Copyright ©2011 John Wiley and Sons.

Analysing change

Whatever mode of representation is used, the basic analytical process is the same: a representation of what is there before the project is prepared, followed by creation of an accurate representation of what will be there if the project proceeds. Analysis of the difference between the current situation and possible future situation requires a systematic account of the existing landscape attributes, an account of the project attributes, and an account of the combined landscape and project attributes after the change. This may be done in a *parametric way* – describing different attributes and the changes that occur one by one – or in a *holistic way*, providing an expert account about the overall change. Experts usually base their synthetic account on a parametric analysis.

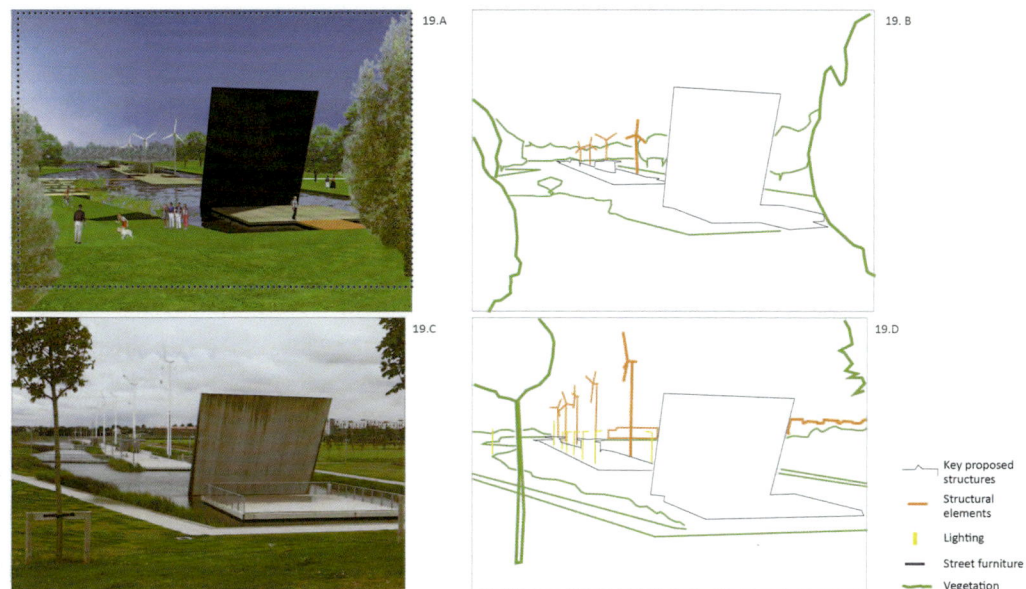

FIGURE 8.6 Gap between illustrations of the project and the reality
This example illustrates the differences between a plan-based visualisation and the actual vegetation condition following project implementation in Father Collins Park, Dublin in Ireland. Visualisation is important, as the growth of trees and shrubs is a slow process, and it is very hard to imagine the future of the landscape. However, visualisations must be as reliable and authentic as possible when making long-term predictions.

Source: Before-and-after images of Fr. Collins Park, Dublin. Visualisation by 'ArArq Ireland/MCO Projects', photography and analytics Melanie Downes.

See also Downes and Lange (2015): What you see is not always what you get: A qualitative, comparative analysis of ex ante visualizations with ex post photography of landscape and architectural projects. *Landscape and Urban Planning*, 142, 136–146.

The analyses can be presented in different ways. A *composite presentation* is a representation of results of an impact assessment of a proposal where different aspects are depicted on separate maps or diagrams, as exemplified in Figure 8.7. The four maps not only explore four separate aspects of the whole; they are also drawn in such a way that when they are placed on top of each other in an overlay technique, they will form a composite proposal map (not shown here). In the example, the different aspects are presented in an overview scale and in a simple form, and thus they can be characterised as diagrams. In a digital analysis using either CAD or GIS it is normal to conceptualise elements as layers that can be turned on and off.

In a *thematic illustration of a proposal*, by contrast, multiple layers of information are presented as overlaid themes on a single map. The map section shown in Figure 8.8 summarises the environmental impacts that will affect the (red) urban areas and the (green) nature areas. Making the individual layers in an overlay

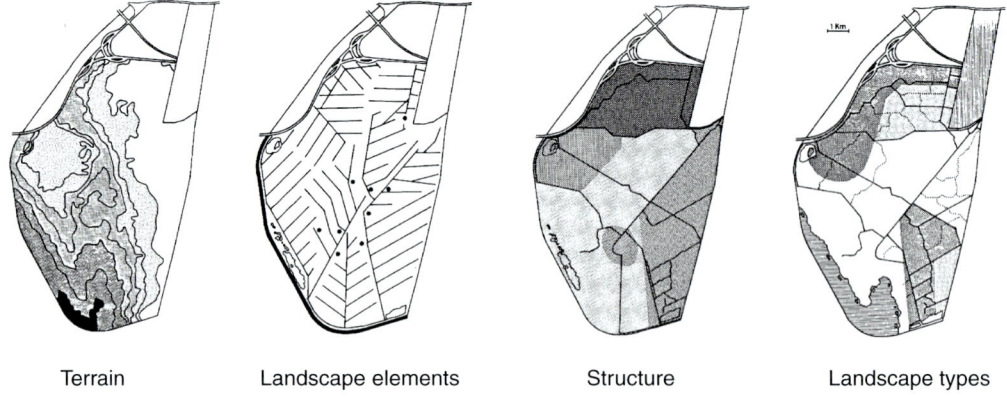

| Terrain | Landscape elements | Structure | Landscape types |

FIGURE 8.7 Separated aspects recreation plan
The four aspects are shown as separate layers. When overlaid they form the composite. In this case from a recreation plan in Copenhagen, the layers were utilised to assess the impacts of a planning proposal, but could also have been used for analysing existing patterns.

Source: Bak (1997): Vestamager – et naturomraade i Koebenhavn. Master's thesis. *Landskab*, 1(97), 18–19.

FIGURE 8.8 Environmental conflicts regional plan
Assessment of a small section of a county in Southern Jutland showing the environmental impact zones of various installations, as well as the extent of sensitive land uses.

Source: Soenderjylland County (1999): *Kortbilag – Regionplan 1997–2008 – Miljoekonflikter, map 6*. Aabenraa.

presentation legible requires a careful selection of map symbols, and the map is easier to read when it is in colour. This map contains a large number of symbols, yet it remains legible. In Chapter 7 on site-selection analysis, the composite classification map shown in Figure 7.14 offers another thematic illustration, but one that portrays the existing landscape rather than a proposal for future landscape design.

Single-theme maps can often be reproduced in a scale that is better suited for overview purposes than a composite map. However, the strength of a composite map is that it illustrates the combination of the themes. Thus, it may at times be preferable to use the two techniques as complementary.

An extreme form of representation in impact assessment is a full-scale model, that is, a model in a scale of 1:1 (a 'mock-up'). One example of this was the proposed expansion of The Royal Danish Theatre in Copenhagen in 1996, when architect Sverre Fehn's 'Theatre Bird' was erected as a full-scale model. Considering the prominent location and the high degree of public interest, this mock-up was an appropriate way to illustrate the potential impacts of the new building (Figure 8.9).

A *graded-zone map* offers a way of mapping how predicted impacts for an environmental factor may change with distance from the proposed project. The noise-zone map shown in Figure 1.6 illustrates the outcome of a technical

FIGURE 8.9 Mock-up building extension, DK
The mock-up erected on the façade of the Royal Danish Theatre in Copenhagen offered the inhabitants a very realistic impression of architect Sverre Fehn's proposal which included a column with wings. This part of the project was subsequently omitted.
Source: Landscape analysis complete pst, www.arkitekturbilleder.dk/bygning-Teaterfuglen-523.

engineering calculation of noise levels that is communicated in a series of zones of different predicted measures of noise, shown in graphic form. However, it also highlights the complexity of measuring impacts that involve people's experience and perceptions, as behind the map with its relatively simple and factual appearance there is an underlying uncertainty in both the prognosis and the interpretation of the noise-zone map. Specifically, do each of the colour-coded zones correspond to the experiences a person would have throughout that zone? And how confident can we be in the mapped location of the boundaries between categories? The categories are a simplification of what in reality are continuously variable phenomena but, just as in other types of modelling, all simplification involves assumptions.

This example illustrates the issues that arise when preparing visualisation maps that are based upon zones intended to indicate different levels of impact – for example, high, medium and low visual impact. Although the broad distinction between levels of impact is plausible and helpful, the determination of the thresholds between zones and their location in space is fraught with uncertainty. At what point as a viewer approaches a proposed project does the visual impact change from medium to high? How accurately can the incremental change be measured? Classification of continuously variable phenomena such as visual impact into levels or degrees of impact can therefore become problematic at a fine scale. Nevertheless, zone maps can be practically helpful in comparing the impact of alternative solutions, and this approach does offer a well-defined basis for assessments and decision-making provided the limitations are acknowledged.

Futures analysis and alternative futures

IA is always oriented to the future, but is typically framed around a specific proposal at a particular point in time. However, as we noted in Chapter 1, landscapes also change as a result of wider dynamics – both natural and socio-economic. The approach developed in IA and EA is being extended and adapted in many countries to undertake much broader assessments of possible future conditions, in order to inform planning decisions. For example, growing awareness of the landscape consequences of current and future climate changes is stimulating public authorities to engage in analysis of the likely impacts and the vulnerability of their territories and cities to changing weather patterns and higher sea levels, and their effect on rainfall, flooding, storms, temperature and drought. The analyses help agencies evaluate and plan climate adaptation and mitigation measures – for instance, establishing new coastal protection or enlarging storm-water systems, avoiding urban expansion into low-lying areas, etc.

Futures analysis is the term used to refer to analysis of possible drivers and effects of larger-scale dynamics or policy decisions (Baker and Landers 2004). This is often described in landscape planning as *alternative-futures* analysis (Shearer 2005; Bryan et al. 2011). An important part of the process is the exploration of different possible pathways into the future. This may involve one or more alternative projections, scenarios, or alternative futures.

A *projection* is a forecast of change based on a defined set of expected relationships, and sets out the future trajectory of a landscape if the current trends continue for a shorter or longer period of time. An example might be, "what would happen to community life in the main street of a town along a major road if authorities decide not to construct a proposed motorway bypass but traffic continues to increase at the current rates?" Or, "what would be the consequences for waterfront neighbourhoods in a coastal city if sea levels rise by a metre?" Or, "what might be the consequences for agricultural landscapes in a region if annual rainfall drops by 20 per cent?" Projections such as these are largely technical analyses, using past and current data to predict a future trajectory, but may be represented in landscape or visual terms, such as a map or visualisation of areas projected to be flooded.

However, there is frequently uncertainty over precisely how future conditions may develop. A *scenario* is a more open assumption about the conditions or decisions that will shape the future, such as current development trends and specific interventions by public and private actors. Landscape scenarios can offer a useful tool for informing and assessing the options for landscape and environmental planning, and are often used in connection with involvement of citizens (Tress and Tress 2003). Scenarios are often presented as 'what if?' questions, such as "What if we promoted irrigation to offset drought?", "What if governments took strong action to reduce greenhouse gas emissions?" and "What if they take minimal action?"

Alternative futures is a term used to illustrate future situations that might result from different projections or scenarios (Shearer 2005). If we assume that sea levels will rise by 0.8m (projection), and no adaptive or mitigation actions were taken (*do nothing* scenario), what will the waterfront neighbourhoods be like in 50 years' time? What would they be like if municipal authorities invested in new sea walls (*protection* scenario). What if they help communities most at risk to move to higher ground (*retreat* scenario)? It is important to note that in the real world, *do nothing* does not result in the status quo. It still results in change, as the landscape is always changing. Do nothing just means we accept whatever happens, and do not attempt to change our responses.

In the following examples of alternative futures, both simple and sophisticated landscape modelling and visualisation techniques are used. The intention in both cases was to help communities and their decision-makers to understand and then adapt to changes that were already under way in their landscapes, but it also helped them assess different possible responses – including do nothing.

Case A: alternative futures, Oppdal

The first case of possible landscape futures illustrates alternative development plans for tourism in Oppdal, Norway. It uses conventional representation techniques to compare two alternative futures with the current situation. In Figure 8.10, the current situation of the existing village of Vangslia in the Oppdal municipality is shown in a hand drawing in the top image. Oppdal church is located in the centre of an open landscape. The alpine pistes and the ski lift are mainly placed in the

171

FIGURE 8.10 Impacts of different development plans, Oppdal
The top drawing shows the existing situation; the middle illustrates how the landscape pattern would have looked if the first plan had been implemented; the bottom illustrates the consequences of the modified plan. Subsequently the municipality of Oppdal has approved developments exceeding what is shown on the bottom drawing. The drawings are from Oppdal Municipality, Cultural Landscape Analysis, a booklet elaborated by Moen and Feste in 1991.

Source: Braataa (1998): Jordbrukets kulturlandskap i kommunal arealplanlegging. In *Jordbrukets kulturlandskap. Forvaltning av miljoeverdier*, p. 227. Universitetsforlaget, Oslo.

forest mosaic above the arable fields. This situation can be compared with each of two alternative futures, each based upon different scenarios for expansion of the village with new homes.

In the centre image, the situation is shown as it would look if the first approved development plan (1991–2002) was implemented. However, in practice this plan was abandoned mainly due to aesthetic concerns as a result of an impact assessment. In a subsequent municipal plan for 1995–2006, permission for new developments was granted based on economic arguments and former investments. It was required that new buildings to the south (the lowest-located buildings) must be low and hidden by vegetation. The bottom drawing shows how the future landscape might be with reduced developments. This alternative was adopted in the municipal plan from 1991. However, it was repealed in the municipal plan from 1995, and in reality more houses were developed. This highlights that alternative-futures analysis can only hypothesise scenarios and the alternative futures they might lead to. They are not actual plans or blueprints.

The presentation technique used in this example resembles the same process as a *before-and-after image* used in landscape analysis (Figures 3.26 and 3.27). With a futures-analysis scenario, the analysts' interpretation of what may happen plays an even greater role in the impression that is conveyed to the reader than does a perspective drawing of a specific proposal, as there is more uncertainty about the likely future development. Furthermore, in a before-and-after evaluation of a proposed urban development the reader is aware that the focus is on the new project. By contrast, in a futures-analysis scenario, a complete landscape future is shown, and it is up to the reader to interpret the representation depending upon their interests. Illustrations of scenarios therefore inevitably include more scope for different interpretations, and are best considered as prompts for discussion rather than precise predictions of the future. The perspective drawing of the present-day situation can be done on-site or drawn from a photograph. The subsequent drawings of the site with alternative proposals have to be constructed on the basis of assembled data, models and policy options.

Case B: alternative futures, Willamette Valley

Alternative-futures modelling and assessment is being increasingly used to help shape larger-scale landscape change – for example, at a district or even regional level – and to help communities decide how to adapt to long-term incremental changes such as urbanisation or climate change. They are also used to test out different policy scenarios. Modelling change at a sub-regional or catchment level can be highly sophisticated and complex. It can also involve a wide range of contributors, and the roles of experts and communities vary across different alternative-futures examples.

One of the most internationally influential and successful models of alternative-landscape futures analysis has been the Willamette Valley project in Oregon, USA (Baker and Landers 2004; Baker et al. 2004). The Willamette Valley is a large and diverse catchment to the south of the city of Portland in Oregon, USA. The river system is a critical conservation resource but there is also a growing economy and demand for housing and development. The alternative-futures project investigated different policy pathways for managing parts of the Willamette River system, comparing *business-as-usual* options with other scenarios such as increased

Pre-EuroAmerican Scenario (PESVEG) ca. 1851

Land Use / Land Cover (LULC) ca. 1990

Plan Trend 2050

Development 2050

Conservation 2050

FIGURE 8.11 Alternative landscape futures, Willamette Valley
Visualisations of alternative futures under different development scenarios.

Source: Hulse, Gregory and Baker (2002): Alternative Futures for Muddy Creek, Oregon. *Willamette River Basin Planning Atlas: Trajectories of Environmental Change*. Used with permission of Oregon State University Press.

development and enhanced conservation. The project involved extensive science studies, public consultations and expert analyses, and made use of landscape mapping and visualisation techniques to investigate the implications of the different scenarios and to represent these to the wider community. A notable feature was the way in which the community was invited to comment upon the projections as they were modelled, so there was a continual *ground truthing* of the science studies with local knowledge.

The project involved a number of important partners, including the US Federal Environmental Protection Agency who were major supporters of the science that underpinned the analyses, and universities that provided expertise in modelling and community engagement. The project extended over a decade, and one outcome of the project has been new conservation policy for the catchment. Figure 8.11 shows visual representations of different landscape futures for a tributary called Muddy Creek, each depending upon a different policy scenario. The digital representations of landscape fulfil the same communication role as the hand-drawn sketches in the Oppdal example, but were based upon extensive scientific modelling, so that they are grounded in many disciplines.

With landscape dynamics such as urbanisation and climate change likely to have increasing effect on communities in all countries, the modelling and representation of effects of change in landscapes and the exploration of the implications of different policy options for alternative landscape futures will become an even more significant part of landscape architectural practice.

9

LANDSCAPE ANALYSIS IN RESEARCH AND PRACTICE

Introduction

The techniques and examples we have shared in previous chapters provide a range of ways to analyse landscapes as part of professional practice in landscape architecture. We have identified two types of application: *situation analyses* – which are aimed at gaining knowledge and understanding of the current landscape, its elements, appearance and functions – and *action-oriented* analysis – guided by particular proposals for landscape change. The examples have covered urban and rural contexts, different scales of analysis from site to landscape to district, and different types of decision-making, including public-policy development, local spatial planning, route and site selection, project development, and impact assessment of proposals.

There are several common features across this diverse range of applications. First, landscape analysis is always about understanding how a landscape has *changed, is changing, may change,* or *should change* – both as a result of different drivers, and in response to particular proposals. Second, landscape analysis creates *new knowledge* and understanding for decision-making – it is undertaken because we need to know more about a changing situation in order to make good choices for the future. Third, landscape analysis is concerned with the *values* that landscapes have for people and communities, and how these may be affected by change. Finally, landscape analysis as described here has been developed largely as a *professional* activity – undertaken by experts in landscape assessment, and communicated through professional reports.

In this final chapter we explore three contemporary developments in landscape analysis which respond to these common features and, in certain respects, challenge them. We first ask how landscape analysis can become more accessible and open to the communities that live and work in the landscapes undergoing change, and consider in particular the emerging idea of landscape democracy, asking how landscape analysis fits within a more open process of landscape decision-making. We then ask how we can improve the way analysis is undertaken, and note how analysis itself has become a focus of scientific investigation, with a growing body of research that examines the process and methods of analysis. Finally, we then turn the argument around and ask how the knowledge created through professional landscape analysis can make a greater contribution to understanding landscape values, change and decision-making, as part of the research activity of the discipline.

Landscape analysis and landscape democracy

Olwig (1996, 2005) has shown how landscape emerged as an approach to spatially managing environmental resources in northern Europe. The earliest-recorded meanings of the concept of landscape relate to a set of locally made and administered rules for landscape management – what we now refer to as customary or common law. Hence from the beginning landscape knowledge was created collectively from the bottom up. However, during the subsequent emergence of the nation state, the idea of landscape became transformed into a synthetic *top-down* view, a way of overseeing land and communities which became formalised in law imposed from above, and in particular styles of representation. Cosgrove (1984) has argued that this synoptic view of landscape and its visual expression through perspective drawings and paintings played an important symbolic role in the emergence of modern capitalism. On this basis, therefore, a historic and contemporary critique of landscape as 'a way of seeing' should be included in a study of how a particular biophysical landscape develops. However, when interpreted in this way, landscape has come to be seen by some scholars as a problematic concept that promotes detachment from land and communities, and expresses and promotes power imbalances within society and across empires (e.g. Barrell 1983; Pough 1990; Mitchell 1992).

In recent decades a counter-view has emerged, drawing upon the earlier meanings of landscape and advocating for a grounded understanding of landscape as a local, directly experienced and collectively made phenomenon (Olwig 1996). The European Landscape Convention expresses the tension between these two perspectives. On the one hand, it is a convention between nation states, expressed at a European level, and hence initiated *top-down*. On the other hand, the way the ELC is implemented seeks to empower communities, requiring both education and participation as fundamental activities. Egoz et al. (2011) have extended this approach and reframed the imperative for recognising people's relationship with landscape within the framework of Universal Human Rights, arguing that there is a fundamental 'right' to landscape, expressed both physically through direct engagement with landscape and through decision-making over its future. This tension between top-down and bottom-up dimensions of landscape highlights the question about the relative role of primary landscape managers, communities and experts in landscape analysis and valuation, discussed in Chapters 1 and 2.

Landscape decisions are taken in different contexts and from different perspectives, and Finn Arler (2008) has proposed a conceptual model of different types of decision-making (Figure 9.1). First, decisions may be taken by the individual land owner who seeks to manage the land for different values, economic resources and practical needs. For rural landscapes this type of decision is mainly taken by farmers, and the landscape decisions are mainly based on *private property management*, by what Arler (2008) terms 'self-determinism'. Those decisions are linked to motives and preferences of the farmer (and family). How he or she manages the farm, both as a producer and a property owner, is described in Chapter 1. An important factor in decisions taken by the individual land owner is the value of the property – both the use value and the market value – which reflects what many other individuals value in that land.

Second, landscapes are also affected by collective actions, by what Arler (2008) terms 'co-determinism'. When residents in an urban neighbourhood or a rural parish cooperate in maintaining the local landscape (a local sports ground, a grove of trees, a village green, a community forest, a common pond, etc.), the motives are linked to common goods and services provided by and for local residents collectively. In such place-based communities (Chapter 2), each actor sees him or herself as citizens, and it is the interaction between the individual owners and users on the one side and the community which shapes the *local democracy,* which may be more or less developed (Figure 9.1).

A third factor in landscape management is the public *policy and planning* represented at various political-administrative levels, from international bodies to national ministries to local municipalities. In relation to landscape values, these

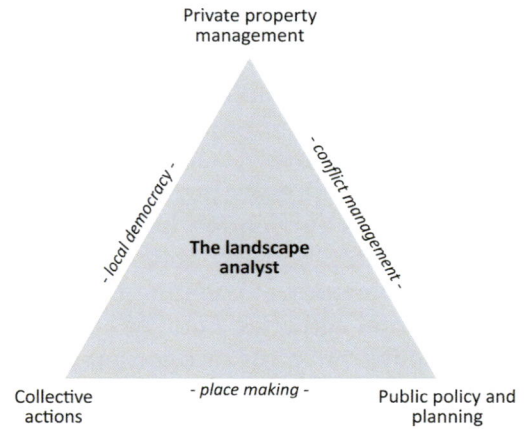

FIGURE 9.1 Conceptual framework of landscape democracy
Three principal agents are interacting in landscape change. The way these three agents interact in practice may with inspiration from Arler (2008) be termed 'landscape democracy'.

public authorities represent the *public interest* in different ways and meanings, as it is related to the protection of common-pool resources such as: clean drinking water, soil conservation and biodiversity, for example; management of cultural heritage features or significant views, etc.; and development of well-functioning and attractive urban and rural places.

To be effective, the public interest must function through policies and plans in two different ways, as indicated in Figure 9.1, namely through *conflict management* and *place-making* (Healy 1998). Managing conflicts between private and public interests – land-use conflicts, for example – is done mainly through land-use regulatory measures and planning approaches such as designations and zoning. Place-making is done partly through overall spatial strategies and plans, and partly through specific projects for the sites in question. Whereas conflict management is organised administratively and legally through submissions, formal hearings, negotiation, contracts and partnership agreements, place-making can be organised through various processes including community meetings and debates, structured strategy-making processes, and more focused workshops.

Altogether, the way the three types of agents interact may be termed 'landscape democracy' (Arler 2008), and the Karby example described in Chapter 2 is an example of a landscape-planning process involving such aspects. Figure 9.1 is a schematic illustration of the principal relationships. Individual agents may of course participate constructively in place-making processes, and the local community may also have quarrels to resolve with public authorities. For the landscape analyst, however, it is very important to locate the nature of the task in a landscape-democracy context. If the task is mainly to provide information needed to mitigate land-use conflicts between visual consequences and individual preferences and the need for the right location of certain developments (see Figure 5.4 as an example), then the analysis should inform all aspects of the conflict. If the task is linked more to place-making (see Figures 3.15 and 3.16) then the analytical dimension becomes an integral part of the landscape-planning and design process.

In every practical context the landscape analyst is working for and sometimes with someone, but this someone is almost always linked to others. The schematic Figure 9.1 on landscape democracy may be used by the analyst to orient him or herself to a range of actors in the context of the task.

Improving landscape analysis – research into process, methods and techniques

As a professional skill, landscape analysis is being continually refined and improved, and there have been a number of texts over the years in which experienced landscape architects and planners have provided guidance to others on their process, methods and techniques. The Scottish landscape planner Patrick Geddes provided an early example in his approach to regional analysis. He formulated the three-stage process of survey, analysis, and synthesis which has since

TABLE 9.1 Levels of analysis: Analysis can distinguish between different levels from the abstract to the concrete.

Level of abstraction	Tools of analysis
Highly abstract	Concepts
	Dimensions
	Attributes
Concrete	Indicators

Source: The levels are taken from Tveit et al. (2006): Key concepts in a framework for analysing visual landscape character. *Landscape Research*, 31(3), 229–255.

been widely used, and developed a specific technique called the 'valley section' (Thompson 2006) as a way to show relationships between natural and cultural factors in a landscape.

Hideo Sasaki (1950) reformulated this process as a teaching approach for design students at Harvard University, in which the first stage of design becomes 'research' in order to 'understand all the factors to be considered', followed by 'analysis' to 'establish the ideal operational relationship of all the factors', followed by synthesis into a spatial solution. Ian McHarg also promoted his 'ecological' method (1967, 1969) as a systematic process, based upon thematic analyses of how particular landscapes have 'become' what they are, what they are best suited for in the future, and how these potential uses are best interrelated. These early examples each provided a 'model' approach to understanding landscape and landscape change in which analysis was fundamental.

The introduction of environmental assessment requirements (Chapter 8) created a need to compare and evaluate different approaches, in order to establish the most effective and defensible ways to analyse landscape change and its consequences. In 1982, for example, Zube, Sell and Taylor offered a classification of approaches to investigate landscape perception, and Daniel and Vining (1983) compared different approaches using several criteria. Subsequent publications have refined and evaluated a widening range of analytical methods and techniques used in landscape analysis. Landscape analysis and assessment has now become part of the core knowledge of the discipline (Deming and Swaffield 2011), and a focus of research published in landscape architecture journals (Vicenzotti et al. 2016).

A recent example is work by Tveit et al. (2006) which analysed a wide range of research on visual landscape quality assessment in order to identify different levels of abstraction in analysis (Table 9.1). This typology was then used to clarify the meanings of a range of commonly used terms such as stewardship, showing how they can be operationalised in analysis and assessment. Professional landscape architects now have a rapidly growing body of knowledge generated by research to which they can turn to inform and improve their practice in landscape analysis. This also opens up the possibility that landscape analysis can be part of a research project, or that outcomes of analysis can contribute towards research.

Landscape analysis as research

Deming and Swaffield (2011) considered four different types of knowledge used in landscape architecture: tacit knowledge, conceptual knowledge, operational knowledge and systematic knowledge (Table 9.2).

'Tacit' knowledge is embedded in the everyday practice of individual landscape architects – it is their expertise – and much landscape analysis is undertaken based upon this expertise. However, it is not accessible to others and is not subject to critical scrutiny, except through professional performance. *Operational knowledge* is when this tacit knowledge is written down into practical 'how to' guidance – for example, as office best practice, professional guidelines, or as examples in educational texts such as this book. *Conceptual knowledge* is the ideas of the profession – concepts that help shape understanding and practice, and that inspire. We have included some conceptual knowledge in this book, intended to help you frame your understanding of analysis.

The fourth type of knowledge, *systematic knowledge*, is that which is produced through research. This is published in journals and other media that follow strict protocols for evaluating and assessing the validity and relevance of the material that is put forward for publication. Systematic knowledge is what creates a discipline rather than a profession, and practitioners seldom feel comfortable engaging with the formal research processes and protocols used by academic researchers. However, the role of systematic knowledge in professional practice is growing, as landscape architects interact with experts and scientists in other disciplines and must demonstrate the scholarly basis for the advice they give to clients and planning authorities. We have included some references and sources of systematic knowledge in this text, but have not specifically highlighted its use or how this

TABLE 9.2 Types of knowledge used in practice.

Tacit	Conceptual
Operational	Systematic

Source: After Deming and Swaffield (2011), incorporating concepts from Nonaka and Takeuchi (1995).

TABLE 9.3 Analysis as part of landscape architectural research: A classification of research strategies in landscape architecture, highlighting in bold those strategies to which landscape analysis might contribute.

Description	**Modelling**	Experimentation
Classification	**Interpretation**	**Evaluation & Diagnosis**
Action Research	Design	Logical Systems

Source: Developed from Deming and Swaffield (2011) Table 1.1.

knowledge is made. However, landscape analysis can both benefit from systematic knowledge (as explained above) and also contribute to its creation.

Deming and Swaffield (2011) have developed a basic classification of different types of landscape-architectural research, and this shows a number of potential ways in which landscape analysis can contribute to knowledge formation. Their classification identifies nine broad types of inquiry. Of these, at least six can involve landscape analysis (Table 9.3).

Description: Much of this text has demonstrated techniques to *describe* natural and human factors in landscape in a systematic way, and Deming and Swaffield include examples – such as mapping users in a park, listing and diagramming visual attributes of seasonal change in a landscape, and recording areas and types of urban woodland – as examples of descriptive research. All of these could be part of a landscape analysis and hence show ways in which landscape analysis could also create useful systematic knowledge. Further examples of descriptive techniques are included in the example below.

Modelling: The measurement of landscape attributes – both biophysical and human responses – can be the basis for creating statistical models of relationships within a landscape (such as preference for different types of scenery), or dynamic spatial models of landscape change. Models to inform particular analysis tasks can therefore contribute to wider cumulative knowledge about landscape functions and dynamics. Building models is a sophisticated and technical exercise, but practices are increasingly using digital visualisation or geographic information systems in their work, and hence developing skills that can be used in research.

Classification: Chapters 6 and 7 demonstrated ways of classifying landscape into different types using different analysis techniques and these are also basic research strategies which are widely used in the discipline. In some classic analysis techniques, such as Lynch's typology of urban structure, the original classification was based upon systematic analysis of people's perceptions of cities, and application of the typology to new locations can create useful new knowledge that has value beyond a specific analysis task. In the UK, landscape character assessments have now built a cumulative knowledge base across England, Wales and Scotland, and similar procedures are being promoted in many countries in Europe. Hence the analyses undertaken to implement the ELC are also building systematic knowledge of the European landscape as a collectively created resource.

Interpretation: *Interpretive* research such as in-depth interviews, analysis of documents, or interpretation of images can all build analytical understanding of particular landscapes and of relationships which may be relevant more widely. For example, Deming and Swaffield include an example of interpretive research in the UK based upon life histories (Bohnet et al. 2003), in which researchers interviewed local key informants and built a narrative that tells a story about how they have managed a particular landscape over an extended period of time. They found that old long-established families are guided by different values to newcomers, and this has significance for how contemporary landscapes are managed and their trajectories of change. Similar investigations as part of a professional landscape analysis could contribute valuable new knowledge, if reported in appropriate ways.

Evaluation & Diagnosis: This is one of the most widely used professional activities that can also create new knowledge. Deming and Swaffield identified evaluation and diagnosis as an important research strategy, and analysis of recent publications suggests it is growing in importance (Vicenzotti et al. 2016). Evaluation and diagnosis involves applying criteria drawn from policy or science to assess a landscape. It may be a landscape under threat, or one undergoing rapid change, or one that is much valued. The crucial feature of this approach to research that is shared with landscape analysis as a professional activity is that the basis for evaluation must be made clear and be relevant to the setting. In these circumstances, analysis of landscape conditions can therefore contribute to research.

Action Research: The term *action research* is used in different contexts and is difficult to precisely define. A general question initiating an action-research process is often "How can this situation be improved?" (Reason and Bradbury 2008, p. 11). It is about supporting concrete actions and learning from both the processes and the results. Action research therefore represents a useful approach to link landscape research with planning practice. The framework of landscape democracy indicated in Figure 9.1 grew out of *action-research* projects such as the Karby example described in Chapter 2, as did part of the landscape-regionalisation processes for Skive municipality described in Chapter 6 (Figures 6.6–6.9). In such projects, researchers, landscape planners, communities and land owners collaboratively investigate a problem or learn more about a landscape. Action research is based upon the presumption that communities have knowledge and skills in analysis of landscape that are essential to developing a robust understanding, and particularly important in developing solutions. Hence researchers enter into partnerships with communities and other key agents, to undertake an investigation and to learn from this. When this is working well, according to Kemmis and Mctaggert (2005, p. 563) 'participatory action research is a social process of collaborative learning realized by groups of people who join together in changing the practices through which they interact in a shared social world in which, for better or worse, we live with the consequences of one another's actions'. Processes like this are highly relevant to many landscape-planning tasks including landscape-analytical tasks.

A critical feature of action research, and of all the different strategies described, is that the process of investigation is fully reported so that people reading the results can understand how they were reached, and if necessary they can be repeated or checked by others. In some landscape-analysis procedures such as character assessment, this transparency of process is also a feature of the technique, usually because of the way procedures are codified in guidance (e.g. the UK Countryside Character Assessment model). The issue of transparency highlights the point that, in order for analysis to contribute new knowledge to the wider discipline, the analysis process needs to be open and the record of findings be public and accessible.

A second advantage of the research approach is that it includes peer review, in which both the methodology and the outcomes are independently reviewed by other experts before being published. Many professional practices undertake peer review of their analysis findings, and some clients now require this, particularly if the outcomes are to be used in public-planning hearings, and if there is a lot of money or investment dependent upon the decision. So this is another way in which professional landscape analysis is converging with research, and could produce research outcomes if the process is appropriate.

An excellent example of research undertaken by a professional practice as part of their consultancy work, which now adds to systematic knowledge of how cities work more generally, has been the series of investigations undertaken by Gehl Architects into the human use and experience of public spaces in cities (Gehl and Svarre 2013). The research started in the 1960s – the decade when Kevin Lynch published his work on the image of the city, and Jane Jacobs (1961) drew attention to the importance of street life and activity in cities. Jan and Ingrid Gehl started investigating how people used public squares and spaces in Italy. Then Jan Gehl turned his attention to understanding how people used the newly pedestrianised street 'Stroeget' in Copenhagen. Over the next 50 years, Gehl and his students and the practice Gehl Architects have applied a range of techniques to observe, record and measure the nature of street life in cities, and what locations and types of place attract people (Gehl and Svarre 2013). The techniques include simple counting of pedestrians, mapping where people gather, tracing their movements, and tracking their routes. They use photographs, keep field diaries and undertake test walks, as well as looking for traces of activity left behind when people are no longer there, such as worn paths in grass.

These research analyses use techniques that any student and professional landscape architect can use, but what makes it valuable as research is the systematic approach to collecting data and its analysis and the publication of the findings. Research into urban space has become a fundamental part of the Gehl Architects design practice, and its subsequent publication in books and articles illustrates one way that design-inspired analysis can create new shared knowledge as part of professional practice.

Conclusion

Communities, clients and public authorities are demanding higher standards of practice and more explicit justification for advice and recommendations, and a research culture is becoming a feature of more design and landscape practices. There can be a number of reasons why practices and practitioners may choose to do this. In the case of Gehl Achitects, the research provided an evidence base for design but over time has also come to be a feature of the practice profile.

Even more fundamental, however, is the value that knowledge creation can bring to professional practice by helping create a professional culture of inquiry. Many of the sections in this text have framed phases or types of analysis in the form of questions, and leading analysts such as Carl Steinitz (1990) frame their analysis process through questions. Inquiry-based analysis is the best way to ensure that the landscape-analysis process is relevant, effective, and critically informed, and is a goal that all analysts, both students and experts, can usefully adopt.

REFERENCES

Alexander, C., Ishikawa, S., Silverstein, M., Jacobson, M., Fiksdahl-King, I., & Angel, S. (1977). *A pattern language*. New York: Oxford University Press.

Andrews, J.N.L. (1979). Landscape preference and public policy. In G.H. Elsner & R.C. Smardon (Eds.), *Our national landscape: proceedings of a conference on applied techniques for analysis and management of the visual resource*. Berkeley, California: Pacific Southwest Forest and Range Experiment Station, USDA Forest service. General Technical Report PSW-35.

Antrop, M. (2000). Background concepts for integrated landscape analysis. *Agriculture, Ecosystems & Environment*, 77 (1), 17–28.

Appleton, J. (1996). *The experience of landscape*. Chichester: Wiley.

Arler, F. (2008). A true landscape democracy. In S. Arntzen & E. Brady (Eds.), *Humans in the land: the ethics and aesthetics of the cultural landscape* (pp. 75–99). Oslo: Unipub.

Arnstein, S.R. (1969). A ladder of citizen participation. *Journal of the American Institute of Planners*, 35 (4), 216–224.

Bak, K.M. (1997). Vestamager – et naturomraade i Koebenhavn. *Landskab* (1), 18–19.

Baker, A.R.H. (2003). *Geography and history – bridging the divide*. Cambridge: Cambridge University Press.

Baker, J.P., Hulse, D.W., Gregory, S.V., White, D., Van Sickle, J., Berger, P.A., Dole, D., & Schumaker, N. (2004). Alternative futures for the Willamette River Basin, Oregon. *Ecological Applications, 14 (2)*, 313–324.

Baker, J.P., & Landes, D.H. (2008). Alternative Futures Analysis for the Willamette River Basin Oregon. *Ecological Applications* 14 (2), 311–312.

Banerjee, T. & Southworth, M. (Eds.) (1990). *City Sense and City Design. Writings and Projects of Kevin Lynch*. Cambridge, Massachusetts: MIT Press.

Barrell, J. (1983). *The dark side of landscape: The rural poor in English painting 1730–1840*. Cambridge: Cambridge University Press.

Berry, R., Higgs, G., Fry, R. and Langford, M. (2011). Web-based GIS Approaches to Enhance Public Participation in Wind Farm Planning. *Transactions in GIS* 15 (2), 147–172.

Bohnet, I., Potter, C., & Simmons, E. (2003). Landscape change in the multifunctional countryside: a biographical analysis of farmer decision making in the English High Weald. *Landscape Research*, 28 (4), 349–364.

Braataa, H.O. (1998). Jordbrukets kulturlandskap i kommunal arealplanlegging. In E. Framstad & I.B. Lid (Eds.), *Jordbrukets kulturlandskap. Forvaltning av miljoeverdier* (pp. 223–232). Oslo: Universitetsforlaget.

Brandt, K. (1998). *Aalborg – en by ved fjorden*. Section for Landscape, Department of Economics, Forest & Landscape, Royal Danish Veterinary and Agricultural University. Master's thesis. Unpublished.

Breuning-Madsen, H. (1992). Den danske jordklassicicering. *Geologisk Nyt*, 2 (92), 15–17.

Bryan, B.A., Crossman, N.D., King, D., & Meyer, W.S. (2011). Landscape futures analysis: assessing the impacts of environmental targets under alternative spatial policy options and future scenarios. *Environmental Modelling & Software*, 26 (1), 83–91.

Butler, A. (2016). Dynamics of integrating landscape values in landscape character assessment: the hidden dominance of the objective outsider. *Landscape Research*, 41 (2), 239–252.

Buttimer, A., (Ed.) (2001). *Sustainable Landscapes and Lifeways. Scale and Appropriateness.* Cork: Cork University Press.

Caspersen, O.H. (2009). Public participation in strengthening cultural heritage: the role of landscape character assessment in Denmark. *Danish Journal of Geography* 109 (1), 33–45.

Caspersen, O.H. & Nellemann, V. (2004). *Landskabsanalyse – pilotprojekt Nationalparken Mols Bjerge*. Forest & Landscape.

Caspersen, O.H. & Nellemann, V. (2009). Landscape character assessment as an instrument for reform: the experience of Danish municipalities. In I. Sarlöv-Herlin (Ed.), *ECLAS Alnarp 2008: new landscapes – new lives: new challenges in landscape planning, design and management* (pp. 109–115). Alnarp: Faculty of Landscape Planning, Horticulture and Agricultural Science, Swedish University of Agricultural Sciences.

Claval, P. (1998). *An introduction to regional geography*. Oxford: Blackwell Publishers.

Copenhagen Regional Council (1982). *Forslag til udpegning af fredningsinteresseomraader. Planlaegningsdokument PD354*. Copenhagen.

Corner, J., (Ed.) (1999*) Recovering Landscape*. Princeton NJ; Princeton University Press.

Cosgrove, D. (1984). *Social formation and symbolic landscape*. London: Croom Helm.

Council of Europe (2000). *European landscape convention and explanatory report*. Strasbourg: The General Directorate of Education, Culture, Sport and Youth, and Environment.

Cullen, G. (1961). *The concise townscape*. (1985 ed.) London: The Architectural Press.

Dam, P. & Jakobsen, J.G.G. (2008). *Historisk-geografisk atlas*. Royal Danish Geographical Society and Geografforlaget.

Daniel, T.C. & Vining, J. (1983). Methodological issues in the assessment of landscape quality. In I. Altman & J.F. Wohlwill (Eds.), *Behavior and the natural environment* (pp. 39–84). Springer US.

Danish Ministry of Environment (1982). *Vejledning i fredningsplanlaegning nr. 2*. Copenhagen.

Danish Ministry of Environment (1983). *Fredningsplanlaegning og kulturlandskab*. Copenhagen.

Danish Ministry of Environment (1992). *Byens Traek. Om by – og bygningsbevaringssystemet SAVE*. Copenhagen.

Danish Ministry of Environment (1993a). *Kommuneatlas Nysted*.

Danish Ministry of Environment (1993b). *Kommuneatlas Holbaek*.

Danish Ministry of Environment (1993c). *Kommuneatlas Middelfart*.

Danish Ministry of Environment (1994). *Kommuneatlas Nyborg*.

Danish Ministry of Environment (1997). *Kommuneatlas Skanderborg*.

Danish Ministry of Environment (2002). *Haandbog: Landskab og kulturmiljoe – Miljoekonsekvensvurderinger i det aabne land (kap 8)*.

Danish Ministry of Environment (2007a). *Vejledning om landskabet i kommuneplanlaegningen.*

Danish Ministry of Environment. (2007b). Bekendtgoerelse af lov om planlaegning nr. 813 af 21. juni 2007.

Danish Ministry of Environment (2011). *Endelig udpegning af risikoomraader for oversvoemmelse fra vandloeb, soeer, havet og fjorde. EU's oversvoemmelses direktiv (2007/60/EF). Plantrin 1, Appendix A: Risk area Holstebro.*

Danish Ministry of Environment (2013). *Kommunernes arbejde med landskabskaraktermetoden, status 2013.*

Danish Nature Agency and Larsen J.B. (2005). *Katalog over skovudviklingstyper i Danmark.* Report. Danish Nature Agency, Copenhagen.

Dansk Landbrugsraadgivning, Landscentret (2008): Visualisation. In Stahlschmidt & Nellemann (2009), p. 86. Copenhagen: Forlaget Groent Miljoe.

Davoudi, S. and Strange, I. (Ed.) (2009). *Conceptions of space and place in strategic spatial planning.* Oxon: Routledge.

Defoe, D. (1719). *Robinson Crusoe.* (2007 ed.) New York: Oxford University Press.

Deming, M.E. & Swaffield, S. (2011). *Landscape architectural research: inquiry, strategy, design.* Hoboken, New Jersey: John Wiley and Sons.

Di Gregorio, A. & Jansen, L.J.M. (2000). *Land Cover Classification System (LCCS): classification concepts and user manual.* Rome: UN Food and Agriculture Organization, 179, Section 1.

Dietz, T., Fitzgerald, A., & Shwom, R. (2005). Environmental values. *Annual Review of Environment & Resources*, 30 (1), 335–372.

Downes, M. & Lange, E. (2015). What you see is not always what you get: a qualitative, comparative analysis of ex ante visualizations with ex post photography of landscape and architectural projects. *Landscape and Urban Planning*, 142, 136–146.

Dragenberg, R. (1999). *Helhedsplan for Assistenskirkegaarden og Ansgaranlaegget i Odense.* Section for Landscape, Royal Danish Veterinary and Agricultural University. Master's thesis. Unpublished.

Drysek, J. (1990). *Discursive democracy: politics, policy, and political science.* Cambridge: Cambridge University Press.

Drysek, J. (2000). *Deliberative democracy and beyond: liberals, critics, contestations.* Oxford: Oxford University Press.

Dwyer, J. & Hodge, I. (2001). The challenge of change: demands and expectations for farmed land. In T.C. Smout (Ed.), *Nature, landscape and people since the second world war* (pp. 117–134). East Linton: Tuckwell Press.

Egoz, S., Makhzoumi, J., & Pungetti, G. (2011). *The right to landscape: contesting landscape and human rights.* Aldershot: Ashgate.

Ehrle, F. (1932). *Roma al tempo di Benedetto XIV; la pianta di Roma di Giambattista Nolli del 1748.* Città del Vaticano, Biblioteca Apostolica Vaticana.

Emmelin, L. (1996). Landscape impact analysis: a systematic approach to landscape impacts of policy. *Landscape Research*, 21 (1), 13–35.

Etting, V. (1995). *Paa opdagelse i kulturlandskabet.* Copenhagen: Danish Forest and Nature Agency, Ministry of Environment and Gyldendal.

European Commission (2006). *Rural Development 2007–2013. Handbook on Common Monitoring and Evaluation Framework Guidance Document.* Brussels: European Commission, DG Agriculture.

European Environmental Agency. (2014). *Distribution of NATURA 2000 sites across the EU, 2012.* Copenhagen: EEA.

European Landscape Convention, C.o.E. (2000). *Den europaeiske landskabskonvention,* Firenze.

Fischer, F. & Forester, J. (Eds.). (1993). *The argumentative turn in policy analysis and planning*. Raleigh, NC: Duke University Press.

Forester, J. (1989). *Planning in the face of power*. Berkeley: University of California Press.

Forman, R.T.T. (1995). *Land mosaics: the ecology of landscape and regions*. Cambridge: Cambridge University Press.

Forman, R.T.T. & Godron, M. (1986). *Landscape ecology*. New York: John Wiley & Sons.

Framstad, E. & Lid, I.B. (1998). *Jordbrukets kulturlandskap. Forvaltning av miljoeverdier*. Oslo: Universitetsforlaget.

Frandsen, K.-E. (1983). *Vang og taegt: studier over dyrkningssystemer og agrarstrukturer i Danmarks landsbyer 1682–83*. Esbjerg: Bygd.

Friedmann, J. (1987). *Planning in the public domain*. Princeton: Princeton University Press.

Fry, G., Tveit, M., Ode, A., & Velarde, M.D. (2009). The ecology of visual landscapes: exploring the conceptual common ground of visual and ecological landscape indicators. *Ecological Indicators*, 9 (5), 933–947.

Gehl, J. & Svarre, B. (2013). *How to study public life*. Washington, DC: Island Press.

GEUS (2016). *Maps of Denmark – height and depth map. Terrain model of catchment area Storaa, DK*. Geological Survey of Denmark and Greenland, GEUS.

Giddens, A. (1990). *The consequences of modernity*. Cambridge: Polity Press.

Gobster, P., Nassauer, J., Daniel, T.C., & Fry, G. (2007). The shared landscape: what does aesthetics have to do with ecology? *Landscape Ecology*, 22 (7), 959–972.

Gosling, D. (1996). *Gordon Cullen – visions of urban design*. London: Academy Editions.

Gustavsson, R. (1986). Struktur i Lövskogslandskap. *Stad & Land*, 48, 108–110.

Hägerstrand, T. (1993). Samhälle och natur. *NordREFO*, (1), 14–59.

Hall, P. & Tewdwr-Jones, M. (2010). *Urban and regional planning*, 5th ed. London: Routledge.

Harrop, D.O. & Nixon, J.A. (1999). *Environmental assessment in practice*. London: Routledge.

Healey, P. (1993). Planning through debate: the communicative turn in planning theory. In F. Fischer & J. Forester (Eds.), *The argumentative turn in policy analysis and planning* (pp. 233–253). London: UCL Press.

Healey, P. (1998). Collaborative planning in a stakeholder society. *The Town Planning Review*, 69 (1), 1–21.

Healey, P. (2009). In search of the "strategic" in spatial strategy making. *Planning Theory & Practice*, 10 (4), 439–457.

Hester, R.T. (1984). *Planning neighbourhood space with people*. New York: Van Nostrand Reinold, Co.

Higuchi, T. (1983). *The visual and spatial structure of landscapes*, 3rd ed. Cambridge, UK: MIT Press.

Holling, C.S. (1978). *Adaptive environmental assessment and management*. London: John Wiley & Sons.

Howard, P. (2011). *An Introduction to Landscape*. Surrey: Ashgate.

Hulse, D.W., Gregory, S.V., & Baker, J.P. (2002). *Willamette River Basin planning atlas: trajectories of environmental and ecological change*. Corvallis, Oregon: Oregon State University Press.

Ingold, T. (2000). *The perception of the environment: essays on livelihood, dwelling and skill*. London: Routledge.

IUSS Working Group WRB (2014). *World reference base for soil resources: international soil classification system for naming soils and creating legends for soil maps* (World Soil Resources Reports No. 106). Rome: FAO.

Jackson, J.B. (1984). *Discovering the vernacular landscape*. New Haven and London: Yale University Press.

Jacobs, J. (1961). *The death and life of great American cities.* Vintage Books.

Jacobsen, P. R., Hermansen, B., & Tougaard, L. (2011). *Danmarks digitale jordartskort 1:25.000. Version 3.1* (Report 2011/40). Copenhagen: GEUS, Geological Survey of Denmark and Greenland.

Jay, S., Jones, C., Slinn, P., & Wood, C. (2007). Environmental impact assessment: retrospect and prospect. *Environmental Impact Assessment Review,* 27 (4), 287–300.

Jensen, K. & Thomsen, H. (1986). *Planlaegning af bynaere moser.* Forest & Landscape, Royal Danish Veterinary and Agricultural University. Master's thesis. Unpublished.

Jensen, K. M. & Kuhlman, H. (1971). *Danmarks Geografi. Kort oevelsesvejledning.* Department of Geography, University of Copenhagen. Unpublished.

Jensen, K. M. & Reenberg, A. (1980). *Dansk Landbrug. Udvikling i produktion og kulturlandskab.* Copenhagen: Geografisk Centralinstitut.

Jensen, L. H. (2006). Changing conceptualization of landscape in English landscape assessment methods. In B. Tress, G. Tress, G. Fry, & P. Opdam (Eds.), *From landscape research to landscape planning* (pp. 161–171).

Joergensen, I., Primdahl, J., & Stahlschmidt, P. (1997). *Landskabsplan for Kvols-Kvosted.* Copenhagen: Department of Economics, Forest & Landscape, Royal Danish Veterinary and Agricultural University.

Joersboe, F. (1999). Vejledning i fremstilling af terraenmodeller. Section for Landscape, Department of Economics, Forest & Landscape, Royal Danish Veterinary and Agricultural University. Unpublished.

Jones, M. (2003). The concept of cultural landscape: discourse and narratives. In Palang, H. and Fry, G. (Eds.). *Landscape Interfaces.* Dordrecht: Klywer Academic Publishers, pp. 21–51.

Kemmis, S. & McTaggart, R. (2005). Participatory Action Research. Communicative Action and the Public Sphere. In Denzin, N.K. & Lincoln, Y.S. (Eds.). *The SAGE Handbook of Qualitative Research.* 3rd edition. London: Sage Publications, pp. 559–603.

Knudsen, T. T. (1999). *Renovering af boligbebyggelsen Folehaven i Valby.* Section for Landscape, Department of Economics, Forest & Landscape, Royal Danish Veterinary and Agricultural University. Master's thesis. Unpublished.

Kristensen, I. T. (2004). Digital visibility analysis. In V. Nellemann, V. J. Abildtrup, M. Gylling, & C. Vesterager (Eds.), *Landbrugsbygninger, landskab og lokal omraadeplanlaegning – metoder til landskabskaraktervurdering og oekonomivurdering* (pp. 57, 70). Hoersholm: Forest & Landscape.

Kristensen, L. S., Primdahl, J., & Vejre, H. (2015). Dialogbaseret planlægning i det åbne land – om strategier for kulturlandskabets fremtid. Copenhagen: Bogvaerket.

Landscape Institute (2013). *Guidelines for Landscape and Visual Impact Assessment,* 3rd ed. London: Routledge.

Linnet, S., Stahlschmidt, P., & Rask, M. (2009). Landskabet som del af kommuneplanlaegningen. *Byplan,* 62 (3), 16–25.

LUC (1999). *South Pennines Landscape Character Assessment.* Bradford: SCOSPA (Standing Conference of South Pennine Authorities).

Lynch, K. (1960). *The image of the city.* Cambridge, Massachusetts: MIT Press.

Lynch, K. (1972). *What time is this place?* Cambridge, Massachusetts: MIT Press.

Mabbutt, J. A. (1968). Review of concepts of land classification. In G. A. Stewart (Ed.), *Land Evaluation* (pp. 11–28). Melbourne: MacMillan.

McHarg, I. (1967). An ecological method for landscape architecture. *Landscape Architecture,* 57 (2), 105–107.

McHarg, I. (1969). *Design with nature.* Garden City, New York: Doubleday/Natural History Press.

Meyer, E. (2005). Site citations: the grounds of modern landscape architecture. In C.J. Burns & A. Kahn (Eds.), *Site matters: design concepts, histories, and strategies* (pp. 93–130). New York: Routledge.

Millennium Ecosystem Assessment (2005). *Ecosystems and human well-being: a framework for assessment*. Geneva: World Health Organization.

Ministry for Environment. (2006). A guide to preparing a basic assessment of environmental effects. MfE: Wellington, New Zealand. www.mfe.govt.nz/sites/default/files/media/RMA/aee-guide-aug06.pdf (accessed 24/11/16).

Mitchell, D. (2001). The lure of the local landscape studies and the end of a troubled century. *Progress In Human Geography*, 25 (2), 269–281.

Mitchell, W.J.T. (1992). *Landscape and power*, 2nd ed. Chicago: University of Chicago Press.

Moeller, P.G., Stenak, M., & Thoegersen, M.L. (2005). Kulturmiljoeregistrering – i praksis. *Fortid og Nutid*, 2005 (3), 192–220.

Moen & Feste (1991). Kulturlandskabsanalyse – samlehefte: Planer for byutvikling Oppdal. In E. Framstad & I.B. Lid (Eds.), *Jordbrukets kulturlandskap. Forvaltning av miljoeverdier*. Oslo: Universitetsforlaget.

Mücher, S. & Wascher D. (2007). European Landscape Characterisation. In B. Pedroli, A. Van Doorn, G. De Blust, M.L. Paracchini, D. Wascher, & F. Bunce (Eds.), *Europe's living landscapes: essays on exploring our identity in the countryside* (pp. 37–43). Zeist: KNNV Publishing.

Nassauer, J. (1995). Messy ecosystems, orderly frames. *Landscape Journal*, 14 (2), 161–170.

Nassauer, J. (1997). *Placing nature: culture and landscape ecology*. Washington, DC: Island Press.

National Cooperative Highway Research Program (2013). *Evaluation of methodologies for visual impact assessments* (NCHRP Report 741). Washington, DC: National Academy of Sciences.

Nellemann, V. & Wainoe, U. (1992). *Vaerdifulde landskaber, Forslag til Regionplantillaeg nr. 4 for Roskilde Amt*. Roskilde County.

Nellemann, V., Abildtrup, V.J., Gylling, M., & Vesterager, C. (2004). *Landbrugsbygninger, landskab og lokal omraadeplanlaegning – metoder til landskabskaraktervurdering og oekonomivurdering* (Rep. No. 23). Forest & Landscape.

Nellemann, V., Andersen, E.B., & Kyhn, M. (2008). *Kommuneplanlaegning for fremtidens landbrugsbyggeri – Favrskov & Randers Kommuner*. Copenhagen: Realdania.

Nellemann, V., Moeller, K.H., Moeller, P.G., Primdahl, J., & Oeberg, A.S. (2015). Strategi for Karby Sogn – landskab og landsby. In L.S. Kristensen, J. Primdahl, & H. Vejre (Eds.), *Dialogbaseret planlaegning i det aabne land – om strategier for kulturlandskabets fremtid* (pp. 66–85). Copenhagen: Bogvaerket.

Nielsen, A.V. (1975). Landskabets tilblivelse. In *Danmarks natur, bind 1, landskabernes opstaaen* (pp. 251–341). Politikens Forlag.

Nijhuis, S., Lammeren, R. and Hoeven, F.v.d., eds. (2011). *Exploring the Visual Landscape. Advances in Physiognomic Landscape Research in the Netherlands*. Delft: ISO Press.

Nonaka, I. & Takeuchi, H. (1995). *The knowledge creating company: how Japanese companies create the dynamics of innovation*. Oxford: Oxford University Press.

OECD (1997). *Environmental indicators for agriculture: concepts and framework*. Paris: OECD.

Oeresundsforbindelsen. (1993). *Oeresund Landanlæg. Projektforslag marts 1993*. Report.

Oeresundsforbindelsen A/S. (1993). *Oeresund Landanlaeg. Projektforslag marts 1993. Arkitektur og landskab*. Oeresundsforbindelsen.

Olsen, I.A. & Stahlschmidt, P. (1975). Egnethedsanalyse for Skovbo Kommune. *Landskab*, (6), 111.

Olwig, K.R. (1996). Recovering the substantive nature of landscape. *Annals of the Association of American Geographers*, 86 (4), 630–653.

Olwig, K.R. (2002). *Landscape nature and the body politic: from Britain's renaissance to America's new world*. Madison: University of Wisconsin Press.

Olwig, K.R. (2005). The landscape of "customary" law versus that of "natural" law. *Landscape Research*, 30 (3), 299–320.

Ostrom, V. & Ostrom, E. (1971). Public choice: a different approach to the study of public administration. *Public Administration Review*, 31 (2), 203–216.

Oxford Dictionaries (2011). *Oxford Dictionaries*. Oxford: Oxford University Press.

Paludan, B., Nielsen, N.H., Jensen, L.N., Brink-Kjaer, A., Linde, J.J., & Mark, O. (2011). *En kogebog for analyser af klimaaendringers effekter paa oversvoemmelser i byer*. Skanderborg: Danva.

Pinto-Correia, T., Primdahl, J. and Pedroli, B. (forthcoming). *European Landscapes in Transition: implications for policy and practice*. Cambridge: Cambridge University Press.

Porsmose, E. (1987). *De fynske landsbyers historie – i dyrkningsfællesskabets tid*. Odense: Odense Universitetsforlag.

Potschin, M. & Haines-Young, R. (2006). "Rio+10", sustainability science and Landscape Ecology. *Landscape and Urban Planning*, 75 (3–4), 162–174.

Primdahl, J. & Kristensen, L.S. (2016). Landscape strategy making and landscape characterisation. *Landscape Research*, 41 (2), 227–238.

Primdahl, J., Kristensen, L.S., & Busck, A.G. (2013a). The farmer and landscape management: different roles, different policy approaches. *Geography Compass*, 7 (4), 300–314.

Primdahl, J., Kristensen, L.S., & Swaffield, S. (2013b). Guiding landscape change: current policy approaches and potentials of landscape strategy making as a policy integrating approach. *Applied Geography*, 42, 86–94.

Primdahl, J. & Swaffield, S. (2010). Globalisation and the sustainability of agricultural landscapes. In J. Primdahl & S. Swaffield (Eds.), *Globalisation and agricultural landscapes: change patterns and policy trends in developed countries* (pp. 1–15). Cambridge: Cambridge University Press.

Pugh, S. (1990). *Reading landscape: country, city, capital*. Manchester: Manchester University Press.

Ramirez, R. (1999). Stakeholder analysis and conflict management. In D. Buckles (Ed.), *Cultivating peace: conflict and collaboration in natural resource management* (pp. 101–126). Washington DC: IDRC and World Bank Institute.

Reason, P. & Bradbury, H. (2008). Introduction. In Reason, P. & Bradbury, H. (Eds.) *The SAGE handbook of action research: participative inquiry and practice*. Los Angeles: Sage.

Reed, M.S., Graves, A., Dandy, N., Posthumus, H., Hubacek, K., Morris, J., Prell, C., Quinn, C., & Stringer, L. (2009). Who's in and why? A typology of stakeholder analysis methods for natural resource management. *Journal of Environmental Management*, 90 (5), 1933–1949.

Repton, H. (1976). *The red books of Humphry Repton, Vols. 1–4*. Basilisk Press.

Ribe County & Vejle County (1998). *VVM-redegoerelse for Udvidelse af Billund Lufthavn*. Ribe and Vejle.

Rippon, S. (2004). *Historic landscape analysis: deciphering the countryside, Vol. 16*. Council for British Archaeology.

Robinson, D.G., Laurie, I.C., Wager, J.F., & Traill, A.L. (Eds.) (1976). Landscape evaluation – the landscape evaluation research project 1970–1975. Centre for Urban Regional Research, Manchester.

Roymans, N., Gerritsen, F., Van der Heijden, C., Bosma, K., & Kolen, J. (2009). Landscape biography as research strategy: the case of the South Netherlands project. *Landscape Research*, 34 (3), 337–359.

Sabatier, P. A. & Jenkins-Smith, H. C. (1993). *Policy change and learning: an advocacy coalition approach*. Boulder, Colorado: Westview Press.

Sasaki, H. (1950). Thoughts on education in landscape architecture: some comments on today's methodologies and purpose. *Landscape Architecture*, 40 (4), 158–160.

Schou, A. (1949). *Atlas over Danmark. Landskabsformerne*, 3rd ed. Copenhagen: H. Hagerup.

Schwartz, S. H. & Bilsky, W. (1987). Towards a unified psychological structure of human values. *Journal of Personality and Social Psychology*, 53 (3), 550–562.

Selman, P. (2004). Community participation in the planning and management of cultural landscapes. *Journal of Environmental Planning and Management*, 47 (3), 365–392.

Selman, P. H. (2006). *Planning at the landscape scale*. London: Routledge.

Selman, P. H. (2009). Planning for landscape multifunctionality. *Sustainability: Science, Practice, & Policy*, 5 (2), 45–52.

Shearer, A. W. (2005). Approaching scenario-based studies: three perceptions about the future and considerations for landscape planning. *Environment and Planning B: Planning and Design*, 32 (1), 67–87.

Sheppard, S. R., Shaw, A., Flanders, D., Burch, S., Wiek, A., Carmichael, J., Robinson, J., & Cohen, S. (2011). Future visioning of local climate change: a framework for community engagement and planning with scenarios and visualisation. *Futures*, 43 (4), 400–412.

Short, M., Baker, M., Carter, J., Jones, C., & Jay, S. (Eds.) (2013). *Strategic environmental assessment and land use planning: an international evaluation*. London: Earthscan.

Skive Municipality (2009). *Landskabsanalyse for Skive Kommune 09 – en intro, juli 2009*.

Smed, P. (1981). *Landskabskort over Danmark*. Brenderup: Geografforlaget.

Soenderjylland County (1999). *Kortbilag: Regionplan 1997–2008 – Miljoekonflikter*. Aabenraa.

Spirn, A. W. (1998). *The Language of Landscape*. New Haven: Yale University Press.

Stahlschmidt, P. (1992). Om rum. *Landskab*, (1), 14–21.

Stahlschmidt, P. (2001). *Metoder til landskabsanalyse*. Copenhagen: Groent Miljoe.

Stahlschmidt, P. & Nellemann, V. (2009). *Metoder til landskabsanalyse*. Copenhagen: Groent Miljoe.

Steenbergen, C. (2008). *Composing Landscapes: Analysis, typology and experiments for design*. Basel: Birkhauser Verlag.

Steenbergen, C. & Reh, W. (1996). *Architecture and landscape*. Bussenn: Prestel.

Steinitz, C. (1986) Foreword. In Forman, R. T. T. & Godron, M. *Landscape ecology*. New York: John Wiley & Sons, p. V.

Steinitz, C. (1990). A framework for theory applicable to the education of landscape architects (and other environmental design professionals). *Landscape Journal*, 9 (2), 136–143.

Steinitz, C., Parker, P., & Jordan, L. (1976). *Hand-drawn overlays: their history and prospective uses* (pp. 444–455). Landscape Architecture.

Stephenson, J. (2008). The cultural values model: an integrated approach to values in landscapes. *Landscape and Urban Planning*, 84 (2), 127–139.

Stevens, S. S. (1946). On the theory of scales of measurement. *Science*, 103 (2684), 677–680.

Stiles, R. (1992a). Determinism versus creativity. *Landscape Design (July/August)*.

Stiles, R. (1992b). The limits of pattern analysis. *Landscape Design* (September).

Strang, G. L. (1996). Infrastructure as landscape [infrastructure as landscape, landscape as infrastructure]. *Places*, 10 (3).

Swaffield, S. R. (2013). Empowering landscape ecology-connecting science to governance through design values. *Landscape Ecology* (2013) 28:1193–1201.

Swaffield, S. & McWilliam, W. (2014). Landscape aesthetic experience and ecosystem services. In J.R. Dymond (Ed.), *Ecosystem services in New Zealand – conditions and trends.* Lincoln, New Zealand: Manaaki Whenua Press.

Swanwick, C. (2002). *Landscape character asessment – guidance for England and Scotland.* Cheltenham: Countryside Agency and Scottish Natural Heritage.

Swanwick, C. (2004). The assessment of countryside and landscape character in England: an overview. In K. Bishop & A. Phillips (Eds.), *Countryside planning: new approaches to management and conservation* (pp. 109–124). London: Earthscan.

Termorshuizen, J. & Opdam, P. (2009). Landscape services as a bridge between landscape ecology and sustainable development. *Landscape Ecology*, 24 (8), 1037–1052.

Tetlow, M.F. & Hanusch, M. (2012). Strategic environmental assessment: the state of the art. *Impact Assessment and Project Appraisal*, 30 (1), 15–24.

Thing & Wainoe (2002). *Ny hoejklasset vej i Frederikssundfingeren: VVM-redegoerelse. Astetisk vurdering og visualisering. Rapport 251.* Danish Road Directorate.

Thompson, C.W. (2006). Patrick Geddes and the Edinburgh Zoological Garden: expressing universal processes through local place. *Landscape Journal*, 25 (1), 80–93.

Tress, B. & Tress, G. (2003). Scenario visualization for participatory landscape planning – a study from Denmark. *Landscape and Urban Planning*, 64 (3), 161–178.

Turner, T. (1991). Pattern analysis. *Landscape Design.* October 1991, 39–41.

Turner, T. (1996). *City as landscape – a post-postmodern view of design and planning.* London: Chapman & Hall.

Turner, T. (1998). *Landscape planning and environmental impact design.* London: Chapman & Hall.

Tveit, M., Ode, A., & Fry, G. (2006). Key concepts in a framework for analysing visual landscape character. *Landscape Research*, 31 (3), 229–255.

United Nations (1992). Rio declaration on environment and development. Report of the United Nations conference on Environment and Development. Rio de Janeiro, 3–14 June 1992. www.un.org/documents/ga/conf151/aconf15126-1annex1.htm (accessed 9/5/2011).

Van Eetvelde, V. & Antrop, M. (2009). Indicators for assessing changing landscape character of cultural landscapes in Flanders (Belgium). *Land Use Policy*, 26 (4), 901–910.

Varming, M. (1970). *Motorveje i Landskabet.* Copenhagen: Danish Building Research Institute.

Vervloet, J.A.J. (1984). *Inleiding tot de historische geografie van de Nederlandse cultuurlandschappen.* Wageningen: Pudoc.

Viborg County (1974). *Landskabsanalyse for Viborg Amt.* Viborg.

Vicenzotti, V., Jorgensen, A., Qviström, M., & Swaffield, S. (2016). Forty years of landscape research. *Landscape Research*, 41 (4), 388–407.

Vägverket (1994). *Öresundsforbindelsen Malmö. Ytre Ringvägen, Järnvägen, Broanslutningen.* Kristianstad: Arkitektur och landskap.

Vos, W. & Stortelder, A. (1992). *Vanishing Tuscan landscapes. Landscape ecology of a Submediterranean-Montana area.* Wageningen: Puduc Scientific Publisher.

Warnock, S. & Brown, N. (1998). EA and visual assessment: a vision for the countryside. *Landscape Design* (April).

Wilson, W. (1887). The Study of Administration. *Political Science Quarterly* Vol. 2, No. 2: pp. 197–222

Winchester, S. (2001). *The map that changed the world: William Smith and the birth of modern geology.* New York: Harper Collins.

Wood, C. (2003). *Environmental impact assessment: a comparative review.* Pearson Education.

Wood, R. & Handley, J. (2001). Landscape dynamics and the management of change. *Landscape Research*, 26 (1), 45–54.

Wylie, J. (2007). *Landscape*. London: Routledge.

Zonneveld, I.S. (1995). *Land Ecology*. Amsterdam SPB Academic Publishng.

Zonneveld, I.S. (1995). *Land Ecology: An introduction to landscape ecology as a base for land evaluation, land management and conservation*. The Hague, NL: SPB Academic Publishing.

Zube, E.H., Sell, J.L., & Taylor, J.G. (1982). Landscape perception: research, application and theory. *Landscape Planning*, 9 (1), 1–33.

GLOSSARY

Action-oriented analysis is analysis that is guided by a specific planning task such as assessment of a proposed development.

Alternative futures is a term used to illustrate future situations that might result from different projections or scenarios (Shearer 2005).

Analysis is the 'detailed examination of the elements or structure of something' (Oxford Dictionaries, 2011).

Biophysical attributes are the specific conditions in a particular landscape such as terrain, elevation, soil types, wetlands and waterway networks, vegetation and habitat, built infrastructure, etc.

Character is 'a distinct, recognisable and consistent pattern of elements in the landscape' (Swanwick 2002) that makes one landscape area different from another.

Characteristics are the 'elements, or combinations of elements, which make a particular contribution to distinctive character' (Swanwick 2002).

Communities of interest are people who share a material, financial, spiritual or other interest in the outcomes of landscape management and landscape change.

Communities of place are the people who live together in a particular place or landscape.

Communities of practice are people who share distinctive knowledge, skills and habits of action.

Composite classification map is a map in which all the thematic layers are combined.

Constraints are limitations on a proposed development due to landscape conditions:

- *Definitive site constraint* is one which logically or absolutely precludes the given development.
- *Relative site constraint* detracts from the options without actually precluding them.

Contours are lines on a map that connect locations with the same topographic elevation above a base datum.

- *Contour density* describes how relatively close together the contour lines are at the given scale, and this indicates how steep the terrain is – its amplitude.
- *Distinct contour density* indicates that the terrain is changing vertically in different directions over short distances.
- *Contour Parallelism* indicates where the terrain is changing in uniform ways.
- Short *contour length* indicates that there are many small humps and hollows.
- *Contour Direction* indicates in what way the terrain is oriented (north, east, etc.).

All moderated from Jensen and Kuhlman (1971):
Danmarks Geografi. Kort oevelsesvejledning.

Development may be a new element or a new object in a landscape, such as a building, a road, a windmill or a power cable. It may also be a new primary land use, such as residential areas, parks, agriculture, etc. It may be a new secondary land use, such as recreational hiking. Finally, it may be a new area designation that reflects the goals of the public administration, such as a nature conversation reserve, or a ground-water protection area.

Environmental assessment (EA), *environmental impact assessment* (EIA*), assessment of environmental effects* (AEE) and *impact assessment* (IA) are processes that have been developed to assess the environmental consequences of 'proposed activities that are likely to have significant adverse impacts on the environment and are subject to a decision of a competent national authority' (United Nations 1992, Annex 1: Principle 17).

Equivalent area classification is classification of landscapes that takes place on one level of generality, and each area constitutes a geographical unit.

Eye-level analysis is a horizontal cross section – or a cross section that follows the movements of the terrain – at eye level.

Figure ground analysis simplifies the vertical dimension of a plan into two layers. The *figure* layer shows the presence of the phenomenon that the analysis intends to highlight. The *ground* layer is the background where the highlighted features are absent – typically this is the surface terrain.

Futures analysis is the term used to refer to analysis of possible drivers and effects of larger-scale dynamics or policy decisions (Baker and Landers 2004).

Geology is the underlying structure of the earth.

Geomorphology is the branch of geology that deals with the earth's surface and refers to the study of surface terrain and its formation.

A *homogeneous region* is an area with homogeneity in its biophysical and cultural character.

Knowledge may be of several kinds (after Nonaka and Takeuchi 1995):

- *Tacit knowledge* is embedded in the everyday practice of individual landscape architects – it is their expertise.
- *Operational knowledge* is when this tacit knowledge is written down into practical 'how to' guidance.

- *Conceptual knowledge* is the ideas of the profession – concepts that help shape understanding and practice, and that inspire.
- *Systematic knowledge* is that which is produced through research.

Land cover is 'the observed (bio)physical cover on the earth's surface' (Di Gregorio and Jansen 2000).

Land use is 'the arrangements, activities and inputs people undertake in a certain land-cover type to produce, change or maintain it' (Di Gregorio and Jansen 2000).

Landscape is 'an area, as perceived by people, whose character is the result of the action and interaction of natural and/or human factors' (European Landscape Convention 2000).

Landscape analysis is an examination of a landscape with the purpose of understanding its character, structure and function, in order to make policy, planning or design decisions concerning its future condition and management.

Landscape character is the particular interaction between the natural factors and the land cover in a landscape area as well as the particular spatial and visual factors that characterise the area and make it different from the surrounding landscapes.

Landscape character assessment (LCA) is an identification, classification and characterisation of landscape character areas, and enable judgements about their state and potentials.

Landscape elements are the 'individual components which make up the landscape', such as trees and hedgerows (Swanwick 2002).

Landscape features are 'particularly prominent or eye-catching elements', like tree clumps, church towers, or wooded skylines (Swanwick 2002).

Natural factors are the fundamental natural drivers that shape the underlying structure and dynamics of landscape systems – climate, geology and geomorphology, hydrology and ecology.

Nested hierarchical area classification takes place on two or more levels, so that each of the general areas is divided into smaller areas on a more detailed level.

Planning is 'linking knowledge to action' (Friedmann 1987).

Potentials analysis is analysis undertaken when the location is given and the analysis question is 'for what functions is the landscape best suited?'

Procedural theories explain how the planning process should be organised (Hall and Tewdwr-Jones 2010).

Projection is a forecast of change based on a defined set of expected relationships, which sets out the future trajectory of a landscape if the current trends continue for a shorter or longer period of time.

Region is 'an area, especially part of a country or the world having definable characteristics but not always fixed boundaries' (www.oxforddictionaries.com).

A *scenario* is a more open assumption about the conditions or decisions that will shape the future – such as current development trends and specific interventions by public and private actors.

Selection is 'the action or fact of carefully choosing someone or something as being the best or most suitable' (Oxford Dictionaries 2011).

Serial vision is a point-by-point depiction of a route through the landscape by means of photos, CAD drawings or free-hand drawings.

Site is 'an area of ground on which a town, building, or monument is constructed' (Oxford Dictionaries 2011).

Site-selection analysis is a systematic search for and selection of possible sites for an intended development.

Situation analyses gain knowledge and understanding of a landscape in advance of any specific proposals, and are not linked to specific plans or actions.

Soil is 'any material within 2 m of the Earth's surface that is in contact with the atmosphere, excluding living organisms, areas with continuous ice not covered by other material, and water bodies deeper than 2 m' (IUSS Working Group WRB 2014).

A spatial analysis is a study of the spatial relationships of a landscape. It deals with the relative location and significance of different patterns, elements and features in the landscape, and how we experience the landscape through our senses and through movement and physical engagement.

Spatial language as defined by Lynch (1960):

- *Paths*: Channels along which the observers move. Depending on scale they can be railroads, roads or trails, etc.
- *Edges*: Linear elements not used as paths. They are boundaries, visual barriers, or linear breaks such as shores or walls. They may be more or less penetrable.
- *Districts*: Medium- to large-size patches which have special meanings or functional significance to the observer; areas with identifying character.
- *Nodes*: Point elements which can be entered and which have strategic significance to the observers – places where people meet, concentrations of events, transportation centres, crossing points, etc.
- *Landmarks*: Point references which are not entered such as a tall distinctive building, a special tree, a special façade or, at larger scale, a mountain. Landmarks are important orientation points for the observer moving in the landscape.

Spatial requirements express whether the size or the conditions of an area are sufficient for a given purpose, and what spatial capacity, capabilities, potentials and sensitivities the structure of the landscape offers for the proposed project.

Stable landscape means that under the current conditions – in terms of use, society and nature – the landscape area appears to have found a harmonious form.

Strategic impact assessment is a 'family of tools' intended to assess the impacts of public policies, plans and programmes before particular projects have been formulated (after Tetlow and Hanusch 2012).

Strength of character is the presence and clarity of the essential landscape elements and spatial-visual factors, that is, key characteristics in the various parts of the area.

Substantive theories explain what planning is or should be about, what the content of good places should be, and what planning solutions should look like.

Synthesis   is putting things together.

Tesserae   are the smallest, homogeneous areas visible at the landscape scale.

Thematic approach   is when the project area is divided into a series of formal single-factor areas.

Topographic approach   is a process of establishing formal multiple-factor homogeneous areas.

Values   are 'concepts or beliefs about outcomes that transcend specific situations, guide evaluation and action, and are typically ordered in relative importance' (Schwartz and Bilsky 1987).

Visual catchment   is the total area that is visible for a person situated at a certain viewpoint.

Zone of visual influence   is the total area from which a building or other object, existing or intended, is visible.

INDEX

absolute constraints 138, 195
action research 183
action-oriented analysis 16, 101, 133, 176
adaptive environmental assessment 156
aerial photography 36, 56, 64, 81, 113, 162, 164
aesthetics 22, 89, 157–65, 173
afforestation 9, 73, 75–6, 122, 126, 128, 132, 149–50, 152, 157
agriculture 22, 35–9, 52, 62, 115, 132–3, 147
Albaek 86, 150
Alexander, C. 137
alignment 39, 104, 143, 145–6, 159, 161–2, 164
alternative futures 170–5
analysing change 166–70
analysis, definitions 5–6
analysis concept 4–6
analysis techniques 3, 64, 76, 88, 100, 182
Anthropocene 2
Antrop, M. 4, 6, 23
archaeology 61–2, 64
area descriptions 103, 110–11, 113, 115–16
Arler, F. 178
Arnstein, S.R. 29, 32
Assessment of Environmental Effects (AEE) 157
AutoCad 49

basic map 69, 73, 75, 104, 109, 114
before-and-after images 71, 162, 164–5, 173
Belgium 100
biased representation 164
biodiversity 7–8, 22, 35, 104, 133, 179

biophysical factors 3, 6–7, 11, 15–16, 62; analysis 33, 39–60; historical analysis 66, 75; impact/futures analysis 157, 162; regionalisation 100; research/practice 177, 182; site selection 136; spatial analysis 79
block diagram 45, 50, 92
bottom-up methods 21, 102, 107, 116, 177
boundary 38, 54, 68, 80–1, 83, 87, 98–9, 103–6, 109–10, 112, 118, 121–2, 138, 152, 170
briefs 129, 134
Brown, N. 137
built infrastructure 6, 15, 33
bureaucracy 20–1, 32
business-as-usual scenarios 174
Butler, A. 100
Buttimer, A. 4

CAD 89, 167
cadastral maps 64–5, 67, 69
capitalism 177
case studies 3, 23–7, 29–31, 39–44, 80–98; impact/futures analysis 157, 159–75; regionalisation 105–6, 109–28; research/practice 179, 181, 183; site selection 133, 135, 142–52
Caspersen, O.H. 39
categorical elevation models 46
characterisation 18, 33, 66, 89, 100–1, 111, 115, 118, 122–3, 162
characteristics 15, 23, 83–4, 100, 106, 109, 125
checklists 11, 15, 82
chronological method 64, 69–71

citizens 9, 18–19, 21, 27–9, 32, 91, 109, 112, 125, 171, 178
classification 6, 16, 18–19, 22, 33–4; historical analysis 66; impact/futures analysis 169–70; land use 36–9, 52; regionalisation 99–104, 106–7, 109–10, 112–13, 115–16, 119, 122; research/ practice 180–2; site selection 131, 133, 135–6, 143–5, 147–50
climate change 2, 10, 33, 35–6, 38–9, 47–8, 53, 62, 153, 170, 173, 175
co-determinism 178
co-management 29
coastal areas 7, 15, 23, 38, 62, 73, 95, 115, 122–3, 170–1
colonialism 8, 63
colour-coding 46, 55, 169–70
common law 177
communities 3–5, 9–10, 21–3, 27–9, 31–2; historical analysis 62, 66; impact/futures analysis 158, 171, 173, 175; land use 36; regionalisation 104; research/practice 176–9, 183–4; site selection 137; spatial analysis 84
community types 27–8
compensation 24
complexity 3, 9, 11–12, 17, 20–1; impact/ futures analysis 162, 165, 170, 173; landscape values 29, 32; regionalisation 103–4, 118, 123; site selection 129, 142; spatial analysis 78, 85, 91–2, 95
composite classification maps 104, 106, 131, 135, 139–40, 143–5, 169
composite presentations 167
comprehensive mapping 71, 73–5
comprehensive time series 75–6
conceptual knowledge 181
condition 2, 5, 8–9, 14, 16, 18–19, 22, 26, 33, 35–6, 44, 46, 52, 60, 71, 77, 79, 86, 95, 100–2, 109–10, 115, 122–6, 129–30, 133, 136, 138, 144–6, 148, 150, 154, 159, 162, 167, 170–1, 183
confidentiality 30
conflict management 21, 28–9, 31, 46, 136–7, 179
conservation 7, 9, 22, 28, 103, 112, 128, 137–8, 174–5, 179
constraints 136–40, 147, 150, 152
continual adaptation 156
contour density 196
contour direction 196
contour lines 13, 46, 48, 55, 59, 105, 114, 196
contour parallelism 196
Copenhagen Royal Danish Theatre 169
Corine Land Cover maps 37

Corner, J. 4, 95
Cosgrove, D. 177
Countryside Character Assessment (CCA) 183
create 3, 6, 15, 21, 36–7, 39, 42, 46, 49, 61–2, 64–7, 69, 79–81, 89, 96–7, 100, 104, 107, 116, 125, 137, 176–7, 180–4
cross sections 48–51, 56, 84–7, 93, 162, 164
Cullen, G. 89
cultural factors 4, 8, 10, 15, 19; historical analysis 61–3, 65, 75–6; impact/futures analysis 157; land use 33, 37, 39; landscape values 22, 28; regionalisation 99–100, 106, 118, 120, 123; research/ practice 179–80; spatial analysis 79, 95
cultural-geographic GIS analysis 118

Daniel, T.C. 180
Danish LCA approach 116–18
databases 36–7, 45, 184
decision-making 11, 18–19, 21, 29, 32, 36, 113, 155–6, 158, 165, 170, 176–8
definitive constraint 138, 148, 150–1
Defoe, D. 1
delineation 103, 105–6, 109–11, 118, 130
Deming, M.E. 181–3
democracy 3, 21, 27, 29, 32, 176–9
Denmark 4, 23–7, 39, 45, 52; historical analysis 61, 63, 65, 67; impact/futures analysis 156–7, 159, 169; land use 55, 60; Ministry of the Environment 89, 109, 113, 116; Nature Agency 55, 60; regionalisation 100–1, 104, 106, 109, 116–28; Road Directorate 159; site selection 149; spatial analysis 85, 89, 93–4
descriptive research 18, 182
design 10–11, 16, 21, 30, 60, 95, 132–3, 157, 180, 184
Design with Nature 142–3
desk 85, 109, 118, 125
development requirements 132–3, 136–40, 143–4
diachronic sections 69
diagnosis 183
digital database 36
digital map 36
digital terrain models 46–7, 162
dimensionality 16, 45–6, 48, 54, 56, 79, 81, 84–5, 87–8, 165
direct methods 29–30
discourse 21, 32
distinct contour density 196
district 80–4, 92–3, 95, 99–100, 104, 106–8, 173, 176, 198
do-nothing scenarios 171
Downes, M. 162, 165

drainage 6, 15, 46–7, 52–3, 95, 133
draping 49
drivers of change 7–9, 33, 35, 63, 76, 134, 170, 176
drones 56
drought 7, 170–1

ecology 4, 15, 19, 33, 35–6; ecosystems 22, 137, 153, 156; ecotopes 102; land use 38, 55; regionalisation 110, 125; research/ practice 180; spatial analysis 79, 81
edge 24, 36, 57, 72–3, 75, 78, 80–3, 85–6, 88, 92–5, 105, 120–1, 198
Egense agricultural plain 120–4, 127–8
Egoz, S. 27, 177
EIA (environmental impact assessment) 153, 156–7, 159–64
elevation 6, 15, 33, 46, 51, 85, 87, 92, 95
empowerment 29
enclosures 103–4
England 35, 61, 81, 102, 106–8, 115–16, 182
Enlightenment 64
environmental assessment 7, 21, 36, 153, 159–64, 170–5, 180
equivalent area classification 102
erosion 7, 36, 52, 63
ethics 32
Europe 8, 10, 20, 24, 37, 61, 63–4, 100, 106, 156, 177, 182
European Commission 6, 20
European Environment Agency (EEA) 37
European Landscape Convention (ELC) 4, 15, 27, 77, 159, 177, 182
European Union (EU) 8, 20, 23, 25, 53
evaluation 18–19, 22–3, 90, 103, 110, 125, 173, 181, 183
Evanstown 166
everyday landscape 22, 66, 116
expectations 1, 22, 32, 147–8, 162, 171
experts 18–19, 21, 24, 29, 31–2; impact/ futures analysis 173, 175; regionalisation 100; research/practice 176–7, 181, 184; site selection 144; spatial analysis 79, 81, 83–4
eye-level analysis 85–8

FAO (Food and Agriculture Organization) 36–8, 52
farmer 7, 9, 23–7, 30–1, 52, 111, 137, 178
feasibility studies 132
feature 2, 15, 18–19, 22–3, 33, 35–6, 38–9, 45–6, 51–2, 54, 58, 60–1, 65, 69, 73, 78–81, 84, 88–9, 94–5, 112, 118, 131, 140, 144, 162, 179, 197–8
Federal Environmental Protection Agency 175

feedback 154
field studies 34, 64, 81, 84–5, 95; impact/ futures analysis 162; regionalisation 106, 109–10, 113, 118, 125; research/practice 184; site selection 138, 142, 144, 149
figure ground 83, 88–9
flooding 7, 10, 23, 37, 47–8, 52–3, 62–3, 138, 170–1
focus groups 30
forests 12, 69, 85, 95, 101; afforestation 9, 73, 75, 122, 126, 128, 132–3, 149–50, 157; historical analysis 61; impact/futures analysis 173; land use 37, 52, 54–6, 60; regionalisation 105, 110–11, 115; research/practice 178
Forman, R.T.T. 102
Framstad, E. 4
Frandsen, K.-E. 67
Frederikssund Motorway 122, 157, 159–64
functional regions 99–100
future site possibilities 136, 141–2
futures analysis 2–3, 5, 9, 16, 36, 48, 63, 102, 141–2, 150, 153–75

Geddes, P. 179
Gehl Architects 184
Gehl, I. 184
Gehl, J. 184
generic model 21, 158
genetic method 6, 33, 39, 66
genius loci 63
Geographic Information Systems (GIS) 39, 48, 110, 112–13, 116; impact/futures analysis 162, 165, 167; regionalisation 118, 125; research/practice 182; site selection 135, 145, 149
geography 7, 34, 45, 61–2, 65, 71; impact/ futures analysis 162; regionalisation 102, 104, 106, 118; research/practice 182; site selection 145; spatial analysis 84, 91
geology 6–7, 33, 35–6, 39, 45, 61, 65, 107, 118
geomorphology 7, 33, 35–6, 39, 45–6, 104, 118, 162
Germany 63
globalisation 8, 10
Godron, M. 102
Google 36
governments 20–1, 27, 29, 153, 171
GPS 95
graded-zone maps 169
Great Britain 100
greenhouse gases 171
ground truthing 175, 177
group methods 30–2

guidelines 128, 156, 181
Gustavsson, R. 55

Hägerstrand, T. 75
Handley, J. 137
Harvard University 180
Healey, P. 137
heritage 8, 10, 19, 60, 118, 157, 164, 179
Hester, R.T. 32
Higuchi, T. 92
historical analysis 3, 6, 15–16, 36, 39;
    impact/futures analysis 165; land use 52;
    methods 61–77; regionalisation 100, 102,
    118; research/practice 177; site selection
    135–6, 144; source materials 63–4
historical series of thematic maps 71, 73
historical series of topographic maps 71–2
holistic method 102, 159, 166
homogeneous regions 39, 67, 85, 99–100,
    102–4; impact/futures analysis 162;
    regionalisation 106–7, 109, 112, 115–16,
    118
horticulture 52, 110
Howard, P. 4
human factors 2, 4, 6–7, 10–11, 15; historical
    analysis 61, 66, 77; land use 33, 35, 37–8;
    landscape values 22, 27; regionalisation
    99–100; research/practice 182, 184; spatial
    analysis 78–9
human rights 27, 177
hydraulic assessment 48, 52
hydrology 15, 33, 35–6, 38–9, 52–3, 100

Ice Age 45
The Image of the City 12, 80–3, 184
impact assessment (IA) 3, 7, 16, 85, 89, 104,
    123, 133, 136–7, 140, 152–76
implementation 126–8
indigenous cultures 28
indirect methods 29, 31
information technology 8
infrastructure 8, 15, 29, 33, 51, 95–8, 129,
    138, 157, 162
inquiry-based analysis 184
interpretation 1, 4, 27, 34, 36, 39, 43, 52, 54,
    62–5, 67, 71, 80–2, 84–5, 89, 96, 104, 123,
    146, 170, 173, 177, 181–2
interpretive research 182
interval scale 12
interviews 30, 63–4, 78, 81
irrigation 35, 171
Italy 63, 184

Jackson, J.B. 4
Jacobs, J. 184
Japan 10, 92

Jones, M. 4
judgement phase 101

Kaloe 39–44, 118
Karby 23–7, 29–31, 179, 183
Karlsson, P. 39
Kemmis, S. 183
key driver 6–8
knowledge types 181
Kristensen, L.S. 100, 103

land classification 99–102, 133
land cover 3, 16, 33–4, 36–9, 54, 102, 104,
    107, 118, 123, 149
land cover classification 37
land use 8, 19, 28, 33–60, 100; impact/futures
    analysis 157, 159; regionalisation 102, 104,
    107, 110, 123; research/practice 179–80;
    site selection 132–3, 136–7, 142, 147–9
land use classification 39
landmark 80–3, 92, 95–6, 121, 198
landscape 4
landscape analysis 3–4, 11–14, 16, 27, 164;
    applications 16–17; areas 116, 118, 122;
    attributes 22, 166; biography 16, 36, 63,
    69, 71, 75–7; change 1–17, 27; character
    3–4, 15, 19, 23, 63, 110–11, 116, 125;
    community types 27–8; democracy 3, 21,
    27, 29, 32, 176–9; ecological classification
    102–3; elements/features 15; framing
    18–32; futures analysis 153–75; historical
    analysis 61–77; impact assessment
    153–75; improving 179–80; judgement
    122–5; land records 64; natural factors
    33–60; policy 10–11; potentials 129–52,
    162, 180; practice 3, 5, 16, 20–1, 34,
    36, 52, 81, 83–4, 129, 154, 165, 176–84;
    regionalisation 99–128; research 176–84;
    services 23; site selection 129–52; spatial
    analysis 78–98; strategy 125–6; values
    17–32, 136, 159, 162, 176–8, 183; worth
    22
landscape architects 21, 27, 32, 34, 52;
    historical analysis 61; impact/futures
    analysis 154, 159, 175; regionalisation 99;
    research/practice 176, 179–80, 184; spatial
    analysis 79, 96
landscape architecture 3, 17, 79, 99, 129,
    176, 180–1
landscape area 16, 38, 99–102, 106–9, 110,
    112–13, 115–16, 143, 147–9
landscape assessment 7, 16, 21, 100, 116,
    157, 176
landscape character area 35, 94–5, 97,
    99–102, 107–8, 114, 116, 118–20, 122, 125,
    135–6, 147, 150, 160–1

landscape characterisation 38, 100, 117, 118–22, 149
landscape concept 4
Landscape Design 17
landscape development 137, 164
landscape ecology 36, 81
landscape implementation 117–18, 126–9, 156, 167, 172–3, 177, 182
Landscape Institute 158
landscape planning 7, 10–11, 16–19, 21, 23, 27, 29, 32, 99, 102, 106, 116, 170
landscape type 15, 109–13, 116, 168
Lange, E. 162, 165
LCA (DK) site selection analysis 149–52
LCA (DK) spatial visual analysis 94–5, 119
LCA (landscape character assessment) 15–16, 22, 33, 39, 66; regionalisation 99–104, 106, 115–28; research/practice 182; site selection 146–7, 149–52; spatial analysis 81, 85, 94–5
leasehold rights 28
legislation 7, 10, 20, 23, 64, 149, 156–7
levels of analysis 180
levels of involvement 3, 26, 29, 102
Lid, I.B. 4
line of sight 94
linear analysis 85
Littorina Sea 42
lived experience 79, 100
local actions 9, 19, 22
local authorities 112, 117–18, 122, 125–6, 128–9, 156, 171, 184
Lynch, K. 11–12, 63, 80–4, 88, 90, 92, 94–5, 101, 106, 182, 184

McHarg, I. 38, 142–3, 145, 180
McTaggert, R. 183
market dynamics 8, 10–11
master plans 118
media 29, 181
Mediterranean areas 61
Meyer, E. 129
Millennium Ecosystem Assessment (MEA) 22
Mitchell, D. 4
mock-ups 169
modelling 12, 47, 89, 165, 170–1, 173, 175, 182
Mols Hills 40–4
morality 22, 28
multidisciplinarity 62, 77, 129, 181

NATURA 2000 Network 20, 23
natural conditions 101
natural factors 3–4, 6–7, 15–16, 22, 33–60, 101–2, 107, 118, 149, 182
Nature Conservation Law 7

nested hierarchical area classification 102, 106–8
nested hierarchical classification 102, 106–15
Netherlands 65, 77
New Zealand 156–7
Nielsen, A.V. 45
Nijhuis, S. 12
node 80–3, 92, 198
noise 100, 131, 135–41, 149, 169–70
Nolli, G. 89, 91
nominal scale 12
non-participatory involvement 29
norms 22
North America 8, 10
Northern Europe 4

OECD 6
Olwig, K.R. 4, 177
Opdam, P. 23
operational knowledge 181
opinion 22, 29, 138
Oppdal 69–70, 171–3, 175
ordinal scale 12
orthophoto 112
overlay analysis 142–6
overlay technique 131, 135, 142–6, 167–9
owners 9, 15, 19, 28–9, 118, 137, 178, 183

parametric method 6, 33, 166
parks 20, 37, 50, 58, 60, 67, 84, 87–9, 131–3, 147, 167, 182
particular visual quality 4, 123–5, 128, 197
peer review 183–4
photomontage 162–5
physiographic GIS analysis 118–19
physiographic regions 118
Pitte, J.B. 61
place names 61, 64
place-making 21, 27, 29, 137, 179
planning 10–11, 16–21, 23, 27, 29; historical analysis 65, 69; impact/futures analysis 153–5, 164, 170–1; land use 35, 39, 48; regionalisation 99–100, 102–4, 109, 112, 115–16, 118, 122–3, 125–6, 128; relevance 63, 67; research/practice 176, 178–9, 183–4; site selection 129–31, 134, 136, 142, 145; spatial analysis 89, 96
planning authorities 28, 136, 156, 181
point-by-point analysis 85, 89
policy objectives 125, 156, 159, 173, 178
political economy 19
Porsmose, E. 65
potentials analysis 131, 133, 135, 197
Potschin, M. 19

practice 3, 5, 16, 20–1, 34, 36, 52, 81–4, 129, 154, 165, 176–84
preference 9, 11, 19, 22, 178–9, 182
preliminary landscape character areas 118
presentation techniques 84, 159, 162, 164, 167, 169, 173
primary land use 39, 132
Primdahl, J. 100, 103
procedural planning 19, 21, 118–28
procedural theories 19, 197
producers 9, 15
professional practice 3, 5, 16, 20–1, 34, 36, 52, 81–4, 129, 154, 165, 176–84
projections 171
property rights 91, 178
protection scenarios 171
protection zones 140
provisioning services 22
public choice theory 21
public participation 9, 21, 29, 32, 177
public policy interventions 8, 10, 21, 176, 178, 184

qualitative analysis 12, 81
quantitative analysis 12, 81
questionnaires 30–1, 63

rainfall 36, 47–8, 52–3
Ramirez, R. 28
Randers Bay 149–52
ratio scale 12
reciprocity 136, 139–40
recreation 8, 15, 26, 37–8, 48; impact/ futures analysis 157; land use 53, 60; regionalisation 126; site selection 132–3, 137, 144, 147
Reed, M.S. 28
regionalisation 99–128
regions 6, 10, 16, 19, 32
regulating services 22
relative constraint 138, 141, 148
Renaissance 64
representation techniques 145, 165–6
representing change requirements 164–6
Repton, H. 164
research methods 3, 15–16, 22, 29–32, 34–5, 45, 67, 69, 158, 176–84
resilience 25, 36, 53
restore 126, 137
retreat scenarios 171
retrogressive method 64, 67
retrospective method 39, 64–7
Rio Declaration 10
rivers 23, 33, 35, 38, 52–3, 71, 95, 115, 173–4

Roymans, N. 76
rural areas 8, 15, 23–4, 60, 80–1, 84, 113, 128, 178–9

SAD (survey, analysis and design) 16
salt marshes 23–6, 37
Sasaki, H. 180
satellites 36
SAVE structural analysis 85, 93
SAVE (Survey of Architectural Values in the Environment) 85, 89, 93
SAVE urban edge analysis 85, 93
scale 2, 4, 6, 8, 10–12; historical analysis 61, 64–5, 71; impact/futures analysis 153, 159, 161, 167, 169–70, 173; land use 35, 45–7, 60; landscape change 16–17; regionalisation 102, 104–7, 109, 115, 118; research/practice 176, 184; site selection 129–30, 135–6, 142, 144; spatial analysis 81–5, 93, 95, 97
Scandinavia 23
scenarios 85, 150, 170–1, 173–5
Schou, A. 45
Scotland 102, 107, 115–16, 182
sea levels 36, 38, 62, 170–1
secondary land use 39, 132
selection 129–52
self-determinism 178
Sell, J.L. 180
Selman, P. 8, 29, 100
sensitive location 136, 140, 164
sensitivity 123, 125, 136, 140, 149–50, 164
sensitivity analysis 149–50
sensitivity study 150
sensory qualities 15
serial vision 89
site constraints 136, 138, 195
site planning 16, 134
site selection 3, 16, 129–52, 159, 169; analysis 79; factors 130–1, 135–43, 145–6, 150; future possibilities 141–2; procedure 133–5; repair patterns 137
situation analysis 16, 63, 67, 101, 176
situational analysis 11
Skive 55, 101–2, 109–15, 183
Skovbo 133, 135, 147–9
slope 34, 38, 42–3, 46, 75, 80, 93, 105, 110, 139–40, 143–5, 148
Smed, P. 45
Smith, W. 35
social learning 29–30
software 36
soil classification 37, 44, 52
soil types 6, 15, 22, 33, 95; historical analysis 61, 64–5; land use 35–7, 39, 46, 52;

regionalisation 100, 104, 109–10, 115, 118; research/practice 179; site selection 133, 138, 144
spatial analysis 3, 6, 10, 15–16, 21–3; impact/futures analysis 159, 161–2; land use 34, 36, 46, 55–6; methods 78–98; regionalisation 100; research/practice 176, 182; site selection 135, 143, 146
spatial language 36, 80–1, 198
spatial requirements 79, 198
spatial visual analysis 79, 85, 94–5, 97, 118–19, 121, 125, 161–2
Spirn, A.W. 61
spot elevation 46
stable landscape 110, 198
stakeholders 9, 19, 27–9, 165
standards 12, 15, 35, 37, 52, 55, 156, 158, 164, 184
statistical analysis 12, 30, 64, 69, 118
Steenbergen, C. 96
Steinitz, C. 11, 81, 184
stewardship 22, 180
Stiles, R. 17
storm water 36, 52, 170
Strang, G.L. 95
strategic impact assessment 156, 159
strategic option 126
strategy phase 101
strength of character 123–4, 198
strength of landscape character 123–4, 198
structural analysis 85
sub-soils 52, 109
substantive planning theories 19, 21
suitability studies 99
supporting services 22
surface shading 46
sustainability 2, 10, 25, 38, 138
Svendborg 102, 105, 116–17, 119–20, 125, 127
Swaffield, S. 181–3
symbol selection 47, 56, 71, 73, 79–85, 87, 92, 95, 135, 140, 169
synthesis 5, 34, 131–3, 179–80, 199
synthetic analysis 85
systematic analysis 181–2, 184
systematic knowledge 181–2, 184, 197

tacit knowledge 181
tax registers 64
Taylor, J.G. 180
technical expertise 21, 32, 171, 182
technology change 8, 10
Termorshuizen, J. 23
terrain 6, 15, 33, 35–6, 39; digital models 46–7, 162; historical analysis 75; impact/futures analysis 160–1, 163–5; land use 45,

48, 51–2; regionalisation 100, 103–5, 107, 109–11, 115, 118, 123; site selection 150; spatial analysis 85, 87–8, 92–3, 95
terrain form 13, 34, 36, 39, 43, 45, 47, 51, 93, 100, 103–4, 107, 112, 115, 118–19, 123, 139, 150
terrain model 36, 42–3, 46–50, 52–4, 85, 161–2, 164–6
tesserae 102, 199
thematic approach 104–6, 199
thematic method 39, 69, 73, 91, 100, 104, 125, 135, 143–5, 167, 169, 180
thematic survey 135
Thing & Wainoe 159
time series 70, 72–3, 75–6
top-down methods 19–20, 102, 107, 116, 177
top-soil 44, 52
topographic approach 106, 199
topographic method 36, 46, 54, 64, 69; historical analysis 71, 73, 75; regionalisation 104, 106, 109, 113; site selection 142; spatial analysis 83
topographical map 46
tourism 8, 62, 171
transparent maps 135
Turner, T. 16–17
Tveit, M. 180

United Kingdom (UK) 4, 35, 65, 99–100, 116, 158, 182–3
United Nations (UN) 10, 36, 155
United States (US) 19, 81, 95, 156, 173, 175
urban-edge analysis 85, 93
urbanisation 8, 10, 53, 77, 80, 153, 170, 173, 175

validation studies 165
valley sections 180
valuation 18–19, 21, 177
values 3, 8, 10–11, 15–32, 38, 62–3, 66, 79, 85, 100, 136, 144, 146, 150, 162, 164, 176–8, 182, 199
Varming, M. 85, 89
vegetated areas 37–8
vertical exaggeration 46, 51
Vervloet, J. 65
video 84, 90
Vining, J. 180
virtual reality 89–91
visibility 46–7, 85–6, 95, 164–5
visibility analysis 85–6, 149–50, 164
visual and aesthetic assessment 157–9
visual appearance 4, 79, 103, 118, 140
visual experience 38, 85, 94–5, 106, 118, 122, 143

visual expression 3–4, 12, 15, 22, 33;
    catchment 85; historical analysis 69;
    impact/futures analysis 164–5, 171, 175;
    land use 38, 46; regionalisation 100, 103–4,
    106, 115–16, 121–3; research/practice 177,
    179–80, 182; site selection 137, 140, 143,
    150; spatial analysis 83, 87, 90; visibility
    analysis 85, 149; visual analysis 79, 85,
    94–5, 118–19, 125, 153, 157–9, 161–2, 170
visual feature 94–5, 118, 162
visual impact assessment 137, 153, 162,
    164–5, 170
visual influence 85–6, 95, 199
visual quality 12, 85, 95, 115–16, 123–5, 128,
    150
visualisation techniques 159, 162–5, 170–1,
    175, 182

Wales 182
Warnock, S. 137

water features 38, 144
wetlands 12, 33, 37, 53–4, 69, 71, 104,
    109–10, 115, 125, 140
Willamette Valley 173–5
Wilson, W. 19
wind farms 129, 137, 165–6
wind turbines 62, 95, 103, 110, 112, 115,
    121, 126, 133, 137, 150–1, 157, 165–6
Wood, R. 137
worksheets 15
workshops 24, 30, 179
World Bank 156
World Reference Base for Soil Resources
    52
Wylie, J. 4

zones of influence 85, 136, 140
zones of theoretical visibility (ZTV)
    164–5
Zube, E.H. 180